CITY OF WORKERS, CITY OF STRUGGLE

Columbia Studies in the History of U.S. Capitalism

Columbia Studies in the History of U.S. Capitalism

Series Editors: Devin Fergus, Louis Hyman, Bethany Moreton, and Julia Ott

Capitalism has served as an engine of growth, a source of inequality, and a catalyst for conflict in American history. While remaking our material world, capitalism's myriad forms have altered—and been shaped by—our most fundamental experiences of race, gender, sexuality, nation, and citizenship. This series takes the full measure of the complexity and significance of capitalism, placing it squarely back at the center of the American experience. By drawing insight and inspiration from a range of disciplines and alloying novel methods of social and cultural analysis with the traditions of labor and business history, our authors take history "from the bottom up" all the way to the top.

Capital of Capital: Money, Banking, and Power in New York City, 1784–2012, by Steven H. Jaffe and Jessica Lautin

From Head Shops to Whole Foods: The Rise and Fall of Activist Entrepreneurs, by Joshua Clark Davis

Creditworthy: A History of Consumer Surveillance and Financial Identity in America, by Josh Lauer

American Capitalism: New Histories, by Sven Beckert and Christine Desan, editors

Buying Gay: How Physique Entrepreneurs Sparked a Movement, by David K. Johnson

Banking on Freedom: Black Women in U.S. Finance Before the New Deal, by Shennette Garrett-Scott

Threatening Property: Race, Class, and Campaigns to Legislate Jim Crow Neighborhoods, by Elizabeth A. Herbin-Triant

CITY OF WORKERS, CITY OF STRUGGLE

HOW LABOR MOVEMENTS CHANGED NEW YORK

EDITED BY JOSHUA B. FREEMAN

This volume is published as a companion to the exhibition *City of Workers, City of Struggle: How Labor Movements Changed New York* organized by and presented at the Museum of the City of New York May 1—December 29, 2019.

This book and the exhibition it accompanies were made possible through the generous support of The Puffin Foundation, Ltd.

The Puffin Foundation, Ltd.

Additional support for this book was provided by Furthermore: a program of the J. M. Kaplan Fund, and other generous donors.

Furthermore:
a program of the J.M. Kaplan Fund

Book Design and Typography
Michael Gericke, Yeryung Ko and Alex Mäkäräinen, Pentagram

Columbia University Press
Publishers Since 1893
New York, Chichester, West Sussex
cup.columbia.edu

Library of Congress Cataloging-in-Publication Data

Names: Freeman, Joshua Benjamin, editor.
Title: City of Workers, City of Struggle: how labor movements changed New York / edited by Joshua B. Freeman.
Description: New York : Columbia University Press, [2019] | Series: Columbia studies in the history of U.S. capitalism | Includes bibliographical references.
Identifiers: LCCN 2018058068 | ISBN 9780231191920 (cloth : alk. paper)
Subjects: LCSH: Labor unions—New York (State)—New York—History. | Labor--New York (State)—New York—History.
Classification: LCC HD6519.N5 C58 2019 | DDC 331.8809747/1—dc23
LC record available at https://lccn.loc.gov/2018058068

♾ Columbia University Press books are printed on permanent and durable acid-free paper.

Printed in the United States of America

ISBN 978-0-231-19192-0

Cover Images

Row 1 (top), left to right

Protest at the construction site of SUNY Downstate hospital, Brooklyn, 1963
Photograph by Bob Adelman;
© Estate of Bob Adelman

Construction workers protest union busting, New York City, 2018
Photograph by Michael Nigro; ©
Michael Nigro/Pacific Press/Alamy Live News

Striking members of ILGWU Local 23-25, New York City, 1982
Photograph courtesy Kheel Center, Cornell University

Row 2 (middle), right

Girl doing homework, New York City, 1924
Photograph by Lewis Wickes Hine; courtesy Library of Congress, Prints and Photographs Division

Row 3 (middle), left to right

Protest against child labor, New York City, 1909
Photograph courtesy Library of Congress, Prints and Photographs Division

Protest at Mt. Sinai Hospital, New York City, 1959
Photograph courtesy Center for Puerto Rican Studies, Hunter College, CUNY

Row 4 (bottom), left to right

Protest at the construction site of SUNY Downstate hospital, Brooklyn, 1963
Photograph by Bob Adelman;
© Estate of Bob Adelman

Bhairavi Desai, director of the Taxi Workers Alliance, 2012
Photograph by Bryan Smith;
© Bryan Smith/ZUMAPRESS.com/Alamy Stock Photo

TWU president Michael J. Quill, 1946
Photograph by Leroy Jakob; NY Daily News Archive via Getty Images

TABLE OF CONTENTS

ILGWU March on
Broadway, 1983
Photograph by
Walter Leporati

Director's Foreword

Whitney W. Donhauser

*Ronay Menschel Director &
President of the Museum of the City of New York*

New York City is known as the nation's finance capital, media capital, arts capital—even as the "capital of the world." But in important ways, it is also the capital of labor. New York was an incubator of the nation's trading economy, its industrial economy, and its financial economy, and each of these was made possible by the brains, skills, and muscle of the city's working people. Here they incubated a variety of labor movements, from the first organizations of craftsmen in the era of the Revolution to the Workingmen's Party of the 1820s, to the American Federation of Labor and the International Ladies' Garment Workers' Union, and on to the Household Technicians of America. The nation's very first Labor Day was held in New York City on September 5, 1882, and today, well over a century later, new organizations like worker centers are re-defining workers' movements yet again.

The Museum of the City of New York's signature exhibition, *New York at Its Core*, argues that New York City is defined by four words—money, diversity, density, and creativity—and the city's history of labor movements has all of these in abundance, as the chapters in this volume show. It is a story full of human drama and struggle, success and scandal, pathos and politics, and it shows how the city's character has been shaped by generations of people fighting for the independence, dignity, and the wellbeing of themselves and their communities. ***City of Workers, City of Struggle: How Labor Movements Changed New York*** began life as a 2019 exhibition of the same name at the Museum of the City of New York. Our gratitude goes to The Puffin Foundation whose generous support made the exhibition and its companion publication possible. Perry, Gladys, and Neal Rosenstein's commitment to preserving the legacy of New York's labor history as well as that of generations of activists through our ongoing exhibition *Activist New York* and its companion programming, publication, and online resources for students and educators enable us to reach countless people with stories that might otherwise have been forgotten. The Puffin Foundation has been a champion of labor rights and causes, and their vision and dedication is inspiring and deeply appreciated.

The exhibition is presented in collaboration with the Kheel Center at the School of Industrial and Labor Relations at Cornell University and the Tamiment Library & Robert F. Wagner Labor Archives at NYU. We are grateful for the leadership of Curtis Lyons and the assistance of Steven Calco at Kheel Center and for the leadership of Timothy Johnson and the assistance of Danielle Marie Nista at Tamiment for making access to their remarkable, rich collections possible. Additional support for this publication was provided by Furthermore: a program of the J. M. Kaplan Fund, and other generous donors.

Huge thanks go to our editor, Dr. Joshua B. Freeman, who shepherded an impressive group of contributing authors with care, vision, and good humor, working closely with the Museum's Deputy Director and Chief Curator Dr. Sarah M. Henry and Director of Publications Susan Gail Johnson. Exhibition curator Steven H. Jaffe contributed editorial assistance and insight as well as lending his research to the book's rich and lively illustrations—drawn from the collections of the Museum and beyond. A dynamic design by Michael Gericke, Yeryung Ko and Alex Mäkäräinen, with the support of Amanda Kesner Walter, at Pentagram reflects the vibrant stories told on these pages. Judy Yonina Gordon, Whitney Harrison, and Sidney A. Carlson White provided valuable editorial assistance. And the project benefited enormously from the guidance and support of Bridget Flannery-McCoy and Stephen Wesley at Columbia University Press.

The contributing authors to this book—several of whom also served as advisers to its companion exhibition—are participants in a vital ongoing reexamination of American labor history that continues to transform our understanding of that history. By expanding the very terms of scholarship to probe the complex relationships among organized labor, politics, economic change, cultural expression, and urban governance; by including previously ignored groups of working people; by widening the definition of labor activism to explore movements outside mainstream unions; and by examining the cultural and social lives of working women, men, children, and families, these historians and social scientists are changing how we view our own New York and how we assess what is at stake in the city's future. We thank them, and we hope you enjoy the fruits of their labor contained within the covers of this book.

Union members join fast-food workers calling for the minimum wage to be raised to $15 an hour and for the right to unionize, 2015

Photograph by Stacy Walsh Rosenstock

"Little Susie at her Work," Gotham Court, c. 1890
Photograph by Jacob A. Riis

CITY OF WORKERS, CITY OF STRUGGLE

Workers' Movements, Workers' Struggles in New York

New York City has been profoundly shaped by its workers and their social and political movements.

Not only have working people built the physical city and driven its economy, but they have helped define its political conversation, its collective culture, and its public sphere. Labor struggles—with employers, within unions, at the ballot box, and against each other—are woven throughout the city's history. And these struggles can be found well beyond famous episodes such as the garment workers' movements of the early 20th century or the tumultuous teachers' strikes of the 1960s. In fact, New York workers' movements, large and small, have inflected every sector, public and private, and changed not just the terms of working people's employment but also the discussion of what makes a good and livable city.

The chapters in this book show that these varied movements and their relationship to one another changed dramatically over time. They shifted as the population of the city shifted—as waves of new arrivals competed, collaborated, and challenged each other. Working people were buffeted by the dramatic rises and falls in the economy and structural shifts in the kinds of jobs that were available in the city, and by the changing nature of work itself. Locally and nationally, their movements both reflected and impacted the political and legal issues and institutions of their times.

These chapters also highlight the ways in which historians of labor have expanded and reexamined their subject. Over the past few decades, scholars have amplified our understanding of how crucially New York's (and America's) labor unions, leaders, and members shaped—and were shaped by—urbanization, party politics, rising and falling economic sectors, a changing workforce, and conflicting visions of what a just society would look like. As the following pages show, historians have also explored how those working people considered marginal or "invisible" to the established (largely white and male) labor movement launched their own hard struggles for better conditions, rights, and legal recognition. Repeatedly new waves of diverse New Yorkers—women, immigrants, people of color, the so-called "unskilled," and the allegedly "unorganizable"—defined their own movements for a better life. They created alternatives (both formal and informal) to organizations dominated by "skilled" white men, while also sometimes fighting for entry into—and status within—established unions. These New Yorkers—notably including domestic workers (both paid and unpaid), casual wage laborers, drivers, office and retail workers, "temps," and sex workers—reshaped the very definition and valuation of work as the city absorbed diverse newcomers. They also fashioned their own distinctive cultures of solidarity, both inside and outside their workplaces. For that reason, rather than treat the "labor movement" as a monolithic entity, this book and the museum exhibition it accompanies seek to explore how plural, diverse "labor movements" changed America's largest metropolis, while also amplifying its national influence.

Changing City, Changing Work, Changing Struggles

The workers' stories told in this book begin in the city's earliest days, when the colonial city was primarily a mercantile and agricultural center, employing a complex combination of free and unfree labor. There, the largest number of enslaved Africans of any North American city worked side-by-side with indentured servants, laborers, and artisans and apprentices following age-old European traditions. As the metropolis grew, slavery finally ended, and the opening of the Erie Canal consolidated the city's role as the fulcrum of North American and Atlantic trade, New York became a major magnet for national migration and international immigration, bringing new people to work for wages in workshops, stores, streets, docks, and households. The city quickly turned into an industrial powerhouse—the largest manufacturing center in the nation—attracting and depending on new arrivals from around the world to run its thousands of factories, small and large. In the 20th century, employment in producing and distributing a staggering variety of New York-made products—from clothing and cigars to pharmaceuticals and printed goods—was augmented by jobs in the wholesale, retail, transportation, office, and government sectors. And, as manufacturing declined and white-collar, service, and freelance jobs grew in the closing decades of the century, expectations surrounding work, opportunity, and power seemed to be rewritten yet again.

Throughout these structural transformations, the pressures of change repeatedly challenged fundamental beliefs: beliefs about the proper relationship between employer and employee, the possibilities of advancement and independence, the distribution of wealth and power, and even the definition of citizenship itself. And working people responded, in a variety of ways, to what they understood to be threats to their welfare, their communities, and their way of life. The result was a series of activist movements, as workers organized, stood up, and fought for their rights and wellbeing.

The task of this book is a complex one, and not only because the twists and turns of this big history are so many. "Labor" itself can mean and has meant so many things to so many people. Both historically and in contemporary discourse, the questions of who is a "worker" has been a subject of strenuous debate. For example, very commonly in colonial and antebellum New York, an artisan might have been an apprentice at one stage of his (or, much more rarely, her) life, a wage worker at another, and a self-employed worker at yet another (perhaps employing others, too). In the 19th century, some people focused on solidarity among those who did "productive work," regardless of whether they were employees or employers, while others focused on the challenges of those working for hourly or piece wages. In the 20th century, permeable boundaries meant that it was common for skilled garment or construction workers to start their own businesses, taking on contracts or subcontracts, perhaps while they still did some wage work on the side (often later going bust and working for others), or for sex workers to go into business as brothel owners while perhaps still engaging themselves in sex for sale. New Yorkers who viewed themselves as entrepreneurs, professionals, or civil servants also grappled with questions of status and identity, sometimes resisting the notion that they were "workers," sometimes fashioning their own kinds of organizations for workplace leverage, and sometimes embracing labor unions as the logical vehicles for negotiating their pay, hours, and work conditions.

Today the complexity continues. As subcontracting again has become ubiquitous, many freelancers, such as livery car drivers, straddle the line between self-employment and wage work. They, along with many public employees, salaried white-collar workers, professionals, homemakers, freelancers, and self-employed people all might consider themselves workers. Accordingly, as a group, the chapters that follow take a deliberately broad perspective on these issues, covering not just "blue collar" manufacturing workers, but groups as varied as enslaved laborers, paid and unpaid household workers, sex workers, and public employees.

Labor and New York's Public Life

The chapters in this book explore many aspects of that history—from the resistance of slaves, to quests for independence by women who embraced sex work or black-market entrepreneurship as an alternative to "wage slavery," to the informal networks and working-class communities that fostered shared identities, mutualism, and creativity. They organized for their own benefit and for their own communities in order to confront the power wielded by employers. At many points in the city's history, they also had more ambitious agendas. In the 1880s an exuberant but unsuccessful campaign to elect the reformer Henry George as mayor attempted to unite workers to transform New York politics. In the 1910s an insurgency of Jewish and Italian shirtwaist and cloak makers dramatically transformed New York's labor movement. Their "uprisings" against poor pay and long hours—and against the workplace conditions that precipitated the deadly 1911 Triangle Fire—helped create a "progressive"–labor coalition, fostered new assumptions about government's role in the economy, and shaped New York politics and public policy for half a century as working people became a potent political force in the city.

Institution-building by unions and labor-affiliated organizations during the 1920s—including housing projects, schools, banks, insurance policies, and cultural programs—helped set the stage for labor's central involvement in the Depression Era's public city. In the 1940s and 1950s, New York truly became "labor's city," with a public cityscape and sensibility shaped by unions and their allies. Union leaders and members supported the city's expanding healthcare and free public university system, sustained a commitment to building housing and community institutions for member families, and made union headquarters and locals a central presence in the city's cultural and political affairs. Under Mayor Robert F. Wagner Jr., municipal employees began to win collective bargaining rights, empowering public-sector unions to become the major players in New York's late 20th-century labor relations and politics.

At the same time, the postwar era brought challenges: Cold War government purges and internal union struggles over Communism, the flight of manufacturing out of the city, tensions over racial inequality during the 1960s, and the city's crippling 1975 fiscal crisis. Still, by the late 20th century, there was no turning back the clock on New York labor as a power player in city, state, and national politics. This power was not without its controversies. Unions and unionists were repeatedly criticized from the outside as self-interested, corrupt, and overly powerful. Working people voiced their own criticisms, particularly on the question of who did or did not get to lead labor organizations. As had been true since the 19th century, racism, nativism, and sexism often held back working people in their own unions as well as in their places of employment. Lacking political and economic power, working women, unpaid women performing domestic services, African Americans, Puerto Ricans, immigrants, and "unskilled" laborers continued or renewed efforts to protect or fortify their standing, either within or outside conventional unions.

The chapters in this volume show the diversity both of workers' experiences and workers' movements in the nation's largest city. They demonstrate that the city's laboring people have been an important part of the dialogue over the very idea of New York. And they show that across time, New Yorkers played a vital role in helping to forge America's varied labor movements. Today, New York remains the most unionized big city in the nation, with a union membership (24 percent of its 2017 workforce) more than twice the national average (11 percent). The city has also become an incubator of "alt-labor" organizations serving new kinds of workers, including undocumented immigrants and wage-earners in the so-called "gig economy." In the face of daunting economic, political, and judicial challenges, working New Yorkers today continue to invigorate multiple labor movements with new strategies and tactics, much as they have repeatedly created and altered such movements over the past three centuries.

14-year-old garment worker with labor activist Flora Dodge La Follette and social reformer Rose Livingston during a garment strike in New York City, 1913

14-YEAR OLD STRIKER - FOLA LA FOLLETTE   ROSE LIVINGSTON

WORK

THE C

COMM

1624

ERS IN
TY OF
ERCE

1898

Workers in the City of Commerce: 1624–1898

New Yorkers have always worked, even before there was a New York. The Lenape, who inhabited Manhattan long before the first Europeans arrived (and gave the island its name), hunted, fished, gathered shellfish, fruits, and berries, grew crops, built the long houses in which they lived, and manufactured tools. The Dutch, who established the first ongoing European presence in what is now New York, did not come to labor as much as to live off the labor of others: the native fur trappers with whom they traded. Yet that required labor, too, to build the rudimentary settlements they established in lower Manhattan and its environs, to feed the growing population, to build, man, and maintain forts and ships, to deliver babies, heal the sick, and bury the dead. For some of that

labor, the Dutch turned to enslaved Africans, the first of whom arrived just two years after the founding of New Amsterdam.

By 1664, when the English took over New Amsterdam by the threat of force and renamed it "New-York," the settlement had grown to nearly 2,000 people, while the Native population had diminished from several thousand to a few hundred as a result of war, disease, and displacement. Despite comprising fewer people than live on many Manhattan blocks today, the new English colony displayed patterns that would remain characteristic of New York all the way up to the present. One was remarkable population diversity, with the Dutch and English joined by Africans, French, Germans, Scots, Irish, and Jews, speaking a babel of tongues. Another was that the work they did was as varied as their origins; there were seamen and soldiers, innkeepers and boardinghouse owners, traders and merchants, coopers and carpenters, brewers, bakers, and butchers, glaziers, tanners, hatters, masons, carters, and laborers. But unlike today, when most work is done by wage labor or self-employment, for its first two hundred years New York relied on a great variety of labor forms, many of them unfree. There were slaves, indentured servants, apprentices, and conscripted laborers alongside the minority of the population that worked for wages.

This diversity of labor arrangements led to a diversity of forms of struggle by women and men dissatisfied with their working and living conditions. For the unfree, running away was, no doubt, the commonest form of protest, although slaves attempted rebellions as well. Workers occasionally used the courts to try to redress grievances. Sometimes, they banded together in formal organizations to improve their lot. The cartmen (wagon drivers who moved goods and supplies around the city) were pioneers in 1667, when they formed a "fellowship," or guild, that contracted with the municipal government at fixed rates for carrying goods. In 1684 the cartmen held an unsuccessful one-week strike to protest new city regulations. Carting also pioneered the other side of solidarity—exclusion—when the city government forbade slaves and free blacks from entering the trade.

Post-Revolutionary New York

The American Revolution led to a spurt of growth in New York and its emergence as the leading city in the nation. On the eve of the independence struggle, New York City (then just Manhattan) had fewer than 22,000 residents. By 1810 it had 96,000, surpassing Philadelphia to become the country's most populous city. Thirty years later Manhattan's population reached 312,000 before leaping to 814,000, just before the Civil War. And it kept growing, so that in 1900, Manhattan housed more than 1.8 million people; together, the five boroughs included 3.4 million.

Immigration accounted for most of the dizzying growth. In the mid-1850s, largely as a result of great waves of German and Irish immigration, a majority of the city's population was foreign born. Later in the 19th century came huge numbers of southern and eastern Europeans. The influx of foreign-born whites contributed to a sharp decline in the relative size of the African-American population, which peaked in the mid-18th century at one-fifth the population in Manhattan and one-third in Kings County, before plunging in 1890 to less than two percent in Manhattan, Brooklyn, and Staten Island, and less than three percent in Queens.

The stupendous growth of New York reflected its central economic place in the Atlantic world and beyond. New Amsterdam and colonial New York thrived because of trade in goods, humans, and money, among England, the Caribbean, North America, and Africa. Not long after the war, as merchants extended trading routes into the Pacific, New

"New York City— Grand Demonstration of Working-men," 1882
Illustration from *Frank Leslie's Illustrated Newspaper,* September 16, 1882

York became the busiest port in the country. The 1825 completion of the Erie Canal, followed by other canals and then railroads, created cheap transportation networks that reached into the heart of the continent. Meanwhile, local infrastructure development, including the 1811 creation of the Manhattan street grid, the leveling of much of the island to speed development, and the building of the Croton Aqueduct, facilitated geographic spread and population growth.

With trade came a position for New York as the leading financial center in the country. That, along with the city's great port, in turn, made it possible to profit from distant labor, much of it done by enslaved peoples. New York became the prime locale for the financing, trading, and transshipment of Southern-grown cotton as well as a national hub of sugar refining, using raw sugar from slave plantations in the South, the Caribbean, and Latin America. The bustling waterfront provided jobs for legions of shipbuilders, sailors, longshoremen, coopers, warehouse workers, and commodity processors, many of whom lived nearby.

In the mid-19th century manufacturing grew increasingly important in the New York economy, facilitated by the large local market, ever more efficient transportation, and the availability of cheap labor from immigrants. By 1880 New York had become the biggest producer of manufactured goods in the country, with Brooklyn, still a separate city, holding fourth place. While there were some large-scale manufacturing enterprises, such as ironworks, shipyards, and refineries, New York shops were typically small or midsize, clustered in districts that specialized in making particular goods.

Simply sustaining and serving the local population also required a large number of workers. Some were in the building trades, local transportation, retail trade, education, or entertainment, licit and illicit. Others worked in homes, as servants, midwives, and caretakers.

Workers' Struggles

A thriving city did not benefit all equally, by any means. Since the earliest days of European settlement, New York has been marked by exceptionally high levels of inequality of income and wealth. Poverty has been a persistent feature.

Throughout the 19th century, workers struggled to better their circumstances and achieve some level of control over their lives. Individually they changed jobs frequently in search of better conditions, set their own pace of work, and restricted their output. Workers also sought improvement through collective action and politics, although some were much better positioned to do so than others.

Soon after the American Revolution, skilled craftsmen came to view their interests as separate from those of the master artisans for whom they labored; these workers began to organize guilds and societies, prototypes of what later came to be called "unions." Some even engaged in "turn-outs" or "stand-outs,"

what today we would call "strikes." But their organizations were fragile and fleeting, disappearing whenever the economy took a downturn or a fight with employers ended badly. Informal networks of collective action were more common, as sailors, domestic workers, and laborers exchanged information about jobs, boycotted bad employers, and created spaces for conviviality and solidarity.

The 1820s and 1830s saw a new round of worker mobilization, extending beyond skilled craftsmen. In 1825 waterfront workers and tailoresses who worked from home went on strike. A welter of worker reform groups popped up, promoting ideas such as the replacement of private property with cooperative enterprise, free education for all, and an end to debt imprisonment. The Workingmen's Party—formed in 1829 as the first partisan group to define itself as explicitly representing workers—took up these causes and more. Four years later, unions formed the first labor federation in the city, the General Trades Union of the City of New York (GTU), which, within a few years, had 52 affiliated groups. The growing labor movement, however, only included some, with African Americans banned from most unions and the GTU opposed to women working for wages.

The New York labor movement collapsed as a result of widespread unemployment that followed the economic crash of 1837. It revived in the 1850s, pressing for higher wages, an eight-hour workday (at a time when workdays of 10 or more hours were common), free land out West, public regulation of housing, and public baths and reading rooms. An 1850 strike by German tailors led to the first strike-related deaths in New York, as two demonstrators were killed by the police. Though broader occupationally than in the past, the labor movement became virtually an all-male enterprise, with female trade unionism essentially disappearing for the rest of the century.

During and after the Civil War, organized labor expanded further. As craft unions—which represented skilled workers in particular occupations—grew, they increasingly came to resemble the labor organizations we have today: led by paid officials, engaging in collective bargaining, and signing written contracts. But not only the employed mobilized. During the economic downturn that began in 1873, both employed and unemployed New Yorkers demanded that the city government employ the jobless on public works and provide relief.

The Great Upheaval

The 19th-century New York labor movement reached its high point in the 1880s. In 1882 labor activists formed a new Central Labor Union (CLU), which, on September 5, sponsored the first Labor Day celebration in the country. The growing number of trade unions were joined by a large local contingent of the Knights of Labor, a hybrid union and reform group that, unlike many labor organizations, was broadly inclusive, welcoming the skilled and unskilled, men and women, whites and blacks. On May 1, 1886, some 45,000 New York workers went on strike, demanding a reduction of the workday to eight hours, in many cases successfully. Then, in response to the jailing of CLU leaders for organizing a boycott of a nonunion brewery and beer garden, the CLU and its allies formed the United Labor Party, selecting reform author Henry George as its candidate for mayor. George called for higher wages, shorter hours, government ownership of railroads and telegraphs, an end to police attacks on peaceful gatherings, and taxing owners of vacant land that might be used for housing. The campaign was a sensation, electrifying working-class quarters. In the end, with more than 68,000 votes, George bested the Republican candidate, Theodore Roosevelt, but lost to Democrat Abram Hewitt. Finally, that year, craft unions nationally founded the American Federation of Labor (AFL), with New York cigar maker Samuel Gompers as its president.

A sharp turn against labor by Catholic Church leaders, the co-opting of some of its proposals by the Democratic Party, internal disagreements, and the depression that lasted from 1893 to 1897 weakened New York labor. However, unlike during previous economic crises, many labor organizations had become strong enough to survive hard times. When, in 1898, Manhattan consolidated with Brooklyn, Queens, Staten Island, and the parts of the Bronx it had not already annexed, workers and their movements were poised to play a major role in the new City of New York.

Artisan Labor in Colonial New York and the New Republic

I n New York City today one can buy artisan bread and beer, shop at an artisan market, and wear artisan jewelry or scents bought from L'Artisan Parfumeur.

But what does "artisan" mean, and why are producers and retailors so keen to identify themselves as such? Our contemporary sense of artisan clearly revolves around trust: it aims to inspire a buyer's confidence in the skills and integrity of the producer of their bread, beer, or perfume. In a world of mass-production by gigantic, global corporations, "artisan" celebrates the authenticity and virtues of the small scale, intimate, and local; an association with these characteristics and qualities is the premium sought by small and, disingenuously, large enterprises.

This positive meaning of "artisan" has deep historical roots in medieval and early modern artisanal or workshop economies. These small-scale enterprises mostly served local customers and were later eclipsed by larger factory producers that competed with anonymous others in international markets. Historians continue to debate the precise character and timing of this transition, which took place over several centuries. Most agree that it transformed the fortunes of tradesmen who comprised as much as 40 to 50 percent of New York City workingmen in the 18th through early 19th centuries. In addition, the shift to factory production changed the relationship of artisans and skilled workers to their wider social context.

In the medieval and early modern eras the separation that we take for granted today between government, society, and something called "the economy" was unthinkable. Instead, villagers, townspeople, county and provincial societies, and emerging national polities, along with their various leaders and administrative institutions, assumed that commerce—especially that associated with the supply of food and other household necessaries—was intimately related to the public good. Accordingly, the private interests and ventures of those who were responsible for making and distributing necessary commodities and services had public consequences and were therefore regulated by formal laws, customary practices, and community expectations.

This meant that city artisans worked to provide for themselves and their families—what colonial Americans called earning their "competence"—and, only after this, to earn a profit. The ability to earn one's living as an independent artisan differentiated free and skilled workers from dependents such as servants and those who worked for others for wages. Artisans also observed regulated public duties; for example, to provide support and training for their apprentices, to produce goods and services of an acceptable quality and standard, and, when required, to sell their wares at set prices. Of course, observance and enforcement of these many and varied regulations and expectations varied enormously, but the assumptions concerning these occupational duties formed part of a broader framework of social obligations on men and women—as householders, masters and mistresses, taxpayers, and militiamen—that they manage their affairs according to the laws and established norms. Public obligations and duties were thus balanced by privileges afforded to particular occupations (such as influence over local markets) and to resident artisans as freemen of the city. One significant privilege enjoyed by city freemen over visitors and strangers was protection from having one's property summarily seized in cases of debt. This bundle of identifications

**Barrel Makers,
1794–1870**
Wood engraving by
Alexander Anderson

———————————

Nineteenth-century
New York artisans,
like those depicted by
Alexander Anderson
for his print-making
business, followed work
traditions dating back to
the colonial era and
early modern Europe.

gave the occupation of baker or butcher or brewer its social meaning and status. Thus the 16th-century English humanist Thomas Starkey counted "artisans (of good occupation)" as essential to "the ground and foundation of this our commonwealth." It was this sense of the word that European colonizers brought to New Amsterdam and, later, New York; its resonances continue to inspire marketing campaigns to this day.

Artisans in New Netherland

The earliest artisans in New Amsterdam likely came as employees of the Dutch West India Company, established in 1621. The Company was a military and trading venture intended to harry the Spanish, with whom the Dutch were fighting a lengthy war for independence, while profiting from New World commerce. New Amsterdam, on the tip of Manhattan Island, was the main port from which the Company planned to administer its monopoly of the fur trade in its northernmost territory, New Netherland. It soon became apparent, however, that illicit trade by locals and interlopers and the considerable costs of supplying the colony made a profit unlikely. The Company eventually threw open the fur trade and promised to govern "according to the style and order

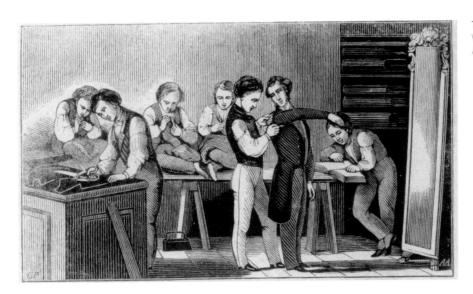

Tailors, 1794–1870
Wood engraving by
Alexander Anderson

of the province of Holland and the cities and manors thereof." Eager to reduce its costs, the Company dismissed all carpenters, smiths, and masons and ordered that they be "left to work for whomever will pay them." The reforms transformed New Amsterdam, drawing in free merchants, farmers, and artisans who complained when officials failed to administer affairs in ways they expected as Dutch citizens.

In 1645 the Company appointed a new governor, Peter Stuyvesant, who worked with local merchants to introduce a civil court modeled on Dutch practice. The court established the burgher right (full citizenship) for registered freemen and extended trade privileges for select occupations. For example, after years of intermittent complaints regarding the supply and quality of local bread, city bakers agreed to bake bread of regulated weights and qualities and to sell it at set prices, in return for special access to city markets and regular reviews of the terms of their trade. In the next decade, the partnership between the Company and its residents and artisans transformed New Amsterdam from a fractious frontier settlement into

an orderly and prosperous seaport town of 1,500 souls.

In 1664 the English conquered New Amsterdam and New Netherland renaming both the city and colony "New-York." As far as the city's government was concerned, however, by signing "Articles of Capitulation," they had preserved their cherished city properties and rights, while simply substituting one distant European overseer for another. Over the next three decades New York became, in many respects, anglicized: newly arrived imperial officials, merchants, and artisans increased the number of English colonists from a dozen or so to 110 in the first 10 years. During the same period, however, the city also welcomed Jewish and French newcomers, including hundreds of Huguenot refugees, giving the still predominantly Dutch town a polyglot and pluralistic feel. New immigrant merchants established powerful families and, in partnership with existing Dutch dynasties, secured lucrative concessions in provincial lands and international trade in return for supporting the crown. The newcomers also included English and French artisans and, in 1670, a promotional pamphlet noted

**Coffee pot,
1756–1760**
Silver and wood, made
by Myer Myers.

Jewish silversmith Myer
Myers belonged to New
York's diverse commu-
nity of English, Dutch,
French, and German
artisans. His colleagues
elected him chairman of
the city's Gold and Silver
Smith's Society in 1785.

and English artisans who felt disad-
vantaged by the Anglo-Dutch mercantile fleet and Stuart regime. Later,
under the new, Protestant succession
of William and Mary, and facing 20
years of war with France and its Indian allies, New York artisans initially
eagerly re-embraced the protection
of the British Empire. But in 1696 the
crown established a Board of Trade.
One of its earliest campaigns was
against Caribbean piracy. New York
shipwrights and other trades had actually benefited from the pirates, who
brought their ships to the city for re-
pair and resupply, frequently paying
locals with much coveted Spanish
silver. Tensions between locals and
imperial officials remained a problem, and New York's governor, Lord
Cornbury, captured the mercantilist
mood when he described the colonies as "but twigs belonging to
the Main Tree" and, as such, "entirely dependent upon and subservient
to England."

Over time, however, the benefits of empire outweighed the
restrictions on local production
and interests. In 1715 the Treaty of
Utrecht settled English and French
differences (for the time being)
and brought peace to the sea lanes,
allowing New York farmers, coopers, dockers, boatmen, sailmakers,
rope makers, and innumerable
others to join the hugely profitable
trade supplying the burgeoning
southern and West Indian slave
colonies. New York City flourished.

that "For tradesmen there are none
but live happily there as Carpenters,
Blacksmiths, Masons, Tailors, Weav-
ers, Shoemakers, Tanners, Brickmak-
ers, and so many other trades."

Below the surface, however, the
city was troubled by religious differences, economic ups and downs, and
fears of French and Indian attack.
Artisans' relationship with the royal
government was similarly complicated. In the wake of the collapse of the
English Stuart monarchy in the 1688
Glorious Revolution, New York wit-
nessed its own uprising, named for
its leader, Jacob Leisler, whose key
city support came from local Dutch

Artisanal Varieties

Thus far, one could be forgiv-
en for thinking that colonial
artisanal skills and production
were the sole preserve of European
immigrant and native-born white men,
but this was far from the case. The
enduring image of an individual
skilled tradesman at work alone or

with his apprentices and journeymen belies the complexity of early modern social relations. Preindustrial productivity, whether on farms or in workshops, was a mostly household affair, combining the labor of husbands and wives, children and kin relations, servants, slaves, and day laborers. Hudson River farmers and city artisans alike relied on servants and slaves to meet the growing demand for local harvests and artisanal products and services. Fugitive slave advertisements regularly listed the skills that would identify a runaway: in 1715 Governor Robert Hunter observed that a recently manumitted butcher's slave had "by his faithful and diligent service...helpt to gain most part of his master's Wealth." Indeed, in the 1730s artisans unable to afford their own slaves complained of their more successful peers and the "pernicious custom of breeding slaves to trades." By the mid-1740s slaves comprised more than 20 percent of the city's population: more than half of city households owned at least one slave, the highest concentration of slave labor in a British colony north of Virginia.

Beginning in the Dutch era women also worked in artisanal trades, especially provisioning and victualling. Although evidence suggests that many were pushed out of the tavern trade following the English takeover and the introduction of new licensing laws. Thereafter the common-law principle of coverture rendered married women, and their property and labor, the possession of their husbands. However, legal prescription rarely, if ever, maps directly on to social practice, and sources such as depositions and account books provide plenty of evidence of married women working as midwives, teachers, and housekeepers, and alongside their husbands as victuallers, bakers, butchers, and shoemakers. The growth of consumption in household goods, as well as the rising interest in English fashions, also provided opportunities for men and women working in luxury trades as silversmiths, furniture makers, seamstresses, milliners, and, especially, shopkeepers, in which trade women may well have predominated. Also, as well as the formal artisanal economy, historians have recovered the work of laboring men and women, servants, and slaves in the informal economy, which provided illicit access to supplies of rum and tobacco, and services necessary for a career in the underground economy as a smuggler or petty criminal.

Another common assumption is that colonial tradesmen dedicated their time to working at their trade in a way largely unchanged since late medieval Europe. This impression is understandable if one focuses on tax lists or the registers of freemen, on which individuals usual identify themselves with a particular occupation or trade. However, the court records concerning artisanal activity tell a different story, demonstrating that from the late 17th century city bakers, butchers, shipwrights, and the rest divided their energies between their formal occupations and all manners of commercial enterprise. Artisans relied on credit to finance ventures exporting furs, tobacco, and plantation supplies, and importing household goods, cloth, and slaves; they bought, sold, and rented property; they farmed and raised livestock; and they (or their wives and female family members) provided housing and domestic services to lodgers and paying guests.

In fact, far from concentrating on one occupation in a workshop,

Builders, 1794–1870
Wood engraving by
Alexander Anderson

city artisans participated in whatever opportunities promised a return. Inevitably some did well and rose up the social scale to become wealthy members of New York society; others did not. By the mid-18th century two men who claimed the occupational title of brewer or shipwright might occupy very different positions in the city's social and economic hierarchy. The established language of civic rights and trade privileges endured, notwithstanding the growing inequalities in artisanal ranks. However, claims for public rights based on artisans' public duties increasingly appeared as a cover for cynical protectionism. In the 1730s city butchers protested

the presence of competitors from the countryside in local markets but were quieted when they secured the right to sublet market stalls on advantageous terms. In 1747, 95 building workers styling themselves as "ancient freemen" petitioned for protection from New Jersey interlopers who came to the city "after the laying of taxes" and then left "carrying away Such Moneys so Surreptitiously got here" without buying any local materials nor so much as "a pair of Shoes." On this occasion the municipal authorities rejected the petition, noting that some had signed twice and that others, who claimed rights as "ancient freemen" were wholly unknown to the city.

Artisans and Politics

Artisans' diverse commercial concerns drew them into political struggles between local landed and mercantile elites who competed for popular support. In the 1730s, the

trial of John Peter Zenger—a printer who was charged with seditious libel for publishing a paper critical of the royal governor—provided a particularly rich example of the growing significance of artisans' political support. The Zenger case was actually a contest between provincial oligarchs over the spoils of patronage, dressed up as a constitutional dispute concerning free speech and English liberties. As the controversy broke, city trade also suffered a series of body blows: a smallpox outbreak prompted the flight of wealthy residents; imperial regulations imposed new import duties and ended a promising trade in the manufacture of hats; local credit collapsed, bringing unprecedented numbers of debtors to the Mayor's Court. Artisans petitioned for debt relief and the protection of local markets. The anti-governor opposition drew upon the contemporary language of radical Whig political rhetoric (named for the parliamentary opponents to the Stuarts in the 1680s) and blamed the city's troubles on a corrupt and inept governor and his party, mobilizing city artisans as "honest" and "virtuous" workingmen against a tyrannical administration.

At mid-century a similar combination of economic distress and appeals to republican and Whig political ideals presaged the arguments that pitched New Yorkers into the American Revolution. The problems began with the fallout from the Seven Years' War, known in the colonies as the French and Indian War (1754–1763). Imperial conflicts had long produced a cycle of boom and bust in colonial seaport economies. Wartime investment brought lucrative contracts for shipbuilders, blacksmiths, coopers, and mariners and for provisioning trades from foodstuffs to clothing, shoes, and weapons. Wars also meant privateering opportunities for large and small investors, bringing booty and specie to the local economy. The

Seven Years' War, the last and greatest 18th-century war between the major European powers in North America, brought unprecedented earnings and growth to New York.

But when Britain won a comprehensive victory over France and Spain, London authorities tightened regulations on colonial trade and acted against smuggling to assist in covering its war debts and administrative charges. The result in New York was a deep recession, worsened by a surge in population driven by European migrants who competed for increasingly scarce artisanal work. London pushed on with new import duties and limits on issues of

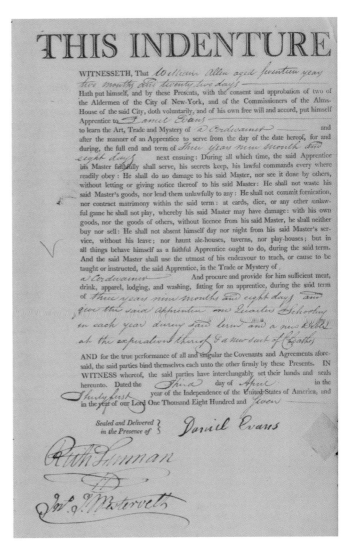

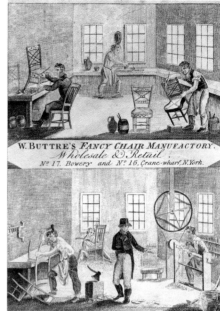

colonial paper money. Amid formal constitutional remonstrances and increasingly riotous street protests, imperial legislators introduced a Stamp Act, taxing paper products to cover the costs of a standing army. What began as colonial resistance to ill-conceived policies morphed into a bitter and principled struggle in defense of cherished liberties. Provincial elites dominated the formal congresses and written protests, but the force of colonial resistance depended on the thousands of artisans and laboring folk who took to the streets, preventing the implementation of imperial reforms.

Reports of mobs rampaging through colonial towns confirmed London officials' already dim view of disaffected American challenges to what they considered reasonable and necessary reforms. In 1765 New York's governor, Cadwallader Colden, reported that the farmers and artisans who comprised the "strength of the Province" were mere "Dupes" of merchant leaders who used them as "Tools for the worst purposes." However, the street protests were far from unruly mobs or mere tools manipulated by the elite, and protestors rapidly developed into organized groups, such as the Sons of Liberty, led by artisans. These "middling" residents had long served as minor public figures, trusted to settle neighborhood disagreements, or as minor municipal officials or jurymen, or in local fire companies. Most of the time they deferred to elite leadership; however, as the imperial crisis deepened, previously unknown artisans and others came to the fore in defense of their traditional liberties and "competence," which they considered foundational to the public good. Patriots from different social classes joined together in a "common cause," each offering their own form of virtuous self-sacrifice: the wealthy relinquished profits from the import trade and served in provincial and later continental congresses; artisans and laborers endured deprivation, enforced consumer boycotts, and served in the militia and, later, the Continental Army.

Revolutionary loyalties are difficult to pin down. Individual motives—

relating to family and county affiliations, religion, and landed or commercial interests—led some artisans to support the patriots and others to remain faithful to the crown. Even within patriot ranks, there was no uniform revolutionary ideology to which all subscribed. American republicanism ranged from radical democratic views infused with class-conscious egalitarianism to conservative and propertied perspectives favoring an independent republic governed by traditional elites. In the early years, key questions—relating to consent, representation, and virtue—were sufficiently malleable to allow for collaboration in the struggle for independence. City artisans' claim to virtue resided in their self-sacrifice and qualities as sober,

self-reliant, and respectable men, while the claims of wealthy merchant grandees rested in their selfless management of the public good. Both were considered essential to the foundation of the republic. However, as wartime shortages, currency inflation, and suffering began to bite (for some, more than others), divisions opened up. Now radical voices cried for the confiscation of loyalist estates and greater democracy in government, believing that "the security of American liberty requires a more equal distribution of property than at present"; conservative Whigs, who were socially closer to loyalist estate owners, feared a wider social revolution and called for restrictions on the franchise and protections for private property rights.

Cabinetmaker's tools, c. 1790
Owned by Stephen Alling Halsey

Stephen Alling Halsey, a cabinetmaker and carpenter in Manhattan during the early 19th century, later became a fur merchant. He gave these tools of his first trade to his son John Jacob.

Artisans and the New Republic

In late 1780s and 1790s the divisions between radicals and conservatives and their constituencies largely persisted: conservative Whigs, led by the patrician merchant-landed elite, became nationalists and then Federalists, and they campaigned for stronger national government to sort out interstate rivalries and public finance, curb the wilder sentiments of "excessive democracy," and project a credible impression to the European powers, whose covetous interest in the potential of North America remained undiminished. The popular and more radical Whigs became the Antifederalists and then Democratic Republicans. They tended to be more suspicious of connections between wealth and power and earnest in their calls for direct representation. Ultimately Federalists came to accept a republic based on principles of consent and popular sovereignty and Republicans supported the Constitution and advocated change by peaceful means. Thereafter both sides competed for the support of city artisans by appealing to the spirit of economic independence captured by the slogan that adorned the "flag of cream colored silk" carried on demonstrations by city skinners, breeches makers, and glovers: "Americans, encourage your own manufacturing."

The struggles between Federalists and Republicans launched America's first political parties and changes over the next two gener-

The Federal Plan Most Solid & Secure
Americans Their Freedom Will Endure
All Arts Shall Flourish in Columbia's Land
And All her Sons Join as One Social Band.

SOCIETY of PEWTERERS

SOLID AND PURE.

ations recalibrated the relationship between skilled workers and wider society, finally supplanting the particularistic claims of colonial artisans with universal claims on behalf of free and waged labor. The development of canals, roads, and railways knit previously disparate farming and urban producers together into regional and national markets that made the United States an international economic power. The availability of credit and new sources of power and technological innovations encouraged investment in industrialization and the employment of workers drawn from a population that rose from four to 32 million by

the eve of the Civil War. The national economic growth brought new markets for city artisans, who refined their working practices, reduced costs, put work out to poorer laborers, and profited from new opportunities. When a French nobleman, Alexis de Tocqueville, toured America in the 1830s he found prosperity among ordinary people that contrasted sharply with the poverty common in French society: "Here freedom is unrestrained," he noted, "and subsists by being useful to every-one."

There were, however, uncertainties as well as opportunities and losers as well as winners. As Tocqueville also

Banner for the Society of Pewterers, 1788
Painted silk

Carried by pewterers in a 1788 parade celebrating ratification of the US Constitution, this banner shows the shared labor of an artisan workshop and the mutual support masters and journeymen believed they owed each other.

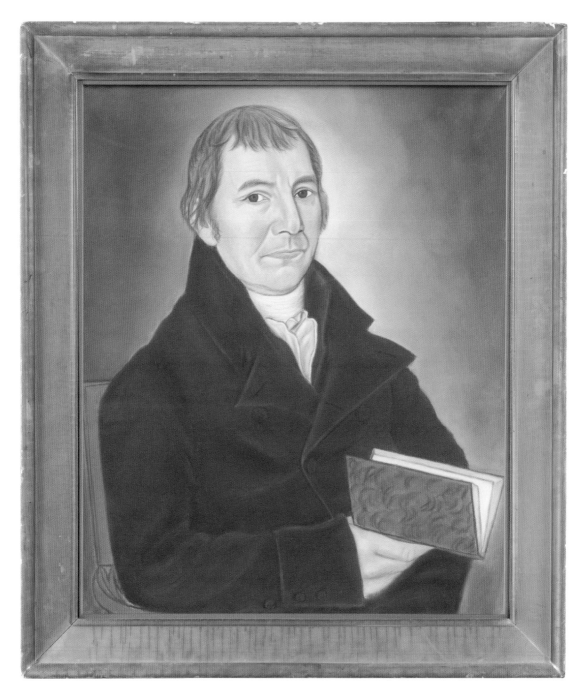

Clarkson Crolius, c. 1817
Pastel on paper by
Micah Williams

Master potter Clarkson
Crolius (1774–1843)
used his family's
successful business to
launch a public career
as a city alderman, state
assemblyman, and early
railroad investor.

noted, American "wealth circulates
with inconceivable rapidity, and
experience shows that it is rare to
find two succeeding generations
in full enjoyment of it." In areas
such as shoemaking, furniture
making, and the garment trades
the division of skilled trades into
simple, repetitive tasks and the
competitive advantages achieved

by larger productive units forced
smaller, independent operators out
of business. As one tailor wrote in
complaint to the *New-York Tribune*:
because one skilled cutter could cut
enough garments for 300 sewers
(usually low-paid German and Irish
immigrants) some city clothiers
produced ready-made garments
so cheaply that it forced "many an

honest and hardworking man out of employment."

But it is important not to be too misty-eyed about the demise of the workshop economy, which, as we have seen, had long pursued opportunities and profits. In fact, it was primarily the labor-intensive trades that experienced the greatest difficulties. Construction trades, baking, butchery, and shipbuilding continued much as before, and new trades, such as plumbing and machinery, flourished under the new circumstances. Nevertheless many artisans and skilled workers perceived the power of the market as a deleterious influence, not just on their living standards, but also on their status as independent producers and virtuous citizens with a crucial role in sustaining republican values of liberty and independence. Thus the febrile democratic politics of the Jacksonian Era featured debates concerning the dangers and possibilities of capitalist production and exchange: workers with no job security and a pittance for pay complained of being no better off than the slaves put to work on southern plantations; not so, their employers retorted, because as waged laborers and equal subjects they were free to choose to work or not according to voluntary contracts. Over time this clash between labor and capital—and justifications of the market economy that depended on the averred virtues of free, waged workers—fed into antislavery debates and a conflict that brought the republic to a bloody civil war.

Price list for stoneware made by Clarkson Crolius, 1813

Jug, c. 1810
Salt-glazed stoneware with cobalt oxide decoration, made by Clarkson Crolius

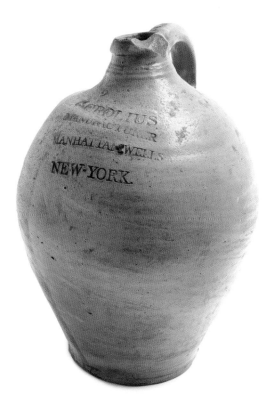

Slave Labor in New York

T he enslavement of people of African descent is a critical part of the first 200 years of New York City's labor history.

By the time the Dutch West India Company had gained the monopoly on New Netherland, founding New Amsterdam in 1624, African slave labor was a proven, foundational path to wealth in the New World. The Company, itself, was a key player in the international African slave trade, supplying slaves to the Dutch colonies of Curaçao, Aruba, Bonaire, and, briefly, Brazil. Although the shipment of African slaves to New Amsterdam was haphazard for the first 30 years of the city's existence, as the Company focused on supplying Caribbean sugar plantations with slaves, African slave labor was key to the colony's labor force, and, over the course of Dutch rule, was the most consistent element of the laboring class there. The slave population increased after 1654 as the Dutch began efforts to develop New Amsterdam into the leading North American slave port. When the British took over the colony in 1664, renaming the colony and the city "New-York," they, too, were commit-

ted to making the city the leading slave trading port in North America, and they continued the employment of enslaved men, women, and children throughout the city.

Although neither the Dutch nor the British were able to make Manhattan North America's leading slave trade port, their commitment to slavery as a labor system imprinted the city's population and labor practices. By the end of the 17th century, New York City had a larger black population than any other North American city. Whites of all classes held an ambivalent stance toward people of African descent. Dependent on slave labor to develop the infrastructure of the colony and for the economic wealth that slavery promised, whites often feared or resented this oppressed class in their midst. Elites, particularly those governing the colony, relied on enslaved men's potential military strength as well as the wealth slave labor brought, but they sought to reinforce enslaved people's status on the lowest rungs

of society at every turn. From the 17th century through the first third of the 19th century, white workers were forced to compete and/or collaborate with enslaved people of African descent. And as the city entered the era of gradual emancipation in 1799, during which time children born to enslaved women would attain full freedom in their mid to late 20s, whites across classes reinforced an enduring legacy of inequality by excluding newly free blacks from more lucrative working-class jobs; limiting citizenship participation, specifically suffrage; and by ignoring the key role enslaved blacks had played in New York's first 200 years.

View of Nieu Amsterdam, undated

This engraving, adapted from an earlier print depicting colonists and enslaved Africans in Barbados, suggests the presence of bound labor in and around the Dutch port of New Amsterdam on Manhattan Island.

Slave Labor in Dutch New Amsterdam

Eleven enslaved men arrived in Manhattan in 1626: Paul D'Angola, Simon Congo, Anthony Portuguese, John Francisco, Gracia Angola, Big Manuel Gerritsen, Little Manual Minuit, Manuel de Reus, Little Anthony, Peter Santomee, and Jan from Fort Orange. These first 11 followed the pattern of enslaved people in most frontier colonies in the Americas, occupying a variety of laboring positions as determined by their owners. In this case, the slave owner was the Dutch West India Company, which used the 11 men to build the infrastructure of the colony, establish farms for food, and assist in defending the colony against Native Americans. The first European colonists lived in makeshift shelters after their arrival in 1625: trenches seven feet deep, lined with timber, and roofed with turf and bark. Enslaved men provided the initial labor to build more permanent structures, including Fort Amsterdam, completed in 1635 with a marketplace, houses, a church, a hospital, and a school within its walls. They also cleared the land, carved out roads, cut timber and firewood, and burned limestone and oyster shells to make the lime used in outhouses and in burying the dead. The Company established *bouweries*, farms just outside the settlement staffed by enslaved

people, over the course of the 17th century. These farms supplied food for the colonists and, eventually, for Caribbean colonies. By 1635 the Company had hired an overseer to set the pace for the enslaved workers, and, by 1639, Company slaves were housed in separate quarters. Slaves owned by individuals and households lived with their owners, sleeping in kitchens, stables, or attics.

As the New Netherland colony grew, the number of enslaved people grew as well, and the labor they performed expanded. There was no part of the colony's work from which slave labor was excluded. Few Dutch citizens wished to travel to the colony since the Netherlands was economically strong, with low unemployment,

Domestic slave, 1794–1870
Wood engraving by Alexander Anderson

As shown here, enslaved New Yorkers often worked as household servants, tending to the needs of their owners' families.

due in part to the nation's successful investments in American slave-labor colonies. Many Europeans who did settle in New Amsterdam preferred to become merchants or landowners, rather than manual laborers, and the Company did not establish the extensive system of indentured servitude in exchange for land that was the norm in the British Chesapeake colonies. The Board of Accounts on New Netherland argued in 1644 that "Negroes would accomplish more work for their masters, and at less expense, than [European] farm servants who must be bribed to go thither by a great deal of money and promises."

Such assumptions by the Company and by owners meant that those Europeans who were laborers in New Amsterdam felt themselves to be in unfair competition with enslaved workers. The Company was the colony's largest employer and paid poor wages; most colonial Europeans worked more than one job. An enslaved worker could be purchased for the same amount as a free laborer's annual wages. In 1628, only two years after the arrival of the first slaves, white workers tried to convince the Company not to train slaves for skilled jobs. In the 1650s European settlers began to argue that Africans were not as competent skilled laborers as Europeans. These attempts to exclude free and enslaved blacks from skilled jobs did not completely succeed, but they did begin a pattern of racializing jobs and skills in Manhattan.

Despite the protests of European workers, New Amsterdam was more dependent on slave labor in the mid-17th century than the southern colonies of Maryland and Virginia, which attracted greater numbers of British indentured servants during this time and had not yet established tobacco plantations rooted in slave labor. By 1638, 100 enslaved people of African

Chimney sweeps, 1794–1870
Wood engraving by Alexander Anderson

In the aftermath of slavery, free African Americans were often forced into the city's most unpleasant and dangerous work. Black children worked as sweeps, risking injury and illness by climbing up inside chimneys to clean them.

descent made up 30 percent of the population; and by the time the British acquired the colony in 1664, 375 blacks, of whom 75 were free, made up about 20 percent of the population. The labor of enslaved people in New Amsterdam extended beyond initial infrastructure and agricultural work. An enslaved man, Pieter, was responsible for the physical punishment, including whipping, maiming, and executions, of those convicted of crimes. And when the colonists went to war against Native Americans enslaved men were expected to participate in the colony's defense. Enslaved people recognized the dependence of the European colonists on their labor and military potential. They used this limited power and their own knowledge to gain some autonomy.

For their part, European colonists also, at times, attempted to appease the slaves. In 1628 the colony brought three enslaved women to New Amsterdam "for the comfort of the Company's Negro men." Given that there were at least 11 enslaved men in the makeshift barracks to which the women were brought, these women should be understood, first, as sexual laborers. The Company may have hoped that by addressing the enslaved men's sexual desires, they would be more quiescent, perhaps less likely to run away to Native American settlements, or to build relationships with European women. It is unlikely that the Company hoped to foster families for the sake of the men or as a way to greater wealth for themselves. At this time few European owners encouraged enslaved people to form families either for moral reasons or as a way to expand their wealth by raising children for sale on the slave market. This was particularly true for individual slave owners in

New Amsterdam who often owned only one or, at most, two slaves and could not afford to buy or house additional enslaved people for "comfort"; indeed, many may have hoped to trade slaves for the greatest profit. Additionally, in the eyes of slave owners, a single-slave household or even a household with two enslaved people would have had difficulty supporting an enslaved child until she was old enough to contribute as a laborer. But despite the limited view of the Company and individual owners, and a sex ratio among the enslaved of 131 men to 100 women, enslaved men and women did form families in New Amsterdam over the course of the 17th century.

In 1644 the first 11 enslaved men used their key role as military laborers and their knowledge of European ways to negotiate for freedom. These men have been identified by historian Ira Berlin as Atlantic Creoles, people of African descent who had gained knowledge of European languages, cultures, and laws, and were able to use this knowledge on their own behalf in ways that would be difficult in the 18th and 19th centuries after the creation of stringent slave codes. These enslaved men had already petitioned the Dutch government for wages they felt the Company had withheld from them unfairly; a few had taken colonists to court for harming livestock they owned and other such offenses. As additional enslaved women were brought to the colony, the men formed families with them that were central to their negotiations for freedom. The men requested freedom not only for themselves, but also because they were "burthened with many children so that it is impossible for them to support their wives and children, as they have been accustomed to do, if they are to continue in service to the Company."

In granting freedom to them and their wives, Company director Willem Kieft and the New Netherland Council both recognized their "many years at service" and that they had "been long since promised their freedom." The men and their families were granted land that became known as the Free Negro Lots, on the site of present-day Washington Square Park. By 1664 the number of black landowners had grown to at least 30 who had been freed under similar conditions by the Company or by individual owners and who lived in multiple locations in lower Manhattan outside the city walls. But the colony retained access to their productive labor by requiring an annual tribute of "thirty skepels (bushels) of Maize, or Wheat, Pease or Beans, and one Fat hog valued at twenty guilders." The men were also "obliged to serve" the Company "by water or land, where their services are required, on receiving fair wages from the Company." Failure to provide these annual tributes or labor could result in re-enslavement. Most important, the Company retained ownership of the men's children: "With express condition, that their children at present born or yet to be born, shall be bound and obligated to serve [the Company] as Slaves."

Slave Labor in British New York

By the time the British took over the colony in 1664, slavery was firmly entrenched in the city and in North America. The British granted the colony to the Duke of York, who had a controlling interest in the slave-trading Royal African Company and sought to make the New York colony a leading market for slaves. Indeed, British rule would coincide with the expansion of slavery in Chesapeake, which reinforced the desire of Europeans in Manhattan to make the port city the slave trade capital of North America. They would not succeed: Newport, Rhode Island, soon became the leading North American center of the slave trade. But the emphasis on African slave imports meant that the New York colony expended little effort encouraging European free or indentured laborers to settle there. As a result, relatively few entered the labor market, which increased the city's reliance on slave labor. Between 1698 and 1738, the slave population increased faster than the white population, and slave values rose, too: in 1687 a healthy male slave sold for £16, and for £100 by 1760. By the early 18th century New York had become the site of the largest urban slave population in North America, a position it would hold until displaced by New Orleans and Charleston in the mid-18th century.

The increased emphasis on slave labor and slave trading in New York was also influenced by the development of tobacco plantations in Chesapeake and the concomitant development of slave codes there. Virginia's and Maryland's slave codes designating slavery as a status only for people of African descent and limiting emancipation and mobility for slaves and the rights of free Blacks were paralleled in New York. In addition, the desire for slave labor on Chesapeake plantations by the early 18th century increased the investment of New York City and other northeastern merchants in the slave trade. Those slaves who New York City merchants could not sell south or to the Caribbean immediately, or even in the longer term, remained in the city as laborers. Slave traders waiting for a lucrative sale hired out their merchandise to New York City employers as a way to make money. New Yorkers owned slaves in larger percentages in the city than would be true in the antebellum South.

In total, 40 percent of New York City households, ranging from those of wealthy elites to artisans with home workshops, owned slaves, usually in small numbers, given the relatively small spaces within which these urban families lived. Enslaved people worked alongside whites in these households, with little personal space, often sleeping in kitchens, attics, or stables. Such conditions limited their ability to form independent families. As under the Dutch, British slave owners did not encourage marriage and childbearing as a way to increase their wealth, as it was more lucrative to invest in slave ships traveling from Africa to the Caribbean and North America. Indeed, some owners attempted to sell enslaved women who had too many children; as one owner said in an ad for the sale of his enslaved female, "she breeds too fast for her owner to put up with such inconvenience." It is unclear who would purchase such a slave, as most Manhattan slave masters actively discouraged their slaves from marrying or having children and appear to have prized infertile women who would focus on providing their households with domestic labor.

As under the Dutch, white workers in some professions pro-

tested the use of slave labor to little avail. The licensed porters, who carried goods and materials on foot throughout the city, complained to the Common Council in 1686 and 1691 that slave owners were circumventing the law that gave them a monopoly on the movement of imported and exported goods by

26

BUTTER-MILK.

. . . .

" *Butter-Mil-leck.*"

A black man, pushing a wheel-barrow before him, cries aloud, "butter-mil-leck." This sells at three cents the quart. It is a wholesome and safe drink in summer ; and, with bread, or wheat flour, boiled and sweetened with sugar or molasses, makes very agreeable diet : and the good house-wife, by hanging it, mixed with other sour milk, over a slow fire, turns it to a curd ; and, with the ad-

The Cries of New York, 1808
Printed by S. Wood

Whether free or working for white owners, African-American vendors were part of New York's early 19th-century street life, as these pages from an early children's book reveal.

dition of a little butter, salt, and sometimes sage, makes what is called pot-cheese. It is made into round balls, and brought to market for sale ; and is good food.

ONIONS.

"*Here's your beauties of Onions : here's your nice, large Onions.*"

THEY are raised in the greatest quantities in Weathersfield, which lies about four miles south of Hartford on

receive, legislation to protect their share of the market. Only cartmen, who hauled goods in horse-drawn carts, succeeded in excluding blacks, slave and free, from their trade. The heavy use of slave labor in New York ultimately limited the migration of European laborers to the city for much of the period before the American Revolution. Fewer European indentured servants listed Manhattan as a destination, compared to Philadelphia and Boston. Although governmental officials and private citizens bemoaned the relative lack of European laborers, little was done to limit the purchase of slaves or the use of slave labor in the years before the Revolutionary War.

The increased reliance on slave labor in British New York and North America led to greater restrictions on enslaved and free black people. New York slave codes established nightly curfews, limited the number of enslaved people who could gather in one place, defined how funerals and other religious services for slaves should be performed, and created a host of other laws that both reflected whites' reliance on slave labor and their fears of this population. The most important restriction was the disappearance of the possibility of manumission, even the limited "half-freedom" that had existed under the Dutch. Half-free blacks had gained full freedom and ownership of their "free Negro plots" as the Dutch turned over the colony to the British. Now fully free, these black landowners resented the new restrictions placed on them by the British. Some sold their land in the city and moved to more rural locales in upstate New York, in a search of greater autonomy. Those who remained in the city largely lost their land by the time of the American

using their slaves. The loss of income left the porters "so impoverished... they could not by their labour get a competency for the maintenance of themselves and families." In 1737 and 1743 New York's coopers (barrel makers) complained that merchants were using their own slaves to build barrels and requested, but did not

Officials worried that in freeing slaves, owners were shifting the costs of caring for aged or disabled African Americans onto taxpayers. When Nicholas Wyckoff of Jamaica, Queens, freed Cato, town functionaries approved, confirming Cato's "ability to provide for himself."

Revolution, and new laws prevented the purchase of real estate by blacks freed after 1712. Enslaved people were too valuable as labor in the city, or as trade goods to be sold south, to be granted freedom, and whites saw the control of free blacks as critical to the control of the enslaved population.

An increase in resistance and rebellion among enslaved people indicated the degree to which British rule differed from Dutch rule. The opportunities for testifying in court against whites, owning livestock, and negotiating greater autonomy, even if not outright freedom, had been replaced by a more rigid system that enslaved people openly opposed. They stole more cash, clothing, and food, and they ran away more frequently than they had under the Dutch. They gathered in small groups despite curfew laws and were sometimes hosted by laboring whites in informal taverns in their homes. On at least two occasions groups of enslaved people rose up in rebellion. In 1712 a group of newly arrived enslaved men and women set fire to an outhouse and then ambushed those whites who turned up to put out the fire, killing nine and wounding seven. New York's colonial militia and British troops quickly put down the rebellion. Six of the rebels committed suicide before their capture. Seventy others were arrested, 26 of whom were convicted and 21 executed.

In 1741 another series of fires led to the discovery of a widespread conspiracy that involved both enslaved blacks and laboring whites. Although relationships between black enslaved and white workers was tense and competitive, their shared work brought them together in interracial taverns, markets, docks, and ships, where they exchanged news and grievances against the city's elite. Some joined interracial criminal circles that fenced stolen goods. Others plotted the overthrow of the colony's elites. Enslaved men who felt they were being kept from their wives and families first openly expressed their displeasure by attempting to burn down the homes of their owners and parts of the city's fort. Investigation into this series of arsons led government officials to an interracial group of laborers who sought to achieve greater economic and political power in the colony. They made their plans in a tavern owned by the Hughsons, a white family that was equally frustrated with the economic situation in New York in the 1740s. In the end, trials resulted in the conviction and execution of 30 blacks and four whites; an additional 70 blacks and seven whites were convicted and banished from the colony, with enslaved blacks sent to Caribbean plantations.

In the aftermath of the conspiracy, New York's elites debated the dangers of slavery, although enslaved laborers were not the only ones implicated in the plot. In the end, white New Yorkers were unable to commit to ending slavery. Not only the labor performed by enslaved people in the city, but also the wealth they represented on the slave market, made it difficult for most slave owners and those who aspired to participate in the slave market to envision ending the system before the Revolutionary War. Even after the war, New York and New Jersey would be the last two northern states to end slavery.

Emancipation and Black Labor

New York ended its dependence on slave labor slowly. The movement against the enslavement of Africans developed among colonial Europeans over the course of the 18th century—most strongly among Quakers—and then accelerated amid the politics of the Revolutionary Era. Vermont, the colony with the smallest number of slaves, incorporated the end of slavery into its new constitution in 1777. Most other provinces or states enacted legislation to end slavery, usually gradually, as Pennsylvania did in 1780. Massachusetts ended slavery by judicial decree in 1784. New York State in 1799 and New Jersey in 1804 were the final northern states to enact policies to end slavery via gradual emancipation legislation. In 1817 New York finally passed legislation

Hot Corn Seller,
from the series
"Cries of New York,"
1840–1844
Watercolor by
Nicolino Calyo

Racism confined most
free African-Ameri-
can New Yorkers to
hard, low-paying labor
following emancipation
in 1827.

The Hot Corn Seller

to end slavery completely by 1827. In 1810 there had been 1,686 enslaved blacks in the city, making up 1.75 percent of the total population; by 1820, there were only 518 enslaved blacks, at .42 percent of the population. In New Jersey, the final few dozen enslaved people were freed by the 13th amendment at the end of the Civil War.

New York's struggle to end slavery enshrined the idea that slave labor and, thus, black people, were marginal to the economy, even as gradual emancipation provided slave owners with access to the labor of the children of enslaved mothers well into their twenties. No slaves were freed by gradual emancipation laws; rather, the children of enslaved mothers gained freedom after serving their mother's owners until the age of 25, if female, and 28, if male. In addition to providing slave owners with access to these children's labor,

these extended apprenticeships to freedom were rooted in the idea that people of African descent had been harmed by enslavement in a way that prevented their immediate and full acceptance into society as workers and as citizens. The New York Manumission Society, founded in 1785 and the central organization advocating emancipation, argued for the immorality of slavery, the need to educate former slaves, and for the incorporation of free black workers into the economy. But many of its elite members were, themselves, slave owners who only slowly released their slaves.

Whites' limited view of the foundational work enslaved people had contributed to New York for nearly 200 years of its history became clear as slavery moved into its final decade. New York State legislators anticipated slavery's end in drafting the racist provisions of the new state constitution in 1821. They revealed their fears of increasing numbers of New York City free blacks, in particular, claiming that they were most likely to "sell their votes to the highest bidder," and to follow the lead "of those...whose shoes and boots they had so often blacked." In other words, black people were unable to think independently as citizens and as voters, and that lack of independence was a result of enslavement as well as black inferiority. A few legislators, including John Jay's son Peter Jay, argued that blacks were not "naturally inferior" and that the impact of slavery on blacks was "fast passing away." Another legislator argued that blacks' service during the Revolutionary War proved that they were worthy of citizenship. But in the end, even as white men of all classes were welcomed into universal manhood suffrage without restrictions, blacks were only allowed to vote if they attained middle-class status through ownership of £200 worth of real estate.

The discounting of the history of blacks' labor under slavery accompanied increased segregation between black and white workers in New York. In the early 1800s, white workers turned to the Jeffersonian Democratic-Republican Party in opposition to the Federalists, who they felt were elitist and controlling. Federalists had largely supported emancipation; white workers thus increasingly disdained blacks as a key voting bloc that could prevent the rise of Democratic-Republicans. As the Emancipation Era wore on, white workers also sought to limit blacks' participation in public politics, disrupting their July 4th parades in celebration of emancipation and forcing blacks to march on July 5th. Finally, white laborers refused to work alongside blacks in skilled jobs, and employers increasingly refused to hire them. Black men and women were largely restricted to badly paid menial labor. As one employer said of his former slave, "The laws set him free and he left me—now let the laws take care of him."

Two hundred and one years after the arrival of the first African slaves in Manhattan and New York State, blacks had gained freedom. But by the time the process of gradual emancipation was largely complete in 1827, the majority of black men and women were limited to the lower rungs of the economic ladder in New York. They were prevented from participation in politics on the same level as whites. Their rightful place among the founding laborers of this country was largely forgotten.

George Cousin, the Patent Chimney Sweep Cleaner, **from the series "Cries of New York," 1840–1844** Watercolor by Nicolino Calyo

George Cousin the patent chimney sweep Cleaner

Sailors Ashore in New York's Sailortown

A visitor to New York during any given year in the late 19th or early 20th century would have encountered tens of thousands of maritime workers who temporarily called the city "home."

While the majority of their work took place at sea, sailors ashore in between voyages had a significant impact on the cultural geography of the city. Having spent months, and sometimes years, laboring away from land, sailors spent their time in the city navigating components of their shoreside lives, such as housing, employment, leisure, and charity and relief services.

Sailortown

By the mid-19th century, New York had become one of the most important port cities in the world. The completion of the Erie Canal in 1825—and the consequent opening of inland markets made accessible via the Hudson River and Great Lakes—combined with a deep and welcoming harbor to make New York an epicenter of international trade and maritime commerce. As the city became increasingly dependent on maritime shipping, an expanding "sailortown" district developed along New York's shorelines. Within this ghettoized district developed dense micro-economies of commercial, cultural, and social exchange that served the needs and desires of a uniquely transient class of maritime laborers.

A tour of New York's sailortown during the mid-19th century would lead down to South Street and Coenties Slip, along the East River underneath a canopy of bowsprits, rope, and sails from vessels that had arrived from all over the world. Bound by the East River and Dover,

New Bowery, Division, and Grand Streets, sailortown encompassed much of the First, Second, Fourth, and Seventh Wards in lower Manhattan. At its lower end, the river bent to the east; at its upper end, the river swung back around Corlears Hook, epicenter for much of the city's shipbuilding during the 19th century. Its streets were perpendicular to the river, on a different axis than any other part of the city, anchored, seemingly, on an entirely separate gravitational plane that gave it the resemblance of a vortex, with its streets, shops, residences, and inhabitants all clinging to an incline that led directly to the waterfront. Its center within a center, the heart of sailortown itself, consisted of the blocks between Cherry and Water Streets, from Cherry Hill (now Franklin Square) to Pike Street.

The lower blocks of the Bowery, which extended away from the waterfront off Catherine Street, were known as the "Broadway of Sailortown." The area contained a mix of high and low culture, famous for its theaters—Thalia, People's, Windsor, National, Harry Miner's—and, of course, its saloons, where a nickel glass of beer came with a cheap lunch. The cheekily named Mariner's Temple, a spot particularly popular with seamen, offered coffee, a stale roll, and pea soup for a penny. Boardinghouses lined every block, especially in the Fourth Ward. Word of infamous dives, such as the Bowery's McGuirk's, spread internationally, through advertising cards carried

South Street near Cuylers Alley, 1887
Collotype by Adolph Wittemann

For over a century, Manhattan's South Street waterfront was a dense zone of ships, docks, warehouses, businesses, saloons, and sailors' boardinghouses.

by seamen across the ocean to other sailors' boardinghouses all over the world.

Within these dense and narrow streets developed thriving networks of longshoremen, boat people, cartmen, waterfront vendors, merchants, importers/exporters, customhouse agents, saloon and grog-shop owners, boardinghouse and brothel keepers, prostitutes, nautical equipment purveyors, sailmakers, cordwainers, coopers, tailors, shellfish hawkers, thieves, shipyard laborers, harbor dredgers, and, of course, merchant seamen. As the shipping industry industrialized during the mid- to late 19th century and into the 20th, divisions of labor at sea became more pronounced, with fewer skilled seamen overseeing the arduous labor of engine-room firemen and wipers, or other backbreaking positions on deck. Often, these divisions were codified along racial and ethnic lines. Sailortown, by contrast, was a bona fide melting pot of humanity. The racial and ethnic makeup of sailors ashore, including men who spilled out of ships from the far corners of the known world, free African Americans, and a hodgepodge of Jacksonian-Era youths drawn from the rural frontiers of the nation to its most rapidly developing city, made New York's sailortown the epitome of 19th-century American metropolitanism.

New York's sailortown was a social, cultural, and economic cauldron, where merchant seamen struggled to maintain control over concepts of liberty and masculinity that they brought ashore and developed within sailortown communities. Sailors' mobility, a cherished right enshrined in the legal tradition of shore leave and a culture of transience that sailors' boardinghouses accommodated, posed a threat to the ideals of stable domesticity and Victorian-Era morality. This essential contrast produced a series of contests for control that sailors waged against exploitive agents of sailortown's economy and zealous waterfront reformers during the late 19th and early 20th centuries.

Sailors' Boardinghouses

At the epicenter of sailors' struggle for control over their own agency while ashore was the sailors' boardinghouse. Boardinghouses were a ubiquitous part of urban life for working people in the United States during the 19th century. By mid-century, the market for room and board for people on the move who did not own their own property, or who were in town temporarily, was booming. Spurred on by the rapid growth of cities and the development of a wage-dependent working class, boardinghouses catered to clientele that was, by definition, mobile, transient, and fundamentally unattached to the conventional anchors of typical home and family life. New York City epitomized these trends. Thomas Butler Gunn, writing in 1857, dedicated an entire volume to the varieties of boardinghouses that he encountered as a young man while living and working in New York. *The Physiology of New York Boarding-Houses* is an inventory of different types of boardinghouses, including "The Artists' Boarding-House," "The Medical Students' Boarding-House," "The Boarding-House Frequented by Bostonians," "The

Irish Immigrant Boarding-House," "The Chinese Boarding-House," and "The Boarding-House Where There are Marriageable Daughters."

In New York boardinghouses loomed large in the public imagination as supposed dens of wayward, unsupervised youths and urban dealers in vice, featured in spectacular national news stories about crime and murder. Merchant seamen became targets of anxieties about urban living by embodying a caricature of subversiveness: inherently transient, diverse in nationality and race, mostly young, unattached men, who were awarded "advance notes" upon signing shipping articles or paid off at the end of their voyages and prone to "sprees" within the labyrinth of sailortown's back-alley brothels and grog shops. Sailors' boardinghouses, specifically, accommodated a population of the city that was marginalized not only by the nature of the sailors' work, but also by their foreignness, the diverse native cultures that they brought ashore with them, and their isolation from the conventions of respectable society.

A review of the 1900 United

CHAPTER XXXI.

THE SAILORS' BOARDING-HOUSE.

IN that quarter of the town containing the two preceding Establishments, and within five minutes' walk of the latter, stands the tenement now claiming our notice. Like the Irish Immigrant Boarding-House, its exterior is that of a low tavern, and of equally repulsive aspect. A fancy marine title over the door, and an American flag stuck out of an upper window—as attractions for sea-faring men—indicate the purpose to which it is devoted.

The landlord claims a Portuguese origin, but his fleshy, aquiline nose, protuberant lips, and small eyes, are unmistakably Hebraical—to say nothing of the remorseless wrinkles of his evil face. He has made a voyage or two in some unknown capacity, and assumes the *bonhommie*

Sailor, 1857
Illustration from the chapter "The Sailors' Boarding-House" in *Physiology of New York Boarding-Houses*, by Thomas Butler Gunn

States Federal Census reveals the profound multicultural diversity for which sailors' boardinghouses provided refuge and cultivation. Census data also reveals that sailors' boardinghouses ranged from small endeavors intended to help support families to large-scale business enterprises. For example, at 109 Cherry Street, a 48-year-old man born in Greece named George Peters and his 35-year-old French wife, Annie, took in six boarders to support their thirteen-year-old daughter and three sons, aged fourteen years, three years, and eight months. The entire family lived in the residence alongside their boarders and a hired cook. Each of the six boarders came from a different country of origin: one was born in New York, one in Russia, one in Sweden, one in Scotland, one in Denmark, and one in Turkey. The boarders ranged in age from 22 to 35 years. They were all single men who had spent an average of two years in the United States. The census lists the occupation for all six men as "Seamen."

Ninety-six Oliver Street was a much larger-scale operation, hous-

ing 61 boarders, all of whom were born in Spain. While it seems that houses with boarders of mixed nationalities were not uncommon, it was also not uncommon for boarders of the same background to congregate together under the same roof, whether of the boarders' own volition or according to the preferences of certain boardinghouse keepers. All 61 of the Spanish seamen were single and of an average age of 27.2 years. Twenty-eight did not speak English, and, on average, the boarders had been in the United States for less than five years.

Within the marketplace of sailortown, boardinghouses provided space and mobility for proprietors and boarders from even the most marginalized racial and ethnic groups. Eighty-nine Roosevelt Street was a black sailors' boardinghouse owned and operated by Henry Young, born in Barbados, and his African-American wife, Margaret, born in New York. The couple had been married 21 years as of 1902, according to a register of licensed sailors' boardinghouses, and together housed 11 boarders, all of whom were recorded as "B" (black) for their race, and all listed "Sailor" as their occupation (except for one "Cook," who also likely worked on ships). The nationalities of the boarders offer insight into the diversity of black seamen at the turn of the 20th century: three boarders were from Barbados, one from St. Thomas, one from St. Vincent, one from the Bahamas, one from France, one from Brazil, and one from Jamaica. All of the boarders except for one were single, with an average age of 29.1 years. Most of them had been in the United States for fewer than two years.

Reflected upon collectively, these snapshots of sailors' boarding-

Bar-room of a sailors' boarding house, 1857
Illustration from the chapter "The Sailors' Boarding-House" in *Physiology of New York Boarding-Houses*, by Thomas Butler Gunn

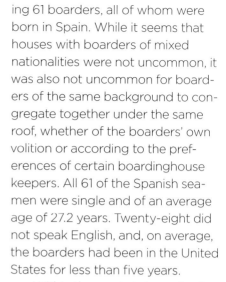

houses in 1900 represent a litany of causes for the anxiety that seamen and their economy of temporary housing in port provoked in the city's upper classes. A 1902 inventory of licensed sailors' boardinghouses reveals that there were 48 total houses registered in Manhattan, with many more, no doubt, operating illegally. Sixteen licensed houses, all on Cherry Street, operated on what would today be fewer than three city blocks. Marked by extreme geographic density at the margins of the city's lower wards, boarders also represented marginal ethnic and racial groups living in pockets of all-male "artificial communities." Further, most of these boarders were newcomers to the United States, some having arrived very recently

and, therefore, were unfamiliar with American social and cultural norms.

"Landsharks," 1857
Illustration from the chapter "The Sailors' Boarding-House" in *Physiology of New York Boarding-House*s, by Thomas Butler Gunn

Employment

Boardinghouses resonated in the nation's collective imagination because they lent clear and graphic evidence to perceptions of a rapidly changing society. The decades of the mid-19th century saw dramatic changes to commerce and agriculture and the seeds of an industrializing economy, including the rise of wage labor and the decline of a local, artisanal trade economy. The decline of the old system of apprenticeship was especially transformative. The erosion of an older paternalistic model, in which masters were expected not only to teach their apprentices a trade, but also to provide room and board, gave way directly to the rise of boardinghouses.

Sailors' boardinghouses were perceived as central sites in the network of crime, deceit, and extortion that marked the notorious "crimping" enterprise. In order to recruit newly arrived sailors to their boardinghouses, keepers frequently dispatched "runners" to the waterfront as soon as a ship coming into port was visible on the horizon. Runners would meet seamen, sometimes even owing out to ships before they reached the piers, in order to entice them to stay at their boardinghouse, often with offers of free or reduced prices on goods and services. Nefarious keepers were notorious for running up bills, falsifying accounts, and imposing bewildering debts on their patrons. Seamen caught in such schemes were forced to sign on for their next voyage and hand over a substantial amount or all of the advance pay to which they were entitled.

Boardinghouses also functioned as important nodes in the local maritime labor market. Due to their position as de facto holding centers for maritime labor pools, boardinghouse keepers often cultivated mutually beneficial relationships with ship captains and recruiters, who were constantly seeking men to crew their vessels. In turn, boardinghouse keepers collected commission fees for their role in supplying crews. For sailors, boardinghouses not only provided temporary room and board and a space for comradery with fellow maritime workers, often of a shared racial or ethnic background, but also functioned as a space for employment negotiations. Although tales of exploitation and nefarious crimps who preyed on naive or inexperienced seamen were based, at least occasionally, on the realities of the sailors' boardinghouse economy, more savvy or veteran sailors just as often made use of their temporary lodgings to structure their time spent ashore and negotiate the terms of their next job.

Conversely, because of their position at the center of sailors' labor negotiations, boardinghouse keepers had the potential to wreak havoc on the local shipping economy. They could distort the local labor market by withholding the supply of men and "tying up the whole port" as a negotiating tactic, as they did in New York in 1884 when legislation threatened to abolish the distribution of allotments except to direct members of sailors' families. Boardinghouses were also perceived as a threat to employers because of their role in corrupting the labor pool with liquor, bad behavior, and sexually transmitted diseases.

Reform

Nineteenth-century agents of maritime reform were among the first responders to the perceived threats that New York's rapidly developing sailortown posed. Beginning in the 1830s an onslaught of funding backed charitable initiatives aimed at providing not just housing, but services and moral betterment for merchant seamen in the Port of New York.

The American Seamen's Friend Society (ASFS), founded and organized in New York between 1826 and 1828, had, by the late 19th century, established a network of sailors' homes and seamen's missions in most of the major port towns and cities in North America, as well as certain ports in Europe, Asia, and Africa. In New York ASFS operated a sailors' home at 190 Cherry Street along the East River from 1842 to 1903 that was capable of housing 300 seamen. In addition, ASFS proposed establishing marine temperance societies in every port city, starting with the Marine Temperance Society of the Port of New-York, founded by members of the Roosevelt Street Mariners' Church in 1833. Also in 1833, Sailors' Snug Harbor opened in Staten Island, funded by a major bequest from Captain Robert Richard Randall, a wealthy former privateer and merchant who died in 1801. Sailors' Snug Harbor provided free lodging and the services of a resident chaplain for seamen who had sailed under the American flag for at least five years. Operations peaked in the late 19th century when more than 1,000 seamen called Snug Harbor home. Meanwhile, in 1843, the Protestant Episcopal Church Missionary Society for Seamen (later the Seamen's Church Institute of New York (SCI)) converted a fer-

Sailors' Snug Harbor, Staten Island, 1899
Photograph by Byron Co.

Snug Harbor residents worked on projects in their retirement home.

ryboat into a chapel and moored it permanently along the East River at the foot of Pike Street, starting a long period of confrontation for control of seamen's patronage amid the boardinghouses and saloons of lower Manhattan.

Reformers were quick to identify the sailors' boardinghouse as their primary target. As early as 1866 the New York State Legislature established by law a Board of Commissioners for Licensing Sailors' Hotels and Boarding Houses in the Cities of New York and Brooklyn. The act, titled "For the better protection of seamen in the port and harbor of New York," appointed representatives from a consortium of corporate bodies with direct economic or philanthropic interest in the eradication of the underground networks of sailortown's economies.

The most audacious effort to eradicate sailortown's underground social, cultural, and economic networks was the SCI's "million-dollar home for sailors" at 25 South Street, opened in 1913. At the heart of the new building were 580 dormitory

THE FLOATING CHURCH OF OUR SAVIOUR, FOR SEAMEN.

rooms, rented out at rates of less than 15 cents per night. It dwarfed all nearby sailors' boardinghouse in its 13-story shadow. During the 19th century, organizations like the ASFS had focused on religious conversions, through either baptisms or temperance pledges that signified the spiritual transformation of an individual's soul. In later techniques,

The Floating Church of Our Savior, for Seamen, **c. 1844**
Lithograph by George Endicott

This chapel was one of several floating churches established by 19th-century reformers seeking to convert New York's sailors to godliness and "clean living."

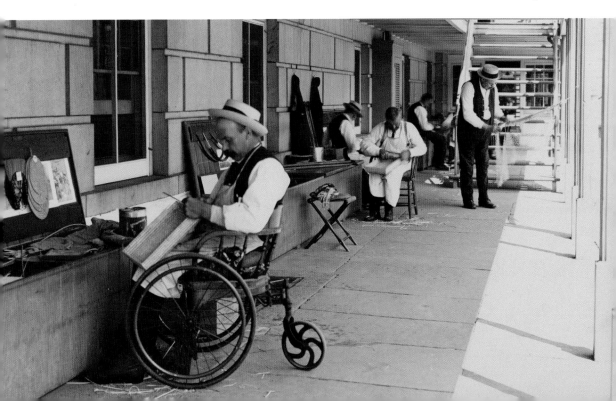

most obvious in the approach of
SCI "House Mother" Janet Roper,
conversions were less overtly spiritual and more focused on a secular,
moralized conversion from transient
waywardness to stable domestic
responsibility, often embodied in a
reconnection and commitment to
a feminine character (mother, wife,
or daughter). It is useful to consider
how SCI demonstrated its own conversions of maritime men, whether
spiritual or domestic, by taking
a closer look at the promotional
photographs that documented the
reformatory architecture of 25 South
Street's early years.

In a photograph shot from the
perspective of a pier directly adjacent to the towering superstructure
of 25 South Street (*page 46, left*),
two men sit at the edge of the
waterfront, their gaze turned inward
toward the building, rather than out
at the East River and harbor. The
background is out of focus and

overexposed, making SCI appear to
be the only option on the horizon.
The cornucopia of sailors' boardinghouses that had dominated sailortown are visually eradicated, despite
persisting in operation for decades
after the opening of SCI's headquarters. Much like the Titanic Memorial
Lighthouse that signals out to ships
at sea from its perch at the apex of
the building in this view, 25 South
Street projects a beacon of hospitality onto the waterfront. For seamen
returning to New York from their
voyages, their destination in port is
now an obvious choice.

Another image depicts a man
inside 25 South Street, clutching a
suitcase and peering warily out at
the cityscape (*page 46, right*). Outside the building appears a modern-
ist jumble of windows and high-rise
buildings, but the sailor is safely
ensconced within 25 South Street.
He still wears his jacket and cap
which, in addition to his suitcase,

suggests that he is newly arrived. The moment of uncertainty upon reaching port, in which the sailor must find safe room and board amid the urban chaos of lower Manhattan, is resolved. He is safe and at home at the Institute. Peering down on the city from his room, the sailor has avoided the temptations and dangers of the city by following the beacon to 25 South Street.

The details of a simple shot depicting a temporarily empty Savings Department reveal several points of SCI's revised maritime ministry strategy (*page 47*). A sign at the far-left side of the frame, likely near the entrance to the bank, reads: "BEWARE OF SHARKS AND CRIMPS OUTSIDE. LEAVE YOUR MONEY HERE. DRAW DAILY AS YOU NEED IT. WE SEND MONEY TO ANY PART OF THE WORLD. REMEMBER THOSE AT HOME." This in-

scription concisely and emphatically summarizes the SCI's intent in providing banking services for seamen. Outside of 25 South Street, crimps and sharks ruled the day. The bank, occupying a sort of liminal space between the streets and the Institute, was there for seamen who wanted to protect their earnings, whether their intent was to make use of it on their own terms, or to remit funds back "home." The sparse interior and collared clerk behind the barred teller window suggest safety, security, and insurance, all qualities that were at a premium when one found oneself on the streets of sailortown.

SCI's Employment Bureau (*page 48*) established direct working relationships with shipping companies in order to take over two of the most critical aspects of sailors' shipping articles: signing on and signing off. Instead of recruiting seamen from

Savings Department in the Seamen's Church Institute building at 25 South Street, 1915–1930

Employment office in the Seamen's Church Institute building at 25 South Street, 1920–1930

boardinghouses to man their vessels, shipping agents could look to SCI's 580 dormitory rooms, which provided an ample supply of men ready to sign on to their next ship. Undercutting the sailors' boardinghouse economy in this way meant that SCI prevented exploitation schemes involving sailors' advance pay or allotment notes. And, of course, SCI's Savings Department provided a repository for such funds, further ensuring that money stayed out of the hands of SCI's old enemies, the crimps. Control over hiring, including the right to sign sailors on and off voyages with companies, remained one of the primary objectives of maritime unions until the 1930s, when union halls finally took control from shipping companies and third parties like SCI. In the meantime, the Institute worked hard to distinguish itself from nefarious hiring practices then prevalent in the city's sailortown.

In a staged scene from a later

era of the Employment Bureau (*page 49*), a suited administrator reviews a sailor's paperwork as a trio of oddly bemused men look on. The younger man, on the right, nonchalantly holds the stub of a cigarette between his fingers and reveals a cluster of tattoos on the back of his hand, visually marking him as a sailor. If this scene is meant to depict a payoff, the sailor who is about to receive his compensation is in the good company of his jovial colleagues, rather than the prey of sailortown's crimps. The well-dressed administrator consults his stacks of paperwork, bestowing on the transaction an air of officiality and legitimacy that contrasts starkly with sailortown's underground networks of labor exchange.

Employment Bureau in the Seamen's Church Institute building at 25 South Street, 1935–1950

Conclusion

Twenty-five South Street marked the culmination of long-standing contests between maritime reformers, exploitive agents of sailortown, and merchant seamen. In New York's sailortown, agents of maritime ministry and legislative reform eventually produced a behemoth structure with the intention of subsuming all forms of competing alternatives for seamen in need of temporary room and board. However, in spite of the impressive resources at reformers' disposal, merchant seamen resisted in struggles for control over the terms of their own social, cultural, and economic mobility in port, sometimes in solidarity with workers from other trades and even allied boardinghouse keepers.

Indeed, seamen had created their own history in New York as agents of labor activism and not just as objects of reform. Sailors resisted early efforts by waterfront reformers, which often aligned with attempts to staunch sailors' collective organizing. In December 1843 a mysterious visitor slid an incendiary handbill underneath the front door of SCI's New Sailors' Home at 338 Pearl Street, inviting the sailors who were present to join in protest in order to raise wages in port from $9 per month to $16. Despite the pleas of the Home's keepers to put aside such matters and keep the Sabbath holy, nearly 600 sailors turned out for a meeting at Burling Slip convened immediately adjacent to ongoing church services, according to the journals of the Home's own chief proprietor and chaplain.

During the New York sailors' strike of January 1869, more than 1,000 sailors marched through Manhattan's

***The Sailors' Strike—
Scene on Peck Slip
Wharf, New York
City,* 1869**
Wood engraving

Over 1,000 seamen
struck for higher pay in
New York in 1869.

lower wards for a full week and a half, demanding higher monthly wages and wage advances. Echoing earlier sailors' strikes in 1802 and 1834, the strikers were joined by artisans from other trades. The 1869 strike has been hailed by one historian as a "major expression of labor militancy by New York's seafarers before the rise of strong maritime unions."

Ethnically homogenous boardinghouses, such as the Spanish sailors' boardinghouse at 96 Oliver Street, served not only as shelter

the East Coast, a coalition of Spanish boardinghouse keepers publicly offered free room and board to striking Spanish firemen. Spanish sailors' boardinghouses were subsequently targeted by surveillance rings and police raids that attempted to undercut the strike's momentum.

These struggles would last well into the 20th century, through organized maritime workers' fight for control over the terms of their own labor. Early maritime unionism (a force on the West Coast since the late 19th century under the leadership of Andrew Furuseth), which previously represented a predominantly white, skilled membership, became increasingly motivated by rank-and-file sailors who demanded recognition of the principles of industrial solidarity, direct control over hiring and relief, and improved working conditions at sea. As economic conditions in maritime shipping tightened dramatically during the 1920s and 1930s, industrial maritime unionism found a home with communist waterfront unions and, eventually, the CIO-affiliated National Maritime Union (NMU).

Old battles over leisure, mobility, employment, and relief that had their origins in early contests for control of the sailors' lives ashore would continue along the waterfront in New York and elsewhere for decades to come.

for boarders, but also as a nexus for shared culture, comradery, and solidarity. During the 1912 Transport Workers' Federation strike, led by maritime workers who called for a general strike to shut down transport industries in port cities along

Housework and Homework in 19th-Century New York City

Housework is never done and is done over and over and over. Today, New Yorkers who flush the toilet or take a shower, turn up the thermostat or turn down the flame on their gas stove, go to the farmers market or order takeout, drop children off for day care or supervise a playgroup, run a vacuum cleaner or leave a check for a cleaning service, wash their underwear in the sink or pick up their laundry on the way home from work seldom have occasion to think about these tasks as labor.

In the 19th century all this work—paid and unpaid—took place in the city's dwellings and sustained daily life. But, in addition to the work of housekeeping, New York's houses also sheltered the most exploited labor in the city: the homework of sweated sewing and tenement production of cigars, toys, or artificial flowers.

Housework was never women's work alone—from a young age boys as well as girls performed daily chores—but women were primarily responsible for maintaining family health and well-being. That a good housekeeper saved money was a re-publican truism and a working-class necessity. Taking boarders to gener-ate cash also remained an essential strategy of New Yorkers' household economies throughout the 19th century, while domestic service had become the city's largest field of employment by mid-century. At the same time, the tens of thousands of women who made and finished goods for the market in their dwell-ings while caring for their families literally worked a double day.

Housework

From the Colonial Era, New York housewives had both super-vised and worked alongside the domestic "help" of slaves, young relatives, and girls formally appren-ticed to housekeeping. When New York passed a gradual emancipation law in 1799, one-fifth of the city's households owned a slave, the ma-jority of them girls or women. The law provided that children born to enslaved mothers after 1799 would remain indentured until early adult-hood, and in 1810 one-third of black New Yorkers continued to reside as workers in white households. By the 1820s New Yorkers were replacing bound or familial "help" with waged workers, but the association of domestic labor with servitude cast a long shadow. Where the ideal of republican independence implied the ability to spare a wife or daughter demeaning labor, the conditions of housekeeping became one of city's starkest markers of class division.

It is impossible to think about the history of housework without con-sidering the house as a workplace. Before 1830 the labor of providing water, heat, and light for urban hous-es differed little from that on farms, but in the city the heaviest and dirti-est work was exposed to public view. New Yorkers got their water from wells, pumps, cisterns, or rain barrels, and they used privies, chamber pots, and slop jars to dis-pose of waste. By the 1810s fireplac-es were giving way to the machinery of cast-iron stoves, but someone had to clean out the ashes, carry in and lay the wood (or, by mid-century, coal), and adjust flues and dampers to maintain fires for both heat and cooking. Since water tanks attached to the more elaborate stoves pro-

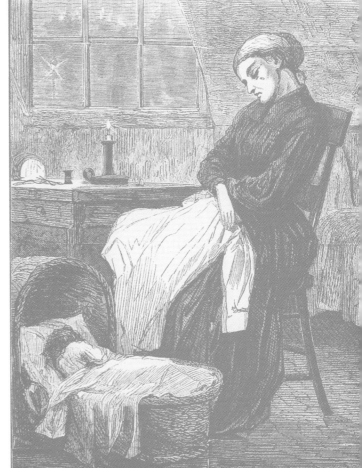

"Women and their Work in the Metropolis" (detail), 1868
Illustration by Stanley Fox from *Harper's Bazar*, April 18, 1868

"**Women and their Work in the Metropolis,**" 1868
Illustration by Stanley Fox from *Harper's Bazar*, April 18, 1868

This magazine engraving evoked the wide variety of wage work that women performed in post-Civil War New York City.

"*I Scrubs*," c. 1890
Photograph by Jacob A. Riis

Investigative reporter Jacob Riis identified the girl in this photograph as "Katie, who keeps house in West 49th Street."

vided hot water for washing, most women lifted kettles or tubs of scalding water a dozen times a day. In the early 19th century, city dwellers turned from candles to oil lamps, which required daily attention to filling, trimming wicks, and cleaning globes. Soot from stoves and lamps accumulated on every surface, which required wiping, sweeping, and mopping, as well as annual rituals of spring housecleaning to scrub floors, beat rugs or upholstery, and whitewash walls and ceilings.

Providing a dwelling's utilities was the first form of domestic labor to be replaced by fixed capital investment, primarily in the form of pipes. Health reformer John Griscom understood the connection. "If houses had water-pipes and drain pipes so that there should be no need of going into the streets to perform the mortifying duty of carrying water and emptying refuse," he observed in 1842, "many highly respectable but poor persons would prefer to do their domestic work themselves," rather than hire servants to preserve their social credibility. Dwellings built after the opening of the Croton Aqueduct in the early 1840s offered running water, though only houses at the top of the market included cellar boilers to heat it. The city's first purpose-built tenements for six or more families, constructed in the late

ELLEN (*loquitur*).—"Yes, Ma'am, I am goin' away this very day. I ain't a-goin' to spile *my* hands making two fires every day. I don't live in nobody's house, where there ain't a Furnace."

1840s, established cold-water flats as standard working-class housing well into the 20th century. The poorest New Yorkers resided in older, subdivided houses whose landlords only hooked up to water and sewer pipes when they thought they could collect higher rents to cover the cost. As late as 1894 Trinity Church, one of New York's largest slumlords, unsuccessfully challenged an 1867 law that required landlords to provide tenant houses with running water (as well as a toilet for every 20 persons). In 1900, when two-thirds of New Yorkers lived in tenements, hundreds of older walk-ups on the Lower East Side still relied on outdoor privies.

New Yorkers' search for better domestic workplaces drove the housing market, as thousands of families changed residence annually, and husbands and wives argued over whether they could afford well-equipped kitchens or rooms with bright windows. The city's wealthiest merchants and bankers established

their daughters' claims in such negotiations by endowing newlyweds with a "modern" dwelling upon marriage. Propertyless yet status-conscious couples in the middling ranks who could not afford rent and a servant's wages deferred "setting up housekeeping" by residing in hotels or well-appointed boardinghouses. After the Civil War the expansion of a salaried middle class of lawyers, accountants, brokers, and managers spurred the construction of apartment buildings, distinguished from tenements by the presence of steam heat, elevators, and plumbing, as well as janitors who kept the works running. The social cachet of these new "French flats" turned on whether or not apartments included "servants' quarters"—at best, 8-by-10-foot rooms off the kitchen (where servants, barred from their employers' bathrooms, washed themselves in the kitchen sink).

Perhaps nothing better captures the full fledging of the labor market

"The Miseries of Mistresses," 1857
From *Harper's New Monthly Magazine*, January 1857

The notion that middle-class and wealthy women were at the mercy of demanding or provocative servants—especially Irish ones—appeared frequently in magazines and newspapers.

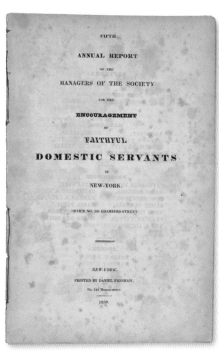

Fifth Annual Report of the Managers of the Society for the Encouragement of Faithful Domestic Servants in New-York, 1830

for domestic service than the organization of an employers' association, the Society for the Encouragement of Faithful Domestic Servants, in 1826, which launched the propertied elite's ceaseless complaints about the servant problem. Modeled after a London society, the New York City managers aimed to tame impertinent domestic workers' "love of change," but quickly discovered that not one of the 2,000 applicants for its placement service had lasted a full year in their previous job. Just as turnover in the housing market represented negotiations between husbands and wives over domestic working conditions, so, too, did servants take into account the qual-

The Intelligence Office, c. 1849
Oil on canvas by William Henry Burr

This Manhattan office scene depicts a prospective employer (right) choosing between two servant women—or deliberating whether to hire both—while a male job broker oversees the transaction.

ity of their workplaces in choosing their employment. Some quit "without notice or reason," as one angry member of the society complained, leaving his wife and daughter "to perform every drudgery above stairs" while he, himself, "had to make office, kitchen and parlor fires, hang on the tea kettles, bring up all the wood and coals, sweep the entries etc."

By 1855 more than 33,000 women were working as domestic servants in Manhattan's 42,668 residential buildings; or, measured another way, there were 260 servants for every 1,000 families. Immigrants constituted 93 percent of this workforce, three-quarters of them young Irish women escaping famine, with Germans, who more often arrived in family groups, composing another two percent. African Americans—fewer than two percent of the city's population—made up more than half of the native-born servants. Most white domestics were between the ages of 14 and 28 and left service upon marriage. Black servants continued to work well into middle age, even after they married and had children. In 1880 two-fifths of the city's female wageworkers worked as servants, and, even as that proportion dropped to one-third in 1900, Greater New York employed more than 100,000 domestics. Both second-generation New Yorkers and new immigrants from eastern and southern Europe preferred jobs in manufacturing, department stores, or offices; however, 89 percent of black women had no choice but to take waged housework. They transformed the job at the end of the century, though, by refusing to "live in," introducing instead the Southern practice of day labor.

The city's wealthiest households hired cooks and children's nurses in addition to chambermaids, but most servants did all kinds of housework. As was true of the vast majority of housewives who could not afford to hire servants, during the course of the day, domestic workers hauled water and fuel; set fires and emptied ashes; cooked, served, and cleaned up after meals; swept and scrubbed floors; dusted and polished furnishings; made beds; changed linen; mended clothes; minded children; nursed the sick; and ran errands up and down flights of stairs (as many as 40 times a day, one servant recalled). The work that went into preparing meals was but one instance of the differentiation of household labor by class. Servants for better-off families or boardinghouses did weekly marketing; received deliveries from butchers; stored provisions in pantry cupboards or iceboxes; cooked three meals a day, with soup, fish, roasted meat, vegetables, fresh baked bread, and pastries for dinner; and washed up numerous pots, pans, plates, cups, saucers, and flatware. Working-class wives scavenged coal or purchased it by the scuttle; bargained daily with neighborhood grocers or peddlers; often bought, rather than baked, bread to spare fuel; and prepared cabbage soups or stews with stringy meat and potatoes in kitchens that doubled as bedrooms, with children underfoot and no space for storage.

When servants had any bargaining power, they demanded that their employers hire out the heaviest work—carrying coal, scrubbing pavements, and, especially, cleaning laundry. In antebellum New York African-American women with families of their own to maintain both carried bundles of dirty clothing, towels, and blankets to wash in cauldrons

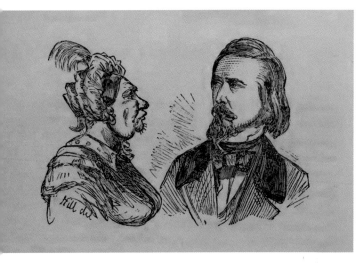

Boardinghouse keeper and boarder, 1857
Illustration from *Physiology of New York Boarding-Houses* by Thomas Butler Gunn

Caricatured and maligned, female boardinghouse keepers were a staple of guidebooks and satirical literature in 19th-century New York.

in their tenant-house yards and did laundry in their employers' basement kitchens. Laundresses filled, lifted, and emptied tubs of steaming water saturated with corrosive soaps and bleaches; scrubbed on washboards; wrung each piece out by hand (or, occasionally, with mechanical wringers); hung laundry to dry; and then, on the following day, used as many as four different kinds of irons to produce the impeccably clean, starched, and pressed shirts, collars, blouses, sheets, and table linens that signified their employers' refinement.

Countless pages devoted to investigating the servant problem produced the same findings decade after decade. Not only was the labor from six o'clock in the morning until ten at night physically exhausting, but servants also described the soul-crushing isolation imposed on them by employers who spoke to them only to chastise or give orders, expected them to wear uniforms ("livery"), prevented them from socializing with their peers, and permitted, at best, only Thursday and Sunday afternoons off. In 1858, when the physician William Wallace Sanger reported that half of the 2,000 prostitutes he interviewed had previously worked as servants,

it was not hard to link their "demoralization" to the "insults" and "indignities" domestics faced from male employers and their sons. Sanger, himself, emphasized that as many as one-quarter of the city's servants were "constantly out of employment" and turned to sex work for better wages until they found a new place. Still, domestics earned six to eight dollars a week with room and board provided—considerably more than seamstresses. Hating the humiliations and drudgery associated with service and changing jobs frequently, New York's servants, nonetheless, deposited more money in the city's mutual savings banks than any other wage-earning group in the city. They had no time of their own in which to spend it.

Although upper-class employers expressed the greatest indignation at their servants' "faithlessness," at mid-century the majority of servants earned wages in households that also took boarders to generate cash. "Two-thirds of New Yorkers are boarders," one journalist joked in 1871, "and three-thirds of the houses take boarders." Boardinghouses, many operated by widows, ran the gamut from quasi-hotels with as many as 20 residents to households that accommodated two or three boarders "in the family way." By the 1870s New Yorkers had designated row houses between 14th and 34th Streets from Second to Eighth Avenue the respectable "boarding district." "I have been in the business thirty years," one widowed proprietor on 23rd Street told a reporter in 1889, "and I tell you to keep a boardinghouse is the most cruel and thankless way a woman can earn her living." She had started out with a house on 14th Street, and, since then, all she could recall was "a stretch

of weary days and sleepless anxious nights," with "continual hoping, striving, and toiling crowned with so small a portion of success....it is all thorns." It was bad enough to be "treated as if she were a sort of an upper servant," the widow said, "even the law seems to be against you. In almost every other business written contracts are made," but boarders had "ample latitude to leave you, perhaps in mid-season with unrentable rooms and no redress." The economic depression of the 1870s had hit the industry especially hard, as middle-class boarders took up "pocket housekeeping" in lodging rooms or flats where wives cooked meals on gas burners.

As boardinghouses declined as an institution for middling households, tens of thousands of immigrant wives continued to provide for boarders, including extended kin and *landsmann*, without the assistance of a servant. Novelists from Abraham Cahan to Anzia Yezierska vividly portrayed the fraught relations between housewives, desperate to add income, and their demanding and unreliable boarders. By the early 20th century housing and health reformers who led campaigns

against overcrowding were surprised to discover that families with annual incomes of $800—considered the minimum for a comfortable subsistence—chose to rent four- or five-room apartments in "new law" tenements, equipped with better utilities, in order to take boarders. Whatever benefits a housewife gained in working conditions, the presence of boarders troubled reformers, not because they meant more labor, but because they were "strangers" intruding into the family circle. It was only when New Yorkers gained better wages that the practice began to decline among white, working-class families with access to industrial jobs.

It is impossible to calculate the value that unpaid and paid housework contributed to New York City's 19th-century economy. We attribute the spectacular rise in real estate values to the constrained supply of land, the level of investment in construction, or the demand generated by population growth, but it was women's labor that both made houses habitable and maintained a neighborhood's social and, hence, economic credibility. Manufacturing censuses counted the output of goods, not "services," and fragmentary statistics on income overlooked both the cash saved by housewives and the cash earned by taking boarders. As labor reformer Helen Campbell observed in 1893, even the millions of dollars that flowed annually through the aggregate hands of servants and laundresses found no entry in studies of gross national product. Historian Jeanne Boydston has argued that the value of domestic work was realized and expropriated by employers who could pay male workers lower wages and count on wives to make up the difference necessary for subsistence. Only since the late 20th century have historians tried to measure the economic value of unpaid household work alongside the value produced in the service sector of restaurants, commercial laundries, hospitals, schools, day cares, janitorial staffs, or "temporary" house cleaners. Still, if scholars have struggled to integrate domestic economy into their understanding of political economy, 19th-century manufacturers had little trouble appreciating the economic value of having household workers cover overhead costs through homework at the same time that they eked out subsistence from exploitative wages.

Homework

Antebellum housekeeping included making and mending men's shirts, women's dresses, and children's clothing, and girls learned the skills of sewing from a very young age. However, by the mid-19th century "homework" associated with the needle carried a very different connotation than "housework." Where shoemakers had long relied on the assistance of wives and daughters to stitch uppers and soles,

Sewing Pants for the Sweater—in Gotham Court, **1890**
Photograph by Jacob A. Riis

Jacob Riis photographed these Italian immigrant homeworkers sewing in their Lower East Side tenement apartment, where the mother finished about 30 knee-pants a day for "a cent and a-quarter a pair."

subcontractors in that trade sent out batches of cut leather to tenant families to finish the shoes. Merchant tailors also turned to outwork to supply the ready-made trade in men's trousers and shirts, shipped to the slave South and agrarian Midwest. Visitors to the poor and health reformers, alike, described the desperate condition of hollow-eyed, starving needle workers, whose piecework wages were reduced even further as clothing manufacturers introduced sewing machines into their lofts after 1855.

Homework exploded as ready-made men's clothing became the city's dominant industry during and after the Civil War, and women in tenements, often assisted by children, sewed seams, hems, collars, or buttonholes for subcontractors. By the late 1870s homeworkers were not only stitching and finishing men's clothing, but also women's underwear, petticoats, and all manner of dress decorations, from fringe and braids to embroidered "frogs" used as clasps. Cigar manufacturers created their own system of homework by leasing entire tenement buildings and renting rooms only to Bohemian cigar-making families whose rent the manufacturers deducted from their piecework wages. When some of these homeworkers joined the Cigar Makers' International Union (CMIU) strike in 1877, they were immediately evicted.

Samuel Gompers, a leader of the CMIU in New York—and, later, the longtime president of the American Federation of Labor (AFL)—rejected a proposal by the union's socialist wing to organize homeworkers, backing, instead, an 1884 law that banned the production of cigars in tenements. Manufacturers hired William M. Evarts, the city's most prom-

inent lawyer; and, one year later, New York's highest court ruled the law unconstitutional in the case *In re Jacobs*. The ban violated a tenement cigar maker's liberty of contract, the judges said, "forcing him from his home and its hallowed associations and beneficent influences to ply his trade elsewhere." For a generation following the *Jacobs* decision, state and federal court judges struck down laws that aimed to improve industrial working conditions.

The hostility of the courts did not prevent New York's legislature from responding to the city's labor movement. Starting in 1887, and with many amendments over the next three decades, New York laws tried to regulate homework by requiring that tenements be inspected and licensed before a manufacturer could send out bundles of finishing work for 41 enumerated goods, from clothing to artificial flowers. At the turn of the century female labor reformers, many active in Florence Kelley's National Consumers League, associated with settlement houses, and members of the National Child Labor Committee, took up and publicized the cause of homeworkers, who earned from four to six dollars a week for 14-hour workdays during the six months of the "busy season."

By 1912, with garment makers' unions gaining strength, homework in the clothing trades had declined. Nonetheless, labor reformers reported that more than 100,000 New Yorkers—especially Italian mothers with young children—continued to make goods in their kitchens. Although, in response to health reformers' warnings about contagious diseases, a 1913 law banned home manufacture of food products and children's clothes, Italian mothers earned their meager piece rates primarily in embroidery

**Family Making
Artificial Flowers,
1910**
Photograph by Jessie
Tarbox Beals

Photographer Jessie
Tarbox Beals noted that
the mother and children
pictured earned 20
cents per gross of artificial roses, averaging two
to three dollars per week,
while their three-room
apartment cost $12 per
week.

and crocheting as well as by making
doll clothes, fly swatters, bonnets,
pinwheels, balloons, kites, buttons,
hair ornaments, pin cushions, and
dozens of knickknacks headed for
dime stores across the country.
Meanwhile, insisting, as they had for
decades, that homework allowed
women to earn "pin money" at
home, manufacturers conceded that
not only did women's homework
save them money on overhead, but
it also allowed them to charge the
same price for goods produced at
half the cost of "inside factory work."
The industrial homeworker "works
from necessity, not for pin money,"
responded Elizabeth C. Watson on
behalf of New York State's Factory
Investigating Commission, "and the
number of hours she works depends
upon her necessity. If she needs
to supplement the family income

by a dollar, she will work just long
enough to secure this dollar. If she
must have more, the hours will grow
longer until they extend far into the
night." Moreover, Watson wrote,
"the homeworker is rarely free from
family responsibility. Usually she
is a mother who must take care of
the children and the home and do
cooking, cleaning and washing for a
large family."

Again and again investigators
described dark, cold rooms with a
single sink and unlit stove, and homeworkers' families subsisting on strong
tea, bread, cheese, and sausages.
At the same time, homeworkers, like
most working-class wives, did their
family's laundry—including diapers—
two or three times a week. Indeed,
one investigator on Manhattan's west
side reported that although "cooking
and sewing are on the decrease"—

often to save the cost of fuel—wives were doing "more and more laundry work." The investigator noted, "The bed is left unmade while the only pair of sheets is being washed and dried; the clothes are boiled on the kitchen stove, filling the apartment with steam." Landlords of new law tenements "put up wash lines on the roof and do not allow them to be attached to the windows. This arrangement is not popular with the women, however, because clothes drying on the roof must be watched to prevent theft," interrupting their other labors.

Change and Resistance

World War I marked a turning point in all forms of housework and homework in New York City. As working-class New Yorkers poured into upper Manhattan, Brooklyn, and the Bronx, they were more likely to find apartments with full indoor plumbing, steam heat, electricity, and washing machines in the building's basement. African-American households, excluded from the broader housing market, continued to take boarders to offset high rents, but the practice steadily declined among second-generation white immigrant families. Manufacturers promoted the labor-saving convenience of new appliances—toasters, refrigerators, vacuum cleaners—as well as packaged foods. The majority of "maids" and "cleaning ladies" ceased to reside in employers' houses, instead doing daywork for multiple households. In 1880 Manhattan and Brooklyn had a ratio of 188 servants to every 1,000 families; by 1920, when only 13.8 percent of female wage earners were household workers, the ratio was 66 per 1,000, and the proportion of laundresses had dropped by a third. At the same time, reformers continued their campaign against homework until it was effectively suppressed by the fair labor standards of the New Deal.

Housework, itself, persisted. The exponential growth of the city's service industries after World War II has rendered the pecuniary value of the labor that maintains families and dwellings fully visible. Meanwhile, even if New Yorkers seldom count their own housework as labor, they know that it's still not done.

Paper flowers produced by a member of the Monturi family, 40 Downing Street, Early 20th century
Collected by the New York Child Labor Committee

Investigators seeking to end child labor collected this sample of artificial flowers made by 14-year-old Annie Monturi in a Downing Street apartment in the early 20th century.

Victims, B'hoys, Foreigners, Slave-Drivers, and Despots: Picturing Work, Workers, and Activism in 19th-Century New York

Nineteenth-century New York was a labor city—and a city that defined work, workers, working-class organizations, and the profound changes they underwent, for the nation.

It was the rapid rise of the city's commercial culture, especially its pictorial print realm, that shaped how labor was perceived—a veritable avalanche of visual media that was produced in New York and disseminated images into more American homes, businesses, social institutions, professional associations, and places of leisure than ever before. And over the course of the century, those public images altered, as their visual codes and characters were invented, adapted, and reinvented. Never static, those ways of seeing informed and influenced Americans' attitudes toward and beliefs about workers and activism.

From Tribulations to Troublemaking

The public visualization of New York workers was limited in the early 19th century. Master craftsmen, journeymen, and apprentices, the "mechanics" (to use the term of the day) who composed the city's various trades, carried flags festooned with emblems heralding their crafts in processions celebrating significant events. Master craftsmen distributed trade cards advertising their products and skills. But for the most part, neither work, nor workers, nor their organized activities—even when the focus of controversy or dispute—were shown in the newspapers and periodicals that comprised the major media of communication and representation during the early republic. This visual silence did not affect labor alone: most news and topical issues rarely appeared in any form other than textual accounts. The cost and labor of illustration was reserved for occasional plates in publications directed to a rarefied, affluent audience.

That situation changed in the third decade of the century with the introduction of lithography, an inexpensive process for producing tonal art via drawing on specially treated stones, and the simultaneous widening of voting for white men in an increasingly contentious political arena. New York quickly emerged as a center of lithographic printing, as numerous firms churned out bucolic prints to decorate homes, portraits of leaders and performers to inspire and delight followers, and topical images and political cartoons to stoke partisan politics.

After the financial panic of 1837 and the ensuing extended economic depression, more than one-third of New York's workforce was unemployed. As the downturn's devastating effects were still being felt, satirical prints in 1838 commented on the hard times, depicting the impact felt by New York's "mechanics." A prime example was the print *Sober Second Thoughts*, drawn on stone by Henry

Sober Second Thoughts, **1838–1839**
Lithograph published by H.R. Robinson

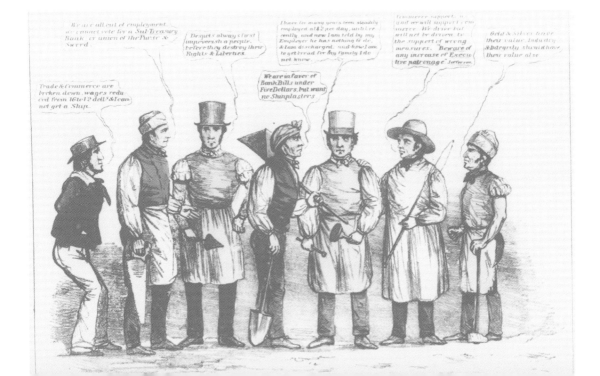

Dacre and published by the Manhattan firm of Henry R. Robinson (the foremost purveyor of political prints in the era). The image showed, perhaps for the first time, a cross section of the city's male workers (*page 65*). Lined up beneath text-heavy balloons, in the static poses and displaying the rigid features typical of antebellum graphic commentary, the seven figures were, nonetheless, immediately recognizable to contemporary viewers by the tools of their trades and their customary dress. Their grievances were equally familiar, ranging from denunciations of the fiscal policies of the Andrew Jackson and Martin Van Buren Democratic administrations (Robinson was an ardent advocate of the Whig Party) to descriptions of hardship and desperation. "Trade & Commerce are broken down, wages reduced from 16 to 12 doll[ar]s & I cannot get a Ship," declared the sailor, while his artisan companion testified, "I have for many years been steadily employed at $2 per day, until recently, and now am told by my Employer that he has nothing to do & I am discharged; and how I am to get bread for my family I do not know."

The theme of undeserved victimization extended beyond pictorial criticisms of monetary policies and depressions. As publishing in every form expanded in antebellum New York City, popular fiction trafficked in narratives that fueled their plots with the shifts in marketing and production that undermined longtime obligations and expectations among master craftsmen, journeymen, and apprentices. Many masters became employers, while journeymen descended into permanent wage work, often reduced to piece-work at home. As the most egregious example, New York's ready-made garment industry became the backdrop of melodramas whose illustrations captured the inherent exploitation. "Fob Visited by a Master Tailor on Broadway" (*page 66, top*), drawn by Charles Dickens's illustrator Hablot Knight Browne (better known by his pen name "Phiz"), from Cornelius Mathews's 1842 satirical novel *The Career of Puffer Hopkins*, rendered, in broad strokes, the growing distinction between masters and journeymen. "Down by three [p.m.], or I cut you off from our shop!" barks the "high and mighty master-tailor from Broadway." His prosperous

F.S. Chanfrau in the Character of "Mose," 1848
Lithograph by E.J. Brown

lone sputtering candle—as in an illustration by Winslow Homer before he gained recognition as a painter (*page 66, bottom*)—the seamstress was imbued with a sentimental narrative. The story of a respectable woman laid low by circumstance merged with the image to embody the exploitation in one of New York's major industries.

Meanwhile, the essential representative of male artisanal labor and urban masculinity was the strident, towering, irreverent, and belligerent New York Bowery B'hoy, epitomized by the character Mose the Fire Laddie. Introduced on stage in the working-class theater district in 1848 by the American actor Frank Chanfrau (*page 67*), Mose was a journeyman butcher, nativist, and volunteer fireman whose power stemmed not from his workplace or any work-related organization, but from the rough, violent, honor-driven gang culture (he was, in one of his catch-phrases, always "spillin' for a muss") that arose out of the collapse of traditional artisanal relations. A product of the Bowery's burgeoning commercial culture, Mose became a sartorial and behavioral model for young urban male journeymen and apprentices. His exploits were carried from the New York stage to other US cities via the dissemination of theater prints and the performances of traveling theatrical companies. Mose's public stature did not diminish until the New York City Fire Department was professionalized in 1865.

outfit, imperious stance, and fancy business address sharply contrasted with the journeyman character Fob's wretched appearance and dismal workshop-home.

But the most durable image of the exploited antebellum outworker was the seamstress, the unskilled woman working in her home, alone or with her family, the foot soldier of the city's ready-made garment industry. Appearing in reform publications, popular literature, pictorial journalism, and, especially, as a character in popular theatrical melo-dramas, the solitary, pallid, usually widowed mother became one of the most familiar figures in the iconography of antebellum work and workers. She also was the quintessential image of the "deserving" poor, in contrast to the "undeserving," primarily Irish indigent immigrants whose moral or innate failings, precapitalist folkways, and corresponding inferior work ethic brought misfortune upon themselves. Usually pictured bent over her sewing in a dark attic apartment, her work illuminated by a

By mid-century, an iconography of New York labor had been established in popular print culture, if not necessarily one truly reflective of the city's workforce. But a significant gap in the visual record of work and workers persisted in that, although very visible organized labor actions

"The Great Meeting of the Foreigners in the Park," 1855
Illustration by Cunnington from *The Crisis or the Enemies of America Unmasked* by J. Wayne Laurens

the Park" (*page 68*) accompanied a chapter describing a labor demonstration in New York's City Hall Park on January 15, 1855, demanding relief for the unemployed. According to the account by the tract's author, J. Wayne Laurens, the crowd of some 8,000 German and Irish demonstrators comprised a "mob of foreigners" whose demands told "the old story—foreign impudence imposing upon American forbearance; and American politicians exhibiting the basest subserviency to Foreign influence." The crowd pictured in the illustration might have seemed benign, but the demonstrators' demand for jobs, as well as the un-American appearance of their clothes and hats, indicated that "in case of refusal intimations of riot and violence to ensue, are distinctly given." With more than half of New York residents immigrants or the children of immigrants, this early visualization of militant labor offered a sinister message.

With the influx of immigrants fleeing the potato famine in Ireland beginning in the mid-1840s, the Irish laborer became the visual standard bearer of New York's unskilled, casual workforce and a pictorial stand-in for urban poverty. Readily recognizable in cartoons and illustrations via simian features, ragged clothes, and bellicose behavior (often fueled by liquor), the figure of the Irish laborer was a derisive admixture of ignorance and imminent chaos. It was one particularly favored as the butt of cartoons that, by the 1850s, were published as wood engravings in weekly illustrated newspapers and a panoply of periodicals devoted to humor. *Vanity Fair* was the most elegant and, for a time, most successful among the humor publications, containing the sharpest wit and some of the best art. By the

occurred, they were almost never rendered visually. The reasons were technological and financial: strikes were covered in the daily press, but newspaper illustrations, in the form of wood engravings, required laborious effort and were impractical for daily reporting, not to mention the fact that illustrations gobbled up valuable space for text or advertisements. Lithography firms tended to produce prints on topical subjects that guaranteed sales, notably disasters. After photography was introduced in 1839, its cumbersome equipment and slow exposure time limited what the medium could capture, and the method for reproducing photographs in print would be unviable until late in the century.

In that light, a crude illustration in an 1855 nativist tract entitled *The Crisis; or the Enemies of America Unmasked* is notable for being one of the first visual depictions of organized working-class action. "Great Meeting of the Foreigners in

"The Irrepressible Conflict," 1862
Wood engraving by Henry L. Stephens from *Vanity Fair*, August 2, 1862

start of the Civil War, the publication also epitomized the sentiments of War Democrats, supporting the war, but reviling Lincoln. Despite *Vanity Fair*'s political affiliation, it bore no love for the Irish working-class supporters of the Democratic Party—while, at the same time, reserving its cruelest, belittling humor for enslaved and freeborn African Americans. Occasionally, its derision accurately captured the state of the city's intra-class relations. Drawn by editor Henry Louis Stephens, "The Irrepressible Conflict" (*page 69*), published in August 1862, played on New York Senator (later Secretary of State) William Henry Seward's 1858 characterization of the fatal conflict between slave and free labor, but referred directly to longstanding tensions between African-American and Irish workers on the city's water-front. "It's lookin' for work ye are?" the cartoon's "Celtic Person" addresses a black longshoreman. "Well, ye may be a man and a brother, sure enough; but it's little hospitality ye'll get out of yer relations on this dock, me ould buck!" A little less than a year after the cartoon was published, white longshoremen and other Irish work-ers targeted African Americans in four days of rioting that began as a protest against conscription and quickly deteriorated into a pogrom.

Hard Times and Outside Agitators

Two significant changes oc-curred in the wake of the Civil War that substantially increased the visibility of New York labor—and especially the labor movement—for the city's and nation's public. The first involved the commercial success of two weekly illustrated newspapers, *Harper's Weekly* and *Frank Leslie's Illustrated Newspaper*, which both emerged in the latter part of the 1850s. The second was the rise of the move-ment for the eight-hour workday.

After years of effort, in the spring of 1872, New York's trade unions escalated their demand for the eight-hour workday and launched a strike wave that, by June, involved more than 100,000 workers, the largest combined labor action to hit an American city up to that time. Not-ing the recent workers' uprising and bloodshed of the Paris Commune, union opponents warned about radical European influences and imminent class warfare. A parade on June 10 to cap an ultimately unsuccessful citywide strike became an opportunity for pictorial media to visualize the "threat" facing the city. *Frank Leslie's* was most active among its peer publications in cover-ing labor activity. Along with most of the daily press, it declared the march

also weighed in regarding the dangers of the eight-hour movement. *The Days' Doings* was not reluctant to use lurid images. A page devoted to the protest included two pictures showing how foreign agitation led to murder in New York's streets, and want and neglect in duped workers' homes. But the largest image featured the exotic figure of Judith Marx, who was identified as an emissary from the European socialist International Workingmen's Association (IWA) and a niece of Karl Marx (*page 70, bottom*). The illustration and its accompanying description denounced "her inflammatory harangue"—highlighted by an oath to

'Conquer capital or die with it,' taken by a number of 'strikers' who had rented a cellar in Orchard Street...under the auspices of a 'Secret Labor Society,' known as 'the Supreme Mechanical Order of the Sun.' [L]ovely as was the speaker, and earnest as were the actors of the occasion, the scene was sadly out of place and time. It might have served its purpose in Europe, or in the Dark Ages, but was utterly opposed to the theory and practice of the City of New York in the Nineteenth Century.

Neither the person, nor presence, of a "Judith Marx" appears in the historical record, but the sexual intrigue she lent to the strike reporting of *The Days' Doings* enhanced the publication's claim that America's class warfare was a European import.

Work and labor actions nationwide were duly illustrated and disseminated after the coverage of the eight-hour movement. But the fact that, following the Civil War, New York was indisputably the locus of pictorial journalism publishing inevitably led

"New York City— The Eight-hour Movement...," 1872
Wood engraving by Matthew Somerville Morgan from *Frank Leslie's Illustrated Newspaper*, June 29, 1872

"The Great Strike— The Seed and Its Fruit...," 1872
Wood engraving from *The Days' Doings*, June 29, 1872

a failure, but submerged the much-bruited threat of violence in a dismissive image (*page 70, top*). Showing a snarling figure on horseback in the background, its engraving nonetheless featured a collection of "foreign" caricatures, whose aggression seemed fixed on the angle of their cigars. *Leslie's* concluded that the marchers were unrepresentative of the city's workingmen. They were a travesty of the true American worker who "certainly did not exhibit the manly bone and sinew of the land."

The less respectable, male-oriented, sensational illustrated weeklies

"The red flag in New York...," 1874
Wood engraving by Matthew Somerville Morgan from *Frank Leslie's Illustrated Newspaper,* January 31, 1874

to the city's workforce, labor organizations, and activism gaining a privileged place in visual reporting. In the process, they inspired a changing cast of working-class pictorial characters for public consumption.

Following the panic of 1873, one-quarter of New York's working population was unemployed. The misery of destitute families and efforts of private charities were covered in illustrated newspapers and magazines. But organized working-class actions calling for government work programs were depicted in visual terms that questioned the legitimacy of demands and the authenticity of activists. Scenes such as *Frank Leslie's* illustration of the police suppression of the January 13, 1874, Tompkins Square demonstration did not evoke sympathy so much as raise alarm (*page 71, top*). "The lower grades of workingmen of New York City, most of them Germans, Frenchmen and Poles" shown fleeing toward the viewer were betrayed by their scruffiness and foreign look as dangerous agitators with an un-American class-conscious ideology. Nonetheless, a month afterward,

"the change in public sentiment" prompted a cartoon in the often crudely illustrated *New York Daily Graphic,* rarely friendly to labor, by the well-known cartoonist Frank Bellew that was critical of the police (*page 71, bottom*).

As the 1870s depression continued, virtually all forms of pictorial publication found it necessary to contend with a new figure, at least nominally tied to labor, appearing

"The police and the Tompkins Square workingmen...," 1874
Illustration by Frank Bellew, from *New York Daily Graphic,* February 16, 1874

THE DAILY GRAPHIC, NEW YORK, MONDAY, FEBRUARY 16, 1874.

FREE SPEECH

Mony.—"It's no use saying any more close, Mr. Policeman, the case is in my hands."
THE POLICE AND THE TOMPKINS SQUARE WORKINGMEN.

in New York. Arising out of the depression, the itinerant, unemployed tramp, moving from city to city along the railroad lines, was a very visible reminder of the exigencies of the economy and a threat to the Gilded Age's cherished notions of civility and order. "The genus tramp," announced an 1876 *Frank Leslie's* editorial, "is a dangerous element in society, and ought to be dealt with accordingly." As depicted in a July 1877 cover engraving showing tramps' early morning disruption of fashionable Madison Square Park's tranquility (*page 72*), the depression's transient victims were no longer willing to haunt only the lowly districts of the city and countryside.

The depression and repression that greeted labor activism, culminating in the July 1877 nationwide railroad strike, drove many labor organizations into silence and secrecy. Media attention, including news illustration, moved away from New York for a number of years to cover western industries and work. But, in 1882, another depression descended on the nation, which sparked a new surge of labor militancy in the face of wage cuts, and the rise of a new national organization, the Knights of Labor. For the next few years, the labor movement's strikes, parades, conventions, and other activities preoccupied pictorial news and commentary, especially in New York. For city residents perusing the weekly pictorial press, humor publications, monthly magazines, and other visual media, labor appeared to be America's, and New York's, most challenging matter.

In contrast to the previous decade, 1880s visual coverage of New York labor bordered on the enthusiastic for a while, beginning with illustrations of the first Labor Day march in September 1882. Similarly, two years later, *Frank Leslie's* illustration of "The great labor parade" of September 1, 1884, notably played up the participants' respectable demeanor, praised the reasonableness of their demands, and, unlike in the 1870s, refrained from rendering their faces or dress using "foreign" stereotypes (*page 73, left*). "All the trades-unions were represented," declared the illustration description.

> A fine, orderly body of men... Banners with inscriptions and pictorial representations, such as that shown in our picture, were very numerous. They set forth the condition of the workingman of to-day, together with maxims calculated to inspire the laborer with a sense of the justice he should demand.

Yet, at the same time, the image of the New York worker was under-

**"New York City—A tramp's ablutions...,"
1877**
Wood engraving from *Frank Leslie's Illustrated Newspaper*, July 21, 1877

"New York City—
The great labor pa-
rade of September
1st...," 1884 (left)
Wood engraving from
*Frank Leslie's Illustrated
Newspaper*, September
13, 1884

"At bay: An incident
of the freight-han-
dlers' strike...,"
1882 (right)
Wood engraving from
*Frank Leslie's Illustrated
Newspaper*, August 5,
1882

going another change. With pictorial reporting on the 1882 freight
handlers' strike on the New York
and New Jersey waterfront, a new
disruptive force was introduced:
the immigrant strikebreaker. Epitomized by an August 1882 engraving
of a lone Italian strikebreaker under
attack by striking workers and sympathizers (*page 73, right*). "[He] has
taken refuge in a corner," elaborated
the description, "and drawing his
knife, he bids defiance to his pursu-
ers, who, much as they would like to
harm him, shrink from coming within
range of the ugly weapon wielded
by a man whose determined air
reminds one of a wild beast at bay."

Like other images of the strike, this
illustration was unsympathetic
about the immigrant's predicament.
Instead, it emphasized his dangerous
"foreign" appearance and behavior.
As Irish workers shed some of their
stereotypes (coinciding with their
broad participation and leadership
in the labor movement), signs of difference settled on immigrants from
Italy and eastern Europe.

Foes of Freedom and Fomenters of Mob Rule

By 1886, the Knights of Labor
had between 700,000 and
one million members across
the country, including 60,000 in
New York. In addition to resurrect-
ing and escalating demands for the
eight-hour workday, trade unionists,
especially in New York, instituted a
new tactic: the boycott. It was an
effective innovation that involved
workers refusing to shop at certain
businesses to win concessions. City
businesses that catered to work-

ing-class consumers were especially
vulnerable, and, as they raised the
alarm, condemnation of the tactic
spread through the popular press,
most visibly via cartoons by some of
the renowned illustrators of the era.

Prominent among them was
Harper's Weekly's Thomas Nast, whose
caricatures had played an instrumental
role in the demise of the Tammany
Hall Democratic Party machine in the
previous decade. Now, in numerous
cartoons, typified by Nast's May

THE ROOT OF THE MATTER.

Boycotter. "You must stop work, because I have a grievance against your employer, no matter whether you have any, or whether your family suffers meanwhile. I must show my power."

"À L'ORGUE"

[Two columns of small illustration caption text, largely illegible.]

"The root of the matter," 1886

Wood engraving by Thomas Nast from *Harper's Weekly,* May 8, 1886

1886 "The Root of the Matter," the labor movement was positioned as the un-American destroyer of individual freedom and an agent of mob tyranny (*page 74*). Brandishing a whip, the boycotter importuned an iconographic worker (identifiable by his tools, apron, and paper cap). "You must stop work because I have a grievance against your employer," he declares, "no matter whether you have any, or whether your family suffers meanwhile. I must show my power." Resembling Nast's caricatures of southern slaveholders a generation earlier, *Harper's Weekly* made the link to boycotters explicit. It denounced trade unionists' adherence to the boycott "at a mere sign from an overseer" and concluded, "No slave-driver upon a plantation ever exercised more cruel power than 'a

walking delegate'" (referring to the peripatetic union official assigned to inspect workplaces and confirm contractual compliance). By the middle of 1886, New York courts ruled that the boycott constituted a criminal conspiracy and indicted more than 100 organizers, many of whom would serve long prison sentences.

This new personification of the labor movement as a figure coercing the "rank and file" took yet another form later in the year when, after the boycott convictions, frustrated New York trade unionists formed the independent United Labor Party (ULP). The city became the site of the most prominent effort among a host of labor-reform political parties that challenged established Democrats and Republicans in fall 1886. Choosing radical Henry George as the ULP candidate for mayor, the coalition offered an already famous face (as the author of *Progress and Poverty,* the most popular book in 19th-century America) to represent the cause. Panicked by class issues subverting the usual New York electoral "horse race," as well as the large crowds and enthusiasm that greeted the insurgent candidate and his pro-labor platform, the city's major businesses, Democratic Party, and Catholic Church hierarchy mounted a concerted attack that incorporated an unusually uniform visual assault on the mayoral candidate (or, as he was often referred to, the demagogue).

For example, the satirical weekly *Puck,* known for its richly composed and sharply rendered full-color caricatures (replacing independently published topical prints in the nation's political culture), leapt into action. But instead of personifying the politicized labor movement (as in the recent image of a boycotter coercing the "honest laboring-man"), now *Puck*'s publisher/artist Joseph Keppler positioned ULP's delusory platform as the target. In "The Mephistopheles of Today," George stands atop the vanquished robber baron Jay Gould while emptying a cornucopia of tempting promises before the mesmerized gaze of an archetypal workingman. But it is all a hallucination wrought by the anarchy-accoutered devil (*page 75*). In the end, the ULP garnered one-third of the vote but could not overcome the working-class electorate's allegiance to the Democratic Party (although the chastened Tammany machine subsequently adopted some labor measures raised in the campaign).

The issue, *Puck* elaborated, was infection brought into the country by immigrants: "The men who applaud Mr. George are mostly the scum of Europe—the men who have made of this hapless city a Botany Bay of voluntary exile—the men who...blacken

the city's fame with riot and disorder whenever there is a strike among factory-hands or car-drivers." While the image of the labor movement as a bomb-toting anarchist was ubiquitous in the aftermath of the May 4 Chicago Haymarket bombing, it was the spring 1886 horsecar strike in New York that unleashed another type of identifiably immigrant terrorist. Although brief, it was the city's most extensive transportation strike up to that time—and whereas previously most strikes were portrayed as a struggle between labor and capital, now a third entity was added, the public. If not always visible, as in *Harper's Weekly*'s panoramic horsecar strike engraving, the public was implicitly the action's blameless victim, reliant on police violence for protection from labor (*page 76, top*).

Yet, for at least one *Frank Leslie's* issue, New York's labor movement was represented in a different way and by a different sort of figure: a

"The Mephistopheles of to-day—Honest labor's temptation," **1886**

Chromolithograph from *Puck*, October 20, 1886

PUCK.

THE MEPHISTOPHELES OF TO-DAY — HONEST LABOR'S TEMPTATION.

Brooklyn-born African-American man. The only black delegate among the 60 members sent by New York's District Assembly 49 to the Knights of Labor's national convention in Richmond, Virginia, Frank Ferrell became the focus of controversy when the delegation defied the city's segregation laws. Featured on *Leslie's* October 16, 1886, cover introducing Knights leader Terence Powderly to the convention, Ferrell embodied a link to the organization's professed goal of "social equality" in a rare,

"The street railroad strike in New York— The police opening the way for a horse-car," 1886
Wood engraving from *Harper's Weekly*, March 13, 1886

"Virginia—Tenth annual convention of the Knights of Labor...," 1886
Wood engraving from *Frank Leslie's Illustrated Newspaper*, October 16, 1886

FRANK LESLIE'S ILLUSTRATED NEWSPAPER

No. 1,621.—Vol. LXIII.]   NEW YORK—FOR THE WEEK ENDING OCTOBER 16, 1886.   [Price, 10 Cents.

GENERAL FITZHUGH LEE.

VIRGINIA.—TENTH ANNUAL CONVENTION OF THE KNIGHTS OF LABOR, AT RICHMOND—FRANK J. FARRELL, COLORED DELEGATE OF DISTRICT ASSEMBLY NO. 49, INTRODUCING GENERAL MASTER WORKMAN POWDERLY TO THE CONVENTION.
FROM A SKETCH BY JOSEPH BECKER.—SEE PAGE 114.

"The tyranny of the walking delegate...," **1889**

Wood engraving from *Frank Leslie's Illustrated Newspaper,* September 21, 1889

THE LABOR DESPOT.

THE supreme tyrant of the labor organizations is the walking delegate, the well-fed, well-paid official who performs the functions of a general overseer, and whose hat is expected to be obeyed without protest or murmur. Not a few of the disastrous strikes of recent years were prolonged, if they were not instigated, by these representatives of the worst elements of discontent. Happily American workingmen seem now to be losing their respect for this class of petty despots, and it is hardly probable that they will be able in future to exercise any such autocratic power as they have so ingeniously employed in the past.

It was the peculiarity of the recent great strike in London that it was spontaneous, that it was based upon a real grievance, was entirely free from coercive excesses on the part of would-be bosses, and that it had, from first to last, the genuine sympathy of the great body of the people. The sole obstacle to a settlement was the obstinacy of the dock companies, upon whom the demand for slightly increased compensation was made by the striking laborers. Against these stubborn dock directors were arrayed the merchants, the shipowners, and all the high officials in church and state, such men as Cardinal Manning, the Lord Mayor, the Bishop of London, and Sir John Lubbock interfering actively in behalf of the strikers, while Lord Randolph Churchill and other men in official life ably championed their cause in public addresses. It was inevitable that, thus sustained, the men on strike should ultimately gain a substantial victory. It will be well if American workingmen shall learn the lesson that, with a just cause, and abstaining from all disorderly and offensive methods, they, too, can depend upon public sympathy, and will be much more likely to win their way than when pursuing an opposite course.

defining image of New York labor idealism (*page 76, bottom*).

As the century waned, another *Frank Leslie's* cover offered a more pervasive portrait of New York's labor movement. The September 1889 engraving, "The tyranny of the walking delegate," showed a trade union official ordering construction workers to abandon a work site (*page 77*). In his appearance—carefully detailing his ostentatious dress, dangling watch fob, mismatched elegant top hat and loudly patterned trousers, smoldering cigar, broad girth, and blunt features—the trade union official no longer had anything in common with the men he was addressing. In the pictorial vocabulary of the time, little distinguished

him from a political boss.

The turn of the century personification of New York labor as a variation on the corrupt denizens of Tammany Hall would not be unchallenged. And the public image of the New York and national labor movement never settled on one type, icon, or symbol. In part, this mutability was due to the growing capacity of working-class organizations to create and control their own images. Assisted by new, cheap methods of image reproduction, including the half-tone process for printing photographs and tonal images, the visualization of New York's work, workers, and activism would continue to be one more among their many critical struggles.

1975

Union City: 1898–1975

Labor Day parades in 20th-century New York (and, in the middle of the century, May Day parades, too) were often impressive affairs. Tens of thousands of workers carrying union banners marched; accompanied by floats, work vehicles, and marching bands, they were cheered on by crowds lining the streets. Politicians made sure to show their faces.

The celebrations reflected a high tide for labor. Worker movements reached their pinnacle of power during the first three-quarters of the 20th century. Union membership swelled: at its peak after World War II, nearly a third of workers in the city carried a union card. Strikes, sometimes massive and occa-sionally violent, became regular occurrences. Union power and militancy boosted the wages, benefits, and security of working people—not just union members, but others, too, as a result of the benchmarks that unions had established. The influence of organized labor extended beyond the workplace into the institutions and public policies that the labor movement helped to sustain, from public housing, rent control, and cheap mass transit to nonprofit health insurance and antidis-crimination laws.

Yet unions, which never represented a majority of New York workers, were just one of many types of organizations through which workers sought to protect them-

selves, improve their circumstances, and shape the city. There were radical—and not so radical—political groups, ethnic organizations, movements against racial discrimination, feminist organizations, tenant and neighborhood associations, and reform societies. Even so, many workers still found themselves with only informal networks of their own making to provide some measure of collective strength.

The Consolidated City

Labor blossomed during the years following the consolidation of the five-borough Greater New York in 1898. A tidal wave of infrastructure investment, some private, some public, boosted the economy and created jobs. Skyscrapers, ever higher, offered new office, hotel, and residential space. Electric-generating plants and an electric grid made better lighting, high-rise elevators, underground trains, and appliances of all kinds possible. Harbor dredging and new piers accommodated ever larger ships. New tunnels and bridges connected rail lines from Manhattan to New Jersey, Queens, and the Bronx, allowing trains from anywhere in the country to reach the new Pennsylvania and Grand Central stations. The subway system, opened in 1904, allowed workers with jobs in the central part of the city to live in distant neighborhoods. Later, the construction of highways and automobile bridges opened up the outer edges of the city.

The infrastructure build-out made possible a continuing population explosion. Already in 1900 the second-largest city in the world, with 3.4 million people, by 1920 New York surpassed London, with 5.6 million residents. Twenty years later the population neared 7.5 million, where it remained, with fluctuations, until the end of the 20th century.

Until the early 1920s the population increase continued to come largely from immigration.

The influx of eastern European Jews increased, alongside an even larger flow from southern Italy. Irish immigration remained substantial, while immigrants from dozens of other countries in Europe and the Americas came in relatively smaller but still significant numbers. However, laws from the World War I Era and the 1920s restricting immigration changed the demographics of the city. Over time, immigrants formed a diminishing proportion of the population, down from 41 percent in 1910 to 29 percent in 1940 and 18 percent in 1970, while their American-born children increasingly set the cultural tone of the city. A growing migration of African Americans from the South and a smaller inflow of Afro-Caribbeans also transformed the city, with the total black population shooting up from just 61,000 in 1900 to 450,000 in 1940, and more than a million in 1960. After World War II, as many white New Yorkers began leaving the city for suburbs and more distant areas, migrants from Puerto Rico, along with a growing black population, kept the overall size of the city's population stable.

As in the past, it was a robust economy, combined with New York's position as a continental and intercontinental transportation hub, that drew so many people to the city. For most of the 20th century New York remained the biggest manufacturing center in the country, even though the so-called "second industrial revolution" (the large-scale production of steel, chemicals, electrical equipment, and automobiles) largely bypassed the city. As in the past, the diversity of the manufacturing sector and of the broader economy contributed to New York's strength. Skilled and unskilled workers could find employment not only in factories, but also in construction, transportation, retail and wholesale trade, entertainment, communications, and service, including in private homes (though racial, religious, and gender discrimination meant some kinds of work were available only to particular groups). The density of the city, with its close clustering of people and work, the solidarities (along with the conflicts) that came from ethnic and racial identification, and the heady mix of ideas and experiences that flowed into the city with the millions of newcomers created a rich brew of collective activity by working people. Their movements not only transformed their own lives, but also helped create the modern City of New York.

Progressive-Era Labor

The two decades after the 1898 creation of the five-borough city saw New York's labor movements blossom in size and influence. As the economy recovered from the depression of the 1890s, union membership grew rapidly, doubling from 125,429 in 1898 to 254,719 in 1904. Craft unions, largely made up of men born in the United States, Germany, and Great Britain (which then included Ireland), provided the spine of organized labor. The building boom allowed construction unions to grow (with some 60,000 members in 1902) and win higher wages and shorter hours through tight organization and strategic strikes. Unions in the printing trades also prospered. Other crafts, old and new, had strong unions, too, from bakers, butchers, and bagel makers to actors, coopers, teamsters, and cigar makers.

New immigrants, shut out of established unions or simply lacking ties to them, fought against employers, sometimes with great militancy, through their own, often ad hoc, organizations. Italian workers building the subway walked off their jobs and fought violent battles against police and scabs, a dynamic also seen in walkouts by longshoremen and transit workers. The Industrial Workers of the World (IWW) tried to organize workers ignored by the craft unions in the American Federation of Labor (AFL), but without much success. More effective was the "new unionism" that emerged in the garment industry, the largest manufacturing sector in the city, which became a template for how to organize polyglot workers of diverse skill levels through groups that linked workers in particular crafts with other workers through umbrella bodies, embraced diverse ethnic cultures, and wedded radical politics with bread-and-butter unionism.

Early-20th-century unions benefited from ties to other working-class organizations as well as to middle-class reform associations. Socialist, anarchist, and communist groups inspired activists, built rich worker cultures, and pressured the mainstream political parties to support labor causes. Cross-class women's groups backed female workers and fought for women's suffrage. Radicals and health reformers pressed for legalizing birth control, an urgent issue for working-class women. Progressive groups worked to end child labor and tenement homework. Interracial and black organizations, including the Urban League, the NAACP, and Marcus Garvey's Universal Negro Improvement Association, all headquartered in New York, aided African Americans and fought discrimination.

By the end of World War I, it looked like a new day for New York workers had arrived. Union membership swelled, new laws regulated working conditions, women won the vote, and a remarkably diverse group of workers—from actors and waiters in Chinese restaurants to transit workers, longshoremen, and building tradesmen—joined a wave of strikes that hit the city in 1919. However, labor's fortunes soon shifted, as a postwar Red Scare and government repression weakened radical organizations and immigrant unions, and as prolabor Democrats were swept out in a Republican electoral tide. Though workers continued to fight through the 1920s, their boldest efforts, including big strikes in the garment and transit industries, largely failed.

Labor Triumphant

The Great Depression hit working-class New Yorkers very hard. Jobs disappeared, incomes plummeted, evictions soared, hunger spread. Yet ultimately, the economic and political crisis helped cement the central role of labor movements in the city. By 1930, workers, employed and unemployed, began to mobilize. They joined radical political groups, rallied to demand that the government provide jobs and relief to the unemployed (as New York workers had been demanding, in hard times, for a century), and physically blocked evictions. When Franklin D. Roosevelt moved into the White House in 1933, bringing to Washington a host of pro-labor progressive New Yorkers, unionizing efforts accelerated under the auspices of both AFL groups and independent unions, many of which ended up in a new national federation, the Congress of Industrial Organizations (CIO). The 1935 National Labor Relations Act (NLRA), sponsored by New York Senator Robert F. Wagner, which guaranteed the right of workers to belong to a union and facilitated the recognition of unions as bargaining agents, gave a further boost to New York unionism.

Labor's newfound clout extended to the polling place. In 1933 workers helped elect as mayor liberal Republican Fiorello La Guardia, who had worked as an attorney for unions and retained close ties to labor. In 1936 unionists and Roosevelt allies created the American Labor Party (ALP), which became a powerful force in both city and state politics. For some three decades, under La Guardia and the Democrats who succeeded him, organized labor was effectively part of the ruling political coalition in the city.

World War II and the postwar years saw a further expansion of organized labor. In 1947 there were 1,107 private-sector union locals in the city, up from 670 in 1904, along with the headquarters of some three dozen national unions. By the early 1950s, at least a million New Yorkers belonged to a union. In the years that followed, another layer of unionists came

with the growth and recognition of unions representing public employees. New York still had a lot of low-wage work. Some of it was unionized, bringing workers (even if their incomes remained modest) greater job security, an end to arbitrary treatment, and a host of benefits, from paid vacations to union-sponsored health clinics and housing projects. However, organized labor maintained a narrow notion of its constituency, all but ignoring many types of workers, particularly women in service jobs, leaving them, as in the past, dependent on informal mutual aid, at best.

At the same time, in the public realm, unions did support many programs that aided workers outside of organized labor. In alliance with tenant organizations, veterans groups, civil rights groups, and progressive professionals, unionists promoted an expansive vision of the role of government, including the provision of affordable housing, low-cost mass transit, public or nonprofit health care, and low-cost cultural events. Many unions also supported efforts to end racial discrimination (though some resisted desegregation in their own industries).

By the early 1970s, three-quarters of a century of labor struggle had helped create a city almost unique in the country, in terms of the voice workers had in shaping the local polity and culture as well as in the range of institutions established to meet the needs of working people. Though the national labor federations had their headquarters in Washington, DC, in many ways, it was New York City that was the center of the American labor movement. New York City was labor's city on a hill, demonstrating how a mobilized working class could shape the community in which it lived, at least when economic and political conditions were there for it to thrive.

The Needle Trades and the Uprising of Women Workers: 1905–1919

In November 1909 young immigrant women who worked in New York City's burgeoning ready-to-wear clothing trade were considering a general strike.

They planned to protest increasingly dangerous conditions and falling wages, as de-skilling and mass immigration reduced the bargaining power of skilled seamstresses. Activists distributed thousands of leaflets in Yiddish, English, and Italian, the languages spoken by most of the city's garment workers, calling them to a meeting on November 22 to decide whether or not to strike. Male labor luminaries—Samuel Gompers, president of the American Federation of Labor (AFL), Socialist Party leader Jacob Panken, and Benjamin Feigenbaum of the Yiddish socialist daily newspaper *Jewish Daily Forward*—were scheduled to speak, along with Irish-American garment worker Leonora O'Reilly. Also on the platform were middle-class women who were allies of the workers, among them Mary Dreier, president of a relatively new cross-class women's worker support group, the Women's Trade Union League (WTUL).

The darkly elegant Great Hall at Cooper Union seemed a natural choice for their meeting. It had seen more than its share of political meetings and spellbinding social justice oratory over the previous 50 years. Presidential candidate Abraham Lincoln spoke there in 1860, arguing that slavery must not be allowed to spread to the western territories. Frederick Douglass defended the Emancipation Proclamation, and, in 1870, Lakota chief Red Cloud condemned the murder and displacement of his people there. Spirited woman suffrage meetings had taken place in the Great Hall for 50 years. Elizabeth Cady Stanton and Susan B. Anthony spoke there, as did "free love" presidential candidate Victoria Woodhull and fiery British suffragist

Meeting of shirt-waist workers at Cooper Union, November 22, 1909
Photograph by Brown Brothers

Labor leader Samuel Gompers (center right, facing audience) presided over the meeting where shirtwaist makers voted to strike.

Emmeline Pankhurst, whose civil disobedience tactics electrified suffragists from London to New York City.

In the first years of the 20th century, New York City's young immigrant working women also gathered regularly in the Great Hall. The Equality League of Self-Supporting Women had held numerous suffrage meetings there. Young women filled the seats, sat on the floor and in the aisles, and stood packed together between the room's many columns, listening intently. Among the speakers were Irish immigrant shirtwaist-maker O'Reilly and a 4-foot-9-inch red-haired cap-maker named Rose Schneiderman. The involvement of working women in the Woman Suffrage Movement had invigorated the long struggle, infusing it with new ideas, with a focus on passing legislation to improve wages and working conditions, and with more than a whiff of the labor socialism that immigrant workers were bringing from Ireland, Italy, and the Jewish towns and cities of eastern Europe.

Worker organizers—mostly young women in their 20s—some male union leaders and progressive middle- and upper-class women spoke at the Great Hall regularly. They decried poverty wages, rampant sexual harassment, and the firetrap sweatshops that were the hallmark of New York City's burgeoning ready-to-wear garment industry.

Among the most powerful of these speakers were four eastern European Jewish immigrant women: Schneiderman, shirtwaist-makers Pauline Newman and Clara Lemlich, and white-goods (underwear) maker Fannia M. Cohn. All four lived and worked in lower Manhattan. In the coming years, they would lead a sustained uprising of women garment workers that, during the 1910s, galvanized and vastly expanded the International Ladies' Garment Workers' Union (ILGWU) and made the

WTUL a national organization. By the end of World War I, 40 percent of women garment workers in the United States would be unionized. It was one of the highest percentages in any American trade, ever.

Schneiderman was a regular at the Great Hall. On March 25, 1905, six years to the day before a fire at the Triangle Waist Company revealed the dangerous working conditions in garment factories, the diminutive 22-year-old Polish immigrant addressed a packed house. She had just led a victorious city-wide cap-makers' strike for which she had mobilized the New York's newest and poorest immigrant workers. Schneiderman urged the crowd to donate generously to help support strikers' families and warned that employers were trying to drive down wages in the trade by hiring children and "raw immigrant girls who would work for next to nothing."

Conditions were worsening in the city's garment trades, Schneiderman told her avidly focused audience that night. That is why their spirit of militancy was growing, she said. So was their political consciousness. "The girls and women, by their meetings and discussions, come to understand and sympathize with each other and, more and more easily, they act together. It is the only hope they have to hold onto what they have now or to better present conditions." Schneiderman concluded that night with characteristic bluntness: "Certainly there is no hope from the mercy of the bosses."

Building to an Uprising

In the years between 1905 and 1909, Schneiderman, Newman, Lemlich, and Cohn, along with O'Reilly, had organized young women workers to protest deteriorating conditions. With the invention and refinement of the industrial sewing machine, operators were forced to speed up their work: a 1905 garment worker was expected to sew twice as fast as her 1900 counterpart. In 1909 a study of factory conditions in women's garment trades found that the "high rate of speed...leaves its impression on even the most robust worker." One of the study's researchers Annie MacLean found young women workers whose nerves were strained to the breaking point, and whose stress manifested in "heavy eyes with deep dark rings, in wrinkled skin and old young faces. The high rate of speed that must be maintained through so many successive hours is undermining the health of thousands of girls in this industry."

Young workers particularly hated the endemic abuse and petty humiliations by foremen and female supervisors. Banned from speaking to each other on the job, forced to work at rates so fast that workers said they did not even have time to think, many felt that they were being turned into machines. "And the bosses," said Lemlich, "they hire such people to drive you! It is a regular slave factory. Not only your hands and your time but your mind is sold." Young workers were furious when colleagues were "immediately fired" for talking on the job. And "at the conclusion of the day's work, the girls were searched like thieves." The dehumanization wore on them, until, as Newman put it, "we were ready to rise."

Anger drove young women like Lemlich and Newman to band

together. Untrained and largely unschooled, these young workers were drawn to both socialism and trade unionism because they were desperate to improve their working conditions. "I knew very little about Socialism," Lemlich recalled. "But the girls, whether Socialist or not, had many stoppages and strikes." Newman, who turned 18 in 1909, argued that political understanding followed action rather than precipitating it. "We of the 1909 vintage knew nothing about the economics...of industry or for that matter about economics in general. All we knew was the bitter fact that, after working seventy or eighty hours in a seven day week, we did not earn enough to keep body and soul together." Coming to consciousness together in the shops, tens of thousands of young immigrant women garment workers would soon amaze the city with their militancy and their resolve.

Shop-floor culture fed the young women's emerging sense of political identity and solidarity. Working alongside older men and women who discussed socialism daily, they began to feel a sense of belonging to a distinct class of people in the world: workers. This allegiance soon became as important as ethnic or religious belonging: being Jewish or Catholic, eastern European, Italian, or Irish. The shops also provided an opportunity for bonding with other young women, alongside whom they labored for 12 hours a day, six or seven days a week. At a time when many other girls their age were in school, garment workers gossiped, read, sang, and dreamed together in overcrowded shops. And they formed tight, deep bonds—as young girls and women sometimes do.

Shared dreams of revolution intensified their bonds. With dashing, bespectacled bravado, Newman captured the imagination of many of her coworkers at the new, modern Triangle Waist Company on Greene St. and Washington Place in Green-

"The Female Slaves of New York— 'Sweaters' and their 'Victims,'" 1888
From *Frank Leslie's Illustrated Newspaper,* November 3, 1888

Sensational press images used the exploitation of women in "sweatshops" to build circulation, but they also helped fuel reform campaigns and early unionization drives.

wich Village. Sometimes, as a letter from fellow worker J. A. H. Dahme to then-16-year-old Newman illustrates, the lines between political commitment and personal love blurred. "Yes, I understand you—understand you to that depth of thoroughness as only one who has long suffered can!...From the deepest, deepest place of my bosom let me utter the words, 'We shall be friends in joy and sorrow!' What is there sweeter in life than the sympathy between woman and woman—what purer than the sincerity of hearts—what greater than the harmony of minds? Yours in friendship and Socialist comradeship."

For young immigrant girls and women, some of whom were living in a strange city and country, thousands of miles from family and familiar surroundings, such bonds were powerful and lasting. From these shop-floor friendships would soon evolve the ties of union sisterhood.

Clara Lemlich, 1909

Clara Lemlich helped launch the shirtwaist makers' strike of 1909–1910. She later became a Communist and an activist for housewives and consumer rights.

Suffragists and Socialists

In the progressive atmosphere of early-20th-century New York City, influential people quickly noticed the militant young workers. Older Socialists, trade unionists, and middle-class reformers offered their assistance. These benefactors helped the young activists sharpen their arguments and find venues to present them. They also provided financial assistance and introduced the young activists to politicians and public officials.

The Socialist Party was a source of mentors for many of these young women. Newman was taken under the wing of Socialist journalist Theresa Malkiel. Armed with a sonorous voice and the certainty of youth, Newman would take "an American flag and a soapbox" from corner to corner on Manhattan's Lower East Side, preaching the gospel of Socialism in Yiddish and English. The teenage orator became one of the neighborhood's most popular attractions. "I, like many of my comrades, believed that Socialism and Socialism alone could and would someday fill the gap between rich and poor," she later recalled.

In 1908, nine years before New York State awarded its women citizens the right to vote, Newman, at 17 years old, ran for secretary of state on the Socialist Party line. *The New*

York Times scoffed at the thought of a "skirted Secretary of State," but Newman loved the experience. So did her audiences of young garment workers who flocked to hear her speak alongside Socialist Party leader Eugene Victor Debs. Involvement in the Socialist Party opened up new worlds to young immigrant women workers, engaging them in discussions of policy and Marxist theory, introducing them to the likes of Debs and other New York Socialist luminaries, including Congressmen Meyer London and many-time candidate Morris Hillquit.

The young workers were also taken under the wing of the city's woman suffrage leaders. Some, such as Alva Belmont, Anne Morgan, and Eleanor Roosevelt, were from the city's wealthiest families; others were progressive academics, such as historian and archivist Mary Ritter Beard. While these allies worked hard to draw young women workers into the suffrage movement, many also pressed them to discard their socialist beliefs, causing tensions that frayed bonds. (Only Roosevelt, of these affluent allies, would remain close to the young workers over the decades to come.)

Cross-Class Women's Alliances

Young garment workers were also drawn into cross-class progressive women's alliances through the WTUL. Founded in 1903 by Jane Addams as an American version of an organization she had encountered in a visit to the slums of London, the WTUL channeled the progressive vision of the country's first generation of women college graduates toward reforming the harsh conditions of industrial shops. The WTUL helped to organize women workers into trade unions, especially where men in the labor movement were resistant or uninterested, and lobbied for labor legislation, first on the state and then the federal level. At first socialist women workers such as Schneiderman, Newman,

Women's Trade Union League, 1910
Photograph by Byron Co.

The WTUL became a vibrant meeting ground for a cross-class coalition of labor activists and feminists, including Helen Marot (second from left, with necktie).

Lemlich, and O'Reilly were suspicious of the motives of middle-class WTUL "allies." Schneiderman said she "could not believe that men and women who were not wage earners themselves understood the problems that workers faced." Then, as activist garment workers sought to build a movement in the years leading up to the general strike call of 1909, the financial and organizational support of the WTUL proved essential. O'Reilly joined first and she convinced Schneiderman and Newman to trust the new alliance. Schneiderman became New York League vice president. Ultimately, she would become president of the New York League and later the national.

Schneiderman and Newman remained central to the organization until its demise in 1955. The WTUL gave these workers a personal as well as professional women's support network. It was there that Newman met her longtime partner, economics professor Frieda Miller, who went on to lead the New York State Industrial Division and, later, the federal Women's Bureau of the Department of Labor, established after World War I and often led by WTUL activists. It was also through the WTUL that Schneiderman would meet and begin a lifelong friendship with Eleanor Roosevelt during the 1920s. That friendship gave the WTUL influence in Franklin D. Roosevelt's administrations as governor of New York and president of the United States.

A Women's Revolution

In many ways, this all began on November 22, 1909, in the Great Hall at Cooper Union. That night, one older male labor leader after another urged the young garment workers not to strike. Union leaders believed that women could not and would not sustain a strike. Middle-class women allies worried that the cost would be too great for immigrant families already living on the edge of destitution. The

meeting started to feel like any other speech-heavy union rally. The young crowd grew restless.

Then, Lemlich—at the time, a 23-year-old Ukrainian immigrant dressmaker—shattered the cautious rhetoric with a firm gesture of impatience, elbowing her way to the front of the room. "I have something to say," she shouted by one account. Others recall her shouting: "I want to say a few words." The crowd demanded that she be allowed to speak and scores of hands physically lifted the slight, young woman onto the stage.

The activist achieved her place in the history books through that act and the speech that followed. She was already famous on the Lower East Side for the bravery she had shown in a strike at her shop earlier that fall. She had been arrested 17 times and had six ribs broken

Women pledging to support the shirtwaist strike and walk the picket line, 1909

by club-wielding police and company guards. She remained unbowed. "Unions are not built easy," she later told her grandson. "Like rain the blows fell on me. The gangsters hit me." When she began to speak to the crowd gathered that night in the Great Hall, she was deeply credible, widely admired for her courage and fierceness.

"I have listened to all the speakers," she began in Yiddish. "I would not have patience for further talk, as I am one of those who feels and suffers from the things described here. I move that we go on a general strike," she shouted. The room was rocked by cheers. Benjamin Feigenbaum of the *Jewish Daily Forward* asked those assembled in the room if they would take the old Jewish oath: "If I forget thee O Jerusalem may my right hand wither, may my tongue forget its speech." That Lemlich's speech was delivered in Yiddish, and that most people in the room knew the Jewish oath and could substitute the word union for Jerusalem as they said that oath as one, dramatically illustrates how Jewish the movement was at that moment. (As workers in the garment trades diversified, the movement would as well. By the 1930s New York City's garment workers' movement was increasingly Italian, Puerto Rican, and Caribbean, as well as Jewish.)

Lemlich's speech sparked a revolution. By the next morning, 15,000 shirtwaist-makers motivated by "an overflow of abuse and exhaustion" had, in journalist Malkiel's words, calmly walked away from the only thing that stood between their families and starvation. During the next few weeks tens of thousands more would join them. It was the largest women's strike in US history. Although it is widely known as the

"Uprising of the 20,000," it is likely that upwards of 40,000 young immigrant women struck between November 22, 1909, and strike's end in February 1910. The Socialist daily newspaper *New York Call* described "excited groups of women and girls standing at the street-corners, gathered in public squares and crowded in the doorways" of the city's streets. The strikers were out at dawn and late into the night, picketing, chanting, blocking traffic, and holding meetings. "Why is every available hall in Lower Manhattan crowded to its utmost?" the *Call* asked. "A hundred voices answer in chorus. 'It's the strike of the 40,000.'"

By the time the Uprising ended, unions had been established in the city's garment industry. But the owners of one factory in particular, the modern, airy Triangle Waist Company, a block from fashionable Washington Square Park, refused to recognize the union. Though owners Max Blanck and Isaac Harris raised wages for Triangle workers

Shirtwaist strikers, "Going out for Better Conditions," 1909

in response to the Uprising, they refused to acknowledge workers' concerns about fire hazards—locked doors, faulty fire escapes, and piles of flammable fabric scraps blocking the aisles between sewing machines.

Triangle and Its Aftermath

On March 25, 1911, a fire broke out in the Triangle factory. It gained force and fury rapidly as it burned the grass-linen fabric from which shirtwaist dresses were made, a shiny, stiff, highly flammable material. Unable to escape in time, some workers burned to death at their machines. Others rushed for the exits, collapsing from smoke inhalation, their inert bodies blocking the doors and preventing others from escaping. Nearly 650 workers on the factory's eighth and tenth floors were able to escape, through the heroic actions of elevator operator Joe Zito and assistance from New York University students who helped those on the top floor walk across to the classroom building next door. But 146 workers died in a little over half an hour, scores jumping, some still on fire, from the building's ninth floor. Their bodies smashed through ineffectual Fire Department nets to the city sidewalks below. It was a warm spring afternoon, and it is estimated that as many as 10,000 New Yorkers watched this horror unfold.

One eyewitness was a social worker and activist in the National Consumers League named Frances Perkins, who lived around the corner and rushed to the scene. Watching the tragedy, Perkins vowed silently that she would devote the rest of her life to preventing future workplace disasters. In the fire's aftermath, she helped to establish New York State's Factory Investigating Commission and ensured that workers, including Newman, were involved in inspections of factories throughout the state. The model was quickly adopted in other industrial states—including Illinois, Massachusetts, and others.

Perkins later became chief labor advisor for Alfred E. Smith, the state representative in whose district the Triangle factory was located, and who had visited the family of every victim. When Smith became governor of New York in 1918 Perkins helped pioneer legislation around wages, hours, and safety standards that paved the way for national New Deal labor protections. Along with Eleanor Roosevelt, who became an avid supporter of the WTUL during the 1920s, Perkins ensured that Franklin D. Roosevelt consulted extensively with Newman, Schneiderman, Irish-American labor activist Maud Swartz, and other workers as governor and then as president. In 1932 Perkins became Roosevelt's secretary of labor, the first woman to serve in a cabinet position. In that post, she became chief architect of the 1938 Fair Labor Standards Act (FLSA), which ensured minimum safety conditions, wage standards, a maximum 40-hour workweek, and overtime pay for workers across the country.

President Roosevelt appointed Schneiderman as the only woman on his National Labor Advisory Board, which negotiated wage and hours standards for industries across the country during the early 1930s. He even invited young garment workers to stay in the White House when they came to Washington, DC,

An officer stands at the window of the ninth floor of the Asch building after the Triangle Fire, 1911
Photograph by Brown Brothers

Who Is Guilty?
To the 140 Victims of the Asch Building Fire, March 25, 1911
Pen, ink, and oil on board by Boardman Robinson

This newspaper cartoon sought to arouse public indignation at unsafe working conditions following the Triangle Fire.

for WTUL conferences. The Roosevelt years marked a symbolic high point in relations between the federal government and women workers, underpinned by the bonds formed in the flames of Triangle and in the decades that followed.

But, if the death toll at Triangle in 1911 made painfully clear the need for workers to press for legislation that could, with the stroke of a pen, improve conditions for millions, the glacial pace at which legislation was passed and the inevitable compromises required to pass new laws convinced garment workers that they needed to continue organizing and striking. New York City's 1909 Uprising sparked a series of garment industry uprisings over the next decade. The movement first spread from New York City to Philadelphia; then to Chicago, Cleveland, Boston, and Kalamazoo, Michigan; and back to Brooklyn in 1913. There, another group of women workers deemed "unorganizable" by male union leadership rose up in a general strike of underwear- and kimono-makers led by white-goods maker Fannia M. Cohn and involving workers who

ILGWU parade banner, 1900

Members of the ILGWU carried this banner in parades, processions, and important meetings.

The spark for this decade-long uprising and the decades of institution-building and legislation that followed was, in many ways, cast that night in the Great Hall, when Lemlich demanded that leadership be ceded to the young women who were the industry's shop-floor workers and who suffered personally from the conditions they were trying to change.

Disgusted by the intransigence of male union leaders who continued to insist, in the face of overwhelming evidence to the contrary, that women were not organizable, these workers voted them out. During the 1910s and 1920s union members elected a more democratic and sex-integrated leadership. Cohn was elected vice president of the ILGWU in 1915, becoming the first woman on a major union executive board.

The ILGWU of Cohn and the women of the 1909 Uprising provided a model that would transform union organizing in the United States. The 1910 Protocols of Peace established collective bargaining and arbitration, laying the foundation for the 1935 National Labor Relations Act (NLRA). Moving away from craft-based, "trade-by-trade" organizing that privileged skilled, white male workers, the new unionism pioneered by the ILGWU and others embraced broader industry-wide organizing: industrial unionism. This model resulted in an unprecedented unionization rate in the garment industry by 1919 and paved the way for the industrial union drives that gave rise to and grew out of the establishment of the Congress of Industrial Organizations (CIO) in 1935.

The city's garment workers continued to organize throughout the 20th century, as the trade became primarily Italian and later Puerto

spoke 35 different languages, including Yiddish, Italian, English, Arabic, Spanish, Chinese, and more.

When union leaders resisted their calls for a general strike in 1913, women workers rioted in lower Manhattan. Thousands took to the streets, smashing down the doors of the New York Hippodrome on Sixth Avenue and 43rd St. on January 5 after ILGWU leaders tried to prevent them from attending the meeting where members would vote about whether to call a general strike. Male leaders insisted that they had to prove to employers that the ILGWU's leaders could control the industry's rank and file. The women were having none of it.

Rican and Caribbean. Organizing efforts continued, even as employers sought to evade unionization by opening up nonunion shops in the US South. In 1982, 20,000 Chinese immigrant garment workers in New York City's Chinatown struck 500 shops in a successful reprise of the 1909 Uprising. They won safety concessions and a day-care center, so that workers did not have to take their children into the factories (a major demand of the strike).

Beginning in the 1980s and intensifying during the 21st century, the garment industry globalized. While labels still had offices in New York City and Los Angeles, manufacturing was increasingly done in far-flung places with limited labor regulations: Bangladesh, Cambodia,

Haiti, Central America, India, China, and Ethiopia. On March 25, 2011, Bangladeshi garment worker and union activist Kalpona Akter, then 37, walked onto the stage of the Great Hall at Cooper Union on the 100th anniversary of the Triangle Fire. From that famed stage, she told the gathered audience, including Lemlich's 95-year-old daughter Rita, about the many parallels between the experiences of New York City garment workers in the early 20th century and those of Dhaka in the 21st, where there have been innumerable factory fires since 2006. "In Bangladesh," she said quietly and fiercely, "it is not 2011. It is 1911." The past is present. And the work of organizing is underway again.

Rose Schneiderman, 1933

WTUL activist Rose Schneiderman went on to become New York State secretary of Labor and an important voice in Democratic Party politics.

Sex Work and the Underground Economy

I n 1928 Baltimore teenager Eleanor Fagan migrated to New York City, hoping to reunite with family and secure employment.

Making her way to Harlem, Fagan reconnected with her mother and obtained a house servant position with a white family. After working for several months for a white woman, who Fagan described as big, fat, and lazy, she believed that there had to be something better than personal service. And, for her, there was better labor: sex work. Fagan viewed prostitution as an escape from low-wage, backbreaking domestic labor. Echoing Fagan's sentiments, one Manhattan sex worker reasoned that she would be a "fool to go out and break my back scrubbing floors, washing, ironing, and cooking and earn six or seven dollars as a part-time worker when I could earn three days' pay, or more, in fifteen minutes."

Fagan's disdain for domestic labor and desire for higher earnings precipitated her entrance into New York's sexual economy. She "didn't want to be nobody's damn maid." At the same time, sex work was not foreign to the Maryland native. Prior

to relocating to New York, a teenage Fagan, who was a rape survivor, school dropout, and the daughter of a prostitute, bartered sex for money at a Baltimore brothel; she was the youngest prostitute at the brothel and catered to those who sought sexual intercourse with adolescent girls.

By the time Fagan became employed at a Harlem brothel in the late 1920s she was an experienced sex worker. She was a strictly $20 call girl with a white clientele. "With my regular white customers, it was a cinch. They had wives and kids to go home to. When they came to see me, it was wham, bang, they gave me the money and were gone. But Negroes would keep you up all the damn night, handing you that stuff about 'Is it good, baby?' and 'Don't you want to be my old lady?'" By 1930, after having spent 100 days in jail on Manhattan's Welfare Island (now Roosevelt Island), Fagan left the urban sex trade, turning to a new passion: music. Taking the stage name Billie Holiday, Fagan would emerge as a world-class blues and jazz singer, using her powerful vocals to speak to varying aspects of women's laboring lives, including prostitution.

Women and Informal Work

Women were integral to New York City's informal economy, a socioeconomic marketplace that, by the early decades of the 20th century, sanctioned the generation of income and exchange of goods and services outside of city, state, and federal regulations. Occupying labor and social spaces traditionally reserved for or dominated by men, women, either as workers or consumers, became part of the city's thriving and, at times, treacherous underground employment sector. Their presence in illegal economic markets broadened prevailing images of female work and refuted societal assumptions that unregulated employment only furnished financial and social opportunities for men. In fact, underground work afforded New York women alternative occupation paths, making it possible for them to imagine and explore new labor and social identities. Gotham women consciously made a place for themselves within New York's early-20th-century informal sector and, in doing so, created labor spaces that allowed them to assume roles as wage laborers, entrepreneurs, and cultural producers.

Their labor shifted and contested (and sometimes reinforced) the racial, gender, class, and sexual politics of the different sectors of New York's informal economy. Moreover, women's income-generating activities reconfigured and, at times, breached normative working- and middle-class ideas about female respectability. Societal norms expected women and girls to display reputable behavior through hard work, Christian values, household duties, sexual restraint, and "modest"

Billie Holiday, 1949
Photograph by Carl Van Vechten

public conduct. In safeguarding their socioeconomic endeavors from customers, competitors, and law enforcers, women who participated in the informal economy assumed public personas that were often aggressive, violent, and/or unbecoming of a "proper" woman.

Varying national and local social, economic, and political factors, including urbanization, European immigration and black migration, economic downturns, personal desires, and mass material consumption, made it possible for early-20th-century women to establish themselves as buyers and sellers of drugs, alcohol, sex, food, clothes, and other illicit and licit products. Factors as varied as abject poverty; race, gender, and class inequities; troubling family dynamics; individual ambitions; and greed motivated different women's decision to engage in precarious work. Coming from diverse racial, ethnic, and socioeconomic backgrounds and geographic terrains, urban women toiled at a myriad of under-the-table jobs. In private residences, at commercial businesses, or on busy New York streets, women labored as unlicensed vendors, confidence artists, fences of stolen goods, and as hostesses, cooks, maids, and entertainers at speakeasies, brothels, and other illegal establishments. Those possessing an entrepreneurial spirit launched street vending, day-care, narcotic smuggling, hair-care, alcohol and sex, and shoeshine enterprises of their own.

Informal work was imperative to women's lives. Pushing beyond the limits of legal work, city women, including poverty-stricken single women and girls, middle-class mothers and wives, church parishioners and pleasure seekers, and formal wageworkers and budding entrepreneurs, viewed informal labor markets as sites that potentially offered financial stability, new labor identities, and occupational control and flexibility. Unreported income-generating activities afforded laborers the opportunity to sustain themselves and their families economically; to combine formal wage labor with off-the-books work; to pursue entrepreneurial opportunities; to purchase fancy clothes and other luxury items; to economically support religious, political, and social institutions; to cope with the death or desertion of their husbands or male companions; and to bypass menial employment as domestics or service workers and city relief during

Polly Adler, 1935

Polly Adler around the time she was arrested for possessing "lewd" motion pictures.

the Great Depression. Rather than seek financial assistance from city and social welfare programs, some women, recognizing the restrictions and surveillance that accompanied the acceptance of charity during the depression, bravely pursued entrepreneurial endeavors. One 1930s unlicensed street vendor admitted that she would rather hustle on the streets than receive city money. "It was hard standing on corners swallowing your pride. But it meant independence. Yes, independence. So many were satisfied with relief. Well, no relief for [me]. Better to stand out here in the [streets] and be your own boss."

Russian immigrant and Manhattan brothel proprietor Pearl "Polly" Adler viewed the urban informal economy, particularly sex work, as an opportunity to escape exploitative labor conditions. Prostitution radically changed her economic future. Born in 1900, Adler immigrated to the United States at the age of 12, settling with relatives in Holyoke, Massachusetts, and later Brooklyn. Like many immigrant girls and women, the uneducated Adler labored as a seamstress and machine operator, earning a $5 weekly wage and experiencing poor working conditions and sexual violence: a factory supervisor brutally beat and raped her after she resisted his sexual advances. The assault resulted in a pregnancy that she made the difficult decision to terminate.

As a young industrial laborer, Adler found it difficult to sustain herself financially, much less afford the city's exciting "cheap amusements." During the late 1910s she entertained an economic proposal that altered the course of her life. A prominent, married bootlegger friend offered to pay her rent in exchange for using

her apartment to commit adultery. Adler welcomed his offer. Shortly after, Adler regularly procured women for the bootlegger and his circle. She earned $100 per week. By the 1920s she had launched a thriving sex business, joining the more than 100 known and suspected brothel houses operating in New York City. Adler aspired to be the "best madam in all America." From the Prohibition Era until the early 1940s, she operated a string of posh parlor houses in Saratoga Springs, New York, and throughout Manhattan. Her Manhattan locations included a brownstone at 63 West 70th Street between Central Park West and Columbus Avenue, and a luxury apartment at the opulent Majestic, a twin-tower apartment building at 215 West 75th Street. Her establishments were well known for

Polly Adler, leaving a police van after her arrest, 1936

Polly Adler left industrial wage work for a career managing high-end brothels.

their glitzy social gatherings, attractive and elegant sex workers, and prominent clientele. "New York's most famous bordello[s]" welcomed businessmen and politicians, such as New York City Mayor Jimmy Walker, high-society urbanites, police officers, celebrities including famed boxer Jack Dempsey, and some of the nation's most notorious criminals. Chicago mobster Al Capone and New York racketeers Arthur "Dutch Schultz" Flegenheimer and Charles "Lucky" Luciano frequently visited Adler's parlor houses. Her fascinating rags-to-riches story is captured in her 1953 memoir, *A House Is Not a Home*.

Dreams of financial bounty also fueled some women's association with New York City's most lucrative criminal enterprises. West Indian immigrant and Harlem resident Madame Stephanie St. Clair was one of the city's wealthiest African-American women entrepreneurs. She participated in the city's illegal and profitable numbers game racket. Part of an international phenome-

Stephanie St. Clair, 1938

non of gambling rackets, New York City's numbers game was a lottery system in which players bet by selecting a set of three-digit numbers for only a penny. Winning numbers were based on the daily closing volume of the New York Stock Exchange. St. Clair was one of a few black women to dominate Harlem's gambling racket during the 1920s and 1930s. White, West Indian, and African-American male numbers bankers, including Jewish-American Bronx bootlegger Dutch Schultz and Danish West Indies immigrant and philanthropist Casper Holstein, typically controlled New York City's numbers rackets. Financing their own independent gambling enterprises, numbers bankers hired individuals to collect gambling slips from players, document slips, count money, and pay winners. Women were part of these enterprises, laboring as number slips collectors, office clerks, and some, such as St. Clair, establishing prominent gambling rings of their own.

St. Clair's rags-to-riches story and lavish lifestyle were captured in both local and national newspapers, including *The New York Times* and the *Chicago Defender*. The Caribbean immigrant had been born on the French island of Guadeloupe in the mid-1890s. Migrating to Harlem in the 1910s, St. Clair, a working-class seamstress, established her gambling operation sometime in the early to mid-1920s. By the Great Depression, she had solidified herself as a powerful and flamboyant numbers banker known as the "Numbers Queen." Newspapers of the day reported that St. Clair had accumulated a personal fortune of more than $100,000, owned several Manhattan apartments, wore expensive clothes and jewelry, and resided in Harlem's exclusive Sugar Hill neighborhood. Her illicit business employed countless gambling collectors, bodyguards, and domestic servants. The Harlem racketeer even had New York City Police Department officers on her payroll. St. Clair boldly carved out space for herself within the city's male-dominated gambling ring, battling dangerous gangsters over the lucrative numbers racket.

For some women, participation in New York City's informal labor marketplace was not primarily about financial survival or becoming wealthy. Economic preservation was not their chief concern. Their desires lay in fulfilling social and sexual pleasures. Personal gratification was a top priority. Inspired by the early-20th-century American culture of cheap amusements, illegal drinking, and sexual experimentation, these women were unapologetic in their quest for pleasure. They were intrigued by boisterous apartment soirées filled with live music, food, and alcoholic beverages and popular night spots, especially those that encouraged partygoers to engage in nonconventional sexual performances. These women interpreted off-the-books labor as a departure from their mundane lives as caretakers and laborers and as a route toward personal fulfillment. Some women's desire for sexual and social excitement was evident in their hosting of private house parties, particularly "buffet flat" parties.

Emerging during the Jazz Age, buffet flats, labeled by some attendees and anti-vice agents as "pussy parties" and "sex circuses," were private house gatherings known for entertaining partygoers with gambling, music performances, food and drink, live sex shows, and prostitution. New York City's racially and ethnically diverse population of blacks, whites, Hispanics, and Asians patronized cross-racial and intra-racial house parties. Buffet flats were also part of the 1930s "pansy" and lesbian crazes, serving as intimate settings for patrons to unapologetically engage in and observe both hetero- and homosexual activities without condemnation. Moreover, buffet flat parties allowed participants to escape, if only for an evening, the daily drudgeries of hard labor, discrimination, respectable politics, and conventional gender norms.

Buffet flats were located in urban enclaves throughout the nation. Detroit, Chicago, Manhattan, and Brooklyn were home to some of the most popular ones. Prominent singers and musicians, such as Bessie Smith and Thomas Wright "Fats" Waller, wrote and sang about buffet flat parties. In 1929 Waller composed "Valentine Stomp," a song about the Daisy Chain, a well-known 1920s New York City buffet flat. Located in Harlem, the Daisy Chain (also known as the 101 Ranch) was operated by married chorus dancer Hazel Valentine. The female proprietor charged attendees to eat, drink, and have sex. One patron described the popular "sex palace" as "a house of prostitution and drinks and everything. Women goin' with women, men goin' with men, nobody paid it any mind, everybody was gay and havin' a ball. [It] was a big railroad flat house, with these rooms over here and rooms over there and a long hall, and you'd see people on the floor gettin' their thing. Everybody got buck naked." Discussing the amusement spot's influence on musicians like Waller, renowned musician William Christopher "W. C." Handy posited that the Ranch's endless flow of alcohol, beautiful women, and sex served as a muse for singers, composers, and songwriters. "If Fats Waller could be locked up in a room at the 'Daisy Chain' with a piano, a bottle of gin, and several beautiful chicks, he would certainly come up with some of the most beautiful music written this side of Heaven."

Consequences of Underground Labor

Newfound labor prospects brought both predictable and unforeseen dangers and obstacles for women. Informal labor was a complex blend of possibilities and restrictions, freedom and surveillance. While many women laborers secured social and financial capital and exercised autonomy over their labor, others experienced physical, emotional, and psychological abuse, labor exploitation, and economic hardships. Arrests and confinement; nonpayment for services; verbal, sexual, and physical harassment by police, consumers, and informal economy competitors; race and gender discrimination; and public shaming by disapproving social activists, moral reformers, relatives, and neighbors characterized many women's laboring experiences. For instance, a homeless teenage girl who occasionally bartered sex for food and money was viciously beaten and nearly raped by a male client in 1937; Harlem gambling racketeer St. Clair constantly received death threats from male competitors; and, in 1938, one street prostitute was arrested and jailed after her Bible-thumping father informed the police about her depraved lifestyle.

Hustling for money or pleasure could result in death. In 1930, 20-year-old Puerto Rican Brooklyn resident and self-professed psychic and healer Palmira Savala was murdered in her home. Working as a full-time supernatural consultant, Savala offered clients psychic and tarot card readings; words of wisdom about relationships, money, and health; and the possibility of care for their physical and mental well-being. She also illegally prescribed and sold medicine to clients, violating state laws that required a license to dispense medicine. Disabled and jobless Brooklynite Lawrence Collins was one of her customers. Desperate to overcome his physical handicap, Collins paid Savala $500 to heal his body. When she failed to restore his health, he demanded she return his money. Unsympathetic to Collins's frustrations and economic circumstances, Savala laughed when Collins expressed dissatisfaction with her services, and refused to return his money. Plagued by long physical suffering and depleted of his life savings, Collins, in a fit of rage, fatally shot Savala and attempted to murder her husband and three-year-old child. Her death illuminates the real and potential dangers many underground laborers encountered and strategized against.

Women underground laborers were savvy survivalists. They challenged labor discrimination, gender and racial oppression, and workplace violence. For instance, some women rendered services only to familiar and regular customers and to individuals within their racial group. In public and private spaces, some women threatened or physically attacked belligerent competitors and clients. Others utilized self-defense tactics, arming themselves with small knives, bats, and other weapons. Fearing for her life, one Brooklyn prostitute fatally stabbed a male client after he brutally assaulted her.

Moreover, women's ability to navigate New York City's informal labor sector was made possible with the establishment of both intra-racial and interracial friendships, social networks, and collaborations. Based on their collective socioeconomic interests and their experiences with poverty and violence, some female informal laborers created

Sophie Lyons, c. 1890
Photograph by
Jacob A. Riis

Sophie Lyons, "a notorious pickpocket and criminal," in a mugshot used by New York police.

laborers schooled one another on street hustling and on their respective occupations. Moreover, women socialized with each other, sharing information about how to protect themselves and their businesses from law enforcement, clients, and fellow underground workers. Late-19th-century criminal, business owner, and mother Fredericka "Marm" Mandelbaum trained and mentored countless young street criminals at her unofficial crime school on Grand Street in lower Manhattan. One of New York City's most influential crime figures of the Gilded Age, Mandelbaum, who stood close to six feet tall and weighed more than 200 pounds,

temporary or permanent mutually beneficial relationships and partnerships with both informal and formal wage laborers. In jailhouses, brothels, nightclubs, rooming houses, and on the city's streets, women forged partnerships and verbal arrangements with men, women, and even children. Such collaborations brought together like-minded individuals interested in creative money-making schemes and survival.

For the sake of individual and collective preservation, informal

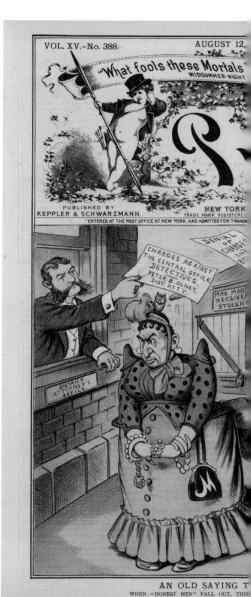

was a highly skilled fence: illegally hawking diamonds, gold, silk, and a variety of other stolen goods. Popularly known throughout the country as the "Queen among Thieves," Mandelbaum had a career that spanned 25 years. Mandelbaum and her team of professional crooks offered budding criminals crash courses in safe-cracking, burglary, blackmailing, pickpocketing, and confidence games. Promising and talented students joined her notorious vice ring.

Native New York City criminal Sophie Lyons was one of Mandelbaum's prize pupils. Referring to her mentor in her 1913 memoir, *Why Crime Does Not Pay*, Lyons, commenting on Mandelbaum's impact on New York City's underworld, noted that "curiously enough, the greatest crime promoter of modern times was a New York woman, Mother Mandelbaum. Alas! I knew her well—too well." National and international newspapers deemed Mandelbaum's protégée, "Princess of Crime." One New York scholar posited that Lyons, whose parents were career criminals, was "perhaps the most notorious confidence artist that America has

ever produced." While maintaining a home with her husband and children, Lyons pickpocketed and defrauded countless New Yorkers and global citizens, separating them from their money, jewelry, and other valuable items. Her criminal career ended in the 1910s. After prison stints in New York and Michigan, the once "Princess of Crime" retired from the criminal world and relocated to Detroit. Surprisingly, the new "Motor City" resident became a leading community anti-vice activist and a staunch critic of her former mentor "Marm" Mandelbaum.

Yet, shared experiences of personal struggle and common interests did not always cultivate supportive networks. Because of the competitive and unpredictable nature of informal labor, hustling became an individual journey rooted in self-preservation. Vying for consumers' pocketbooks, rival and jealous informal workers gossiped and created vicious rumors about their competitors. For some, the contest over economic survival, pleasure, and urban space even resulted in violent confrontations.

"An Old Saying Twisted" depicting Fredericka "Marm" Mandelbaum, 1884

Illustration by Frederick Burr Opper from the cover of *Puck*, August 12, 1884

A successful receiver of stolen goods and mentor to female criminals, "Marm" Mandelbaum gained public notoriety in the late 19th century.

Conclusion

Underground laborers in New York City certainly struggled to negotiate a terrain between their visions of occupational autonomy and the realities of informal labor, between self-sufficiency and economic dependence, and between self-perception and societal views that often mischaracterized their working lives. These Gotham women worked, lived, and socialized on the margins, and outside normative perceptions of female labor. Part of a community of workers, urban

women used the city's burgeoning underground sector as an unconventional route toward fashioning new economic and social possibilities for themselves. Despite the potential dangers of informal work, city women's diverse levels of participation in New York's underground economy symbolized a long-standing commitment to securing economic permanence, personal ambition, and labor autonomy.

Here Comes the CIO

At 3:00 p.m. on January 23, 1937, 150 workers at the Kent Avenue powerhouse in Brooklyn, which supplied electricity to the New York City subway and trolley systems, did not leave the plant upon finishing their shift.

Instead they began a "stay-in" to protest the firing of two pro-union engineers. When the next two shifts ended, workers likewise remained in place. Soon armed company guards, union supporters, and scores of policemen converged on the waterfront site. If the workers shut off the power, some two million commuters would be stranded. Seeking to avert chaos, New York City officials intervened, negotiating an agreement that led to the rehiring of the fired engineers and the evacuation of the plant.

The powerhouse workers, no doubt, were influenced by the dramatic sit-down strike then in progress against General Motors under the leadership of the United Automobile Workers (UAW) and its parent body, the Committee for Industrial Organization (CIO). The UAW victory against one of the most powerful corporations in the world set off a nationwide burst of labor militancy that extended to some unlikely quarters in Gotham. In March, workers at more than a half-dozen five-and-dime stores in Brooklyn and Manhattan occupied their workplaces demanding higher pay and union recognition. Hundreds of supporters rallied outside the struck stores. When the police arrested strikers at two Woolworth stores, the workers simply reoccupied them after being released from court. Again, the city stepped in, with Mayor Fiorello La Guardia helping the workers win a big victory. In late April it was the sailors' turn to sit down. The crew of the passenger liner SS *President Roosevelt* refused to sail when the ship's owner insisted on hiring seven men who had failed to support an earlier strike.

The nascent worker groups that led the transit, retail, and seamen's strikes soon became national unions with charters from the CIO. The CIO had been formed two years earlier by a group of American Federation of Labor (AFL) unions seeking to

organize workers in nonunionized industries on an industrial basis, that is, including all workers at a workplace in the same union, rather than dividing them up into separate craft groups. In early 1937 the CIO began chartering unions on its own. The following year it cut ties with the AFL and changed its name to the Congress of Industrial Organizations.

Sit-down strike at Woolworths, 14th Street, 1937

Popularized by CIO industrial workers in the midwest, sit-down strikes became a tactic for New York powerhouse, retail, maritime, and other workers.

The New York Roots of the CIO

New York City was not a place most Americans thought of when they thought of the CIO. Instead, they envisioned cities like Pittsburgh, Detroit, Akron, and Flint, with their giant steel, electrical equipment, automobile, and rubber factories, owned by companies like United States Steel Corporation, General Motors, Ford Motor Company, General Electric Company, and Goodyear Tire and Rubber Company. These huge corporations, at the core of the American economy, had managed to keep out unions until, after a series of dramatic clashes, they succumbed to the CIO, laying the basis for an extraordinary improvement in the working-class standard of living and providing an electoral base for the New Deal and liberal policies for decades to come.

New York City, though by far the largest manufacturing center in the country, had few large factories. Instead, it housed myriad small and medium-size shops in a wide range of manufacturing industries, including garment making, printing, food processing, electrical equipment, machine making, chemicals and pharmaceuticals, and leather. Its diversified economy also included substantial employment in transportation, finance, services, entertainment, and wholesale and retail trade. Yet, even though it did not look like a typical CIO town, New York played a large role in the creation of the CIO. In turn, the CIO, though never as large in New York as the AFL, left its mark on the city's labor movement, its politics, and its path of social development.

The United Mine Workers of America (UMW), which, even while it belonged to the AFL, always had practiced inclusive, industrial unionism, played the leading role in launching the CIO. Frustrated by the failure of the AFL to seize the organizing opportunities created by the Great Depression and the New Deal, UMW president John L. Lewis convened the founding meeting of the CIO and served as its first president. His most important allies were based in New York: the International Ladies' Garment Workers' Union (ILGWU) and the Amalgamated Clothing Workers of America (ACWA). During the Progressive Era, the garment unions had emerged as prime practitioners of "New Unionism," which combined inclusiveness, militancy, left-wing politics, and multiculturalism with the AFL's focus on contracts and workplace gains. ACWA president Sidney Hillman developed a wide range of contacts in reform and political circles, as he came to see the need for government economic regulation to protect workers and stimulate the economy, breaking with the AFL principle of "voluntarism" that rejected state intervention in the labor market. The

garment unions pioneered extensive benefit programs for their members, from unemployment insurance to health care and low-cost housing, while promoting high wages as not only helping individual workers, but also creating consumer demand that would maintain national economic prosperity. Their outlook, programs, and networks helped define the CIO and marshal support for the massive uprising of workers it shepherded.

The garment unions, like the UMW, also played a critical role in providing money and organizers to newly formed CIO groups, including the steelworkers, textile workers, rubber workers, and automobile workers unions. The ILGWU alone gave $345,000 (nearly $6 million in current dollars) to the steelworkers and textile workers groups. Although the ILGWU left the CIO in 1938, the ACWA remained a CIO stalwart throughout its history and always represented the largest group of CIO members in New York. Hillman served as a top leader of the federation and its most important liaison with the New Deal until his death in 1946. The International Fur and Leather Workers Union (IFLWU), a smaller union that had once been part of the AFL, also moved over to the CIO.

The two largest CIO affiliates nationally, the United Automobile Workers (UAW) and United Steelworkers (USW), had a very modest presence in New York City, but the third of the big three CIO unions, the United Electrical, Radio and Machine Workers of America (UE), had local roots. In 1930 a small group of New York machinists founded the Metal Workers Industrial Union. It was an affiliate of the Trade Union Unity League (TUUL), a Communist Party union federation created after a de-

ILGWU's David
Dubinsky (left),
ACWA's Sidney
Hillman (right)
speak with UMW's
John Brophy (cen-
ter), who became
the first national
director of the CIO,
1936

cision by the party to stop working within the AFL. By 1933 the Metal Workers had small groups in Brooklyn, Manhattan, and Queens, as well as outside of the city. As the coming of the New Deal and the passage of the 1933 National Industrial Recovery Act (NIRA) stimulated union organizing, additional independent and TUUL-affiliated unions sprang up in the electrical equipment, radio, and machinery industries. In 1935 they joined forces and, after a series of reconfigurations, became the UE, with James Matles, the leader of the New York machinists, serving as one of its top officers. Matles's old group, Local 475, won contracts with many of the largest machine manufacturers in Brooklyn, including Mergenthaler Linotype Company,

Intertype Corporation, and American Machine and Foundry, as well as with many smaller shops. Other New York UE locals organized radio manufacturers, companies in the emerging electronics industry, and defense contractors such as Sperry Gyroscope Company.

Other CIO unions also had New York City roots. The Retail, Wholesale, and Department Store Union (RWDSU) grew out of the amalgamation of various independent and TUUL-led unions in New York retail and wholesale trade. Many retail and wholesale workers, including salespeople, pharmacists, and clerks, were generally thought of as white-collar workers, not the usual CIO profile. But their work conditions and pay were often abysmal, especially after the economy nosedived in 1929. Some were well educated, with hopes of professional careers or owning their own businesses, before the Depression forced them into jobs they might have otherwise spurned.

The first flashes of retail worker rebellion took place in 1934, when employees at S. Klein and Ohrbach's, low-end department stores on Union Square, sought out the TUUL Office Workers Union and went on strike. For months, strikers and their supporters disrupted the stores with rallies, picket lines, and stunts, such as releasing mice on the selling floors, before returning to work after winning minor concessions. Nineteen thirty-seven brought five-and-dime store strikes. Within a year workers at more upscale, uptown department stores, including Macy's, Gimbels, and Bloomingdale's, won

union contracts, too. Joining them in the new CIO union were Local 1199, an organization of drugstore workers, and Local 65, which represented wholesale workers and became the largest RWDSU affiliate.

The Transport Workers Union of America (TWU) similarly came out of Communist union organizing efforts, though it was never officially part of the TUUL. Like the groups that were, it succeeded because Communist organizers proved effective in articulating worker grievances and building alliances with activist workers of various political stripes. In the TWU case, immigrant workers with ties to the Irish republican movement, influential in the heavily Irish transit workforce, helped legitimate the radical-led union. In just three years, from 1934 to 1937, the TWU won contracts for almost

Seamen in a hiring hall under a National Maritime Union banner, 1941
Photograph by Arthur Rothstein for the Farm Security Administration—Office of War Information

With many members in New York City, the CIO National Maritime Union became the dominant seamen's union on the east and Gulf coasts.

all New York City subway, elevated, trolley, and bus workers and began organizing workers outside of the city. Michael J. Quill, an Irish immigrant subway change-maker, became president of the national union and, along with Hillman, the best-known CIO leader in New York.

Parallel developments occurred on the waterfront. Sailors, disgusted with the inept and inert AFL sailors' union, joined forces with Communist organizers to create the Marine Workers Industrial Union, before changing course in 1935 and rejoining the AFL group. Acting as an organized caucus, they soon seized the initiative through a series of strikes. In May 1937 they bolted the AFL to form the CIO National Maritime Union (NMU), which became the dominant seamen's union on the east and Gulf coasts.

The bulk of CIO members in New York City belonged to these unions, but there were others as well. By 1947 there were 273 CIO-affiliated union locals in the city. The national unions to which they were attached included the American Newspaper Guild, United Furniture Workers of America, Marine Cooks and Stewards Union, Industrial Union of Marine and Shipbuilding Workers of America, United Packinghouse Workers of America, Textile Workers Union of America, United Office and Professional Workers of America (UOPWA), United Public Workers of America (UPWA), United Transport Service Employees, and Utility Workers Union of America. There were even eight locals of a CIO Barbers and Beauty Culturalists Union. In January 1946 the CIO claimed to have 600,000 members in New York City (though, no doubt, that number was significantly inflated). With the UE, ACWA, NMU, TWU, Furriers, RWDSU, and some smaller CIO groups all having their national headquarters in New York, the city played an outsized role in the labor organization.

The CIO—New York Style

Diversity of membership was one of the distinguishing characteristics of the CIO in New York City. Far from being strictly a union of blue-collar workers, the New York CIO included legions of white-collar, professional, and public employees. Though white men made up the bulk of the membership—especially first-and second-generation Jewish, Italian, and Irish immigrants—there were substantial numbers of women scattered among such unions as the Amalgamated Clothing Workers, RWDSU, UE, UPWA, and UPOWA; a large bloc of African Americans in the maritime unions; and smaller numbers of African Americans in other unions.

Some New York unions deviated from the CIO template of a single unit for a single work site. The ACWA, Fur and Leather Workers, NMU, and TWU all had locals or sub-units organized by craft, occupation, or ethnicity, as well as by employer, joined together through joint boards or other structures, an approach that combined parochial bonds with broader solidarity. Several New York CIO unions, including the NMU, Local 1199, and Local 65, had hiring halls where members went to get jobs, a powerful device, usually associated with the AFL, for creating

RIGHT TO ORGANIZE

COLLECTIVE BARGAINING

5 Day Week

SHORTER HOURS

ABOLITION OF Child Labor

HIGHER WAGES

Social Security

VOTE AMERICAN LABOR PARTY VOTE
ROOSEVELT and LEHMAN
JOINT BOARD DRESSMAKERS' UNION, Locals 10·22·60·89

American Labor Party campaign poster, 1936
Artwork by William Sanger

New York's American Labor Party reflected the new industrial militancy that also fueled the rise of the CIO. Artist William Sanger included an African-American woman in this group of confident worker-voters.

union loyalty by largely taking employment decisions out of the hands of employers.

The New York CIO was also distinguished by the heavy influence of the political Left, especially the Communist Party. At least through the end of World War II, and in some cases well beyond, local units of the UE, Fur and Leather Workers, TWU, NMU, UPWA, Newspaper Guild, American Communications Association, United Shoe Workers of America, Furniture Workers, Teachers Union, and RWDSU were led by officials in, or close to, the Communist Party. Together they represented the majority of CIO members in New York. Though in most of these unions the actual number of Communist workers was small, the central role party members had played in organizing them, the competence of Communist-oriented leaders, and

the liberal, if not left-wing, inclination of many New York workers allowed the party to play an outsized role. Socialists and other non-Communist leftists were a lesser presence, but could be found in the Amalgamated Clothing Workers, Newspaper Guild, and some other unions.

The Communist bloc consolidated its influence with the 1940 formation of the Greater New York Industrial Union Council. Joseph Curran, president of the NMU, who worked closely with Communist leaders in his own union, served as the council president, with its day-to-day operations overseen by Saul Mills, a former newspaper reporter and Newspaper Guild activist. The council served as the official voice and coordinating body for the CIO in New York. It provided money and personnel for affiliated unions during organizing campaigns and strikes and acted as the CIO's local political arm, lobbying City Hall and holding rallies and demonstrations promoting such CIO positions as maintaining price and rent controls after World War II, opposing transit fare hikes, and outlawing racial and religious discrimination. A few unions, most notably the NMU, aggressively fought racial discrimination on the job, while others shied away from strong action, fearing that they would alienate white members.

CIO leaders had a capacious view of the role unions should play in civic life. During World War II, the Industrial Union Council and individual CIO unions threw enormous energy into supporting the war effort through rallies, war bond drives, and fund-raising for war relief. Many individual CIO unions had extensive social, recreational, and cultural programs, from classes for members and their children to baseball and bowling leagues and, in the case of the Fur and Leather Workers, operation of a summer resort. The CIO even established its own charity organization and social service program.

The New York CIO plunged into electoral politics even before the Industrial Union Council had been established. In 1936 the garment unions joined forces with President Franklin D. Roosevelt's political lieutenants to create the American Labor Party (ALP) to provide a vehicle for left-wing voters who supported the president but would never vote Democratic. Several CIO unions affiliated with the party, which took on greater weight when it provided the winning margin for Mayor La Guardia in his reelection bid in 1937. . That year five ALP candidates were also elected to the City Council, including Mike Quill, who served on and off until 1949. A few other CIO activists won office over the years, such as Local 65 organizer Kenneth Sherbell, elected to the state assembly in 1946. CIO political activity helped advance a liberal political agenda and ensured a sympathetic hearing from officials elected with CIO support.

Cold War Fratricide

The CIO emerged from World War II in strong shape, organizationally and politically, but soon it was rent by ferocious battles tied to the Cold War. Even before the war, there had been internal and external criticism of Communist unionists. Anti-communist caucuses operated inside the TWU and the NMU, aided by Catholic labor activists. In 1938 a congressional committee held hearings in New York City at which various union leaders were charged with being members of the Communist Party, leading Quill to quip that he "would rather be called a Red by the rats than a rat by the

Michael J. Quill (left) with John L. Lewis (center) after a meeting with Mayor La Guardia, 1940
Photograph by George Rinhart

Reds." During the war, the political battling continued, with the ILGWU leading a break from the ALP to form the anti-communist Liberal Party.

After World War II ended, the combat intensified. In the NMU it began with a fight among the Communist leaders in the union. By 1947 full-scale war had broken out, with Curran allying himself with critics of the Communists and resigning as head of the Industrial Union Council. National developments upped the pressure on the Communist left. The 1947 Taft-Hartley Act required union officers to declare that they were not members of the Communist Party in order for their unions to participate in federally supervised recognition elections or enjoy the protections of federal labor law. While, at first, almost all CIO leaders refused to sign oaths, they soon began complying, with some unions even raiding Communist-led groups, knowing that they could not participate in a recognition election.

The 1948 presidential election completed the political fissure in the CIO. Philip Murray, who had replaced Lewis as CIO president in 1940, made support for Harry Truman a test of loyalty, denouncing the left-wing third-party candidacy of former Vice President Henry Wallace. After Truman's victory, Murray and his allies began moving against the Communist-led unions.

As pressure grew, some New York unions switched sides. In March 1948, Quill broke with his Communist colleagues in the TWU and, after a bitter battle, won control. In the NMU and Newspaper Guild, anticommunist forces also took over. But in other unions, Communist leaders and their allies held firm and maintained membership support. When the national head of the RWDSU

ordered all local officers to sign Taft-Hartley affidavits, New York City locals of the union—with more than 30,000 members—walked out, establishing a new organization.

In late 1948 the national CIO dissolved the Industrial Union Council. The next year, the UE walked away from the CIO. In response, the CIO chartered a new union, the International Union of Electrical Workers (IUE), leading to years of jurisdictional battles. It also expelled a group of national unions that re-

Retail workers picket Oppenheim Collins, 1948

Arguing that officers of the CIO Retail, Wholesale, and Department Store Union (RWDSU) had not signed the Taft-Hartley non-Communist pledge, Oppenheim Collins refused to negotiate with them. Here, striking union members picket in front of the storefront, which bears a sign reading "The issue is Communism."

"'True Blue' Platform," c. 1948

Cartoons like this one by a CIO artist suggested that purging "reds" was really a ploy by rival unionists out to plunder union treasuries.

fused to change their political stand, including the Fur and Leather Workers, UPWA, and UOPWA.

Federal and local governments also mobilized against left-wing unions. Congress held new hearings in New York City in an effort to weaken them. The Truman administration barred the UE from representing workers at defense contractors, including New York firms such as Sperry Gyroscope and Sylvania Electrical Products. Several high-level left-wing unionists were arrested for immigration violations commit-

"TRUE BLUE" PLATFORM
1. GET RID OF THE "RED" STUFF.
2. THEN GET HOLD OF THE GREEN STUFF.

LOCAL 450 TREASURY

"TRUE BLUE" CANDIDATES

COMMITTEE FOR THE ELECTION OF ABLE CANDIDATES

ted years earlier and forced to leave the country, including John Santo, the TWU director of organization; Irving Potash, manager of the New York Furriers Joint Council; and Ferdinand Smith, secretary of the NMU and one of the highest-ranking black trade unionists in the country. For its part, the New York City government fired members of the UPWA from the Welfare Department and other agencies and stopped dealing with the union.

Some former CIO unions managed to continue more or less intact, notably the Fur and Leather Workers and the former RWDSU units, which, except for Local 1199, merged into a new entity called District 65. The UE lost many shops to the IUE and other unions, but hung on. Most of the other groups disintegrated. Even survivors found their isolation difficult. With many of their leaders disenchanted with the Communist Party, in the mid-1950s the remaining left-wing unions found their way back into mainstream groups: Local 1199 and District 65 rejoined the RWDSU, the Fur and Leather Workers merged with the AFL Amalgamated Meat Cutters, and the New York–New Jersey district of UE joined IUE (though elsewhere in the country UE continued to operate as an independent entity).

Toward Merger

When the CIO expelled the Communist-linked unions, it promised to aggressively organize workers in the economic sectors that those unions represented. But that largely failed to happen. As a result, organization of public employees in New York stalled for more than a decade and no significant gains grew from the modest progress the UOPWA had made in organizing workers in the financial industry. When department stores began setting up suburban branches, efforts to organize them largely failed. The only significant institutional advance of the CIO after its split came with the creation of the Communications Workers of America out of a loose federation of independent telephone industry unions.

In the early 1950s the CIO remained a powerful political force in New York City through a reconstituted Greater New York CIO Council, headed by Quill. Now allied with the Democratic Party rather than the ALP, the CIO, sometimes in coordination with the AFL, mobilized massive campaign efforts. It was particularly important in the 1953 election of Mayor Robert F. Wagner Jr. CIO leaders used their ties to Wagner to advocate for labor causes, including the extension of collective bargaining to city employees. The CIO opposed an increase in the sales tax, pressed for an increase in the minimum wage and its extension to

Greater New York CIO Council sample voter's card, undated

GREATER NEW YORK CIO COUNCIL
Voter's Card

Name John Doe

Address 1 8. 1 21. Boro Man.

Assembly District (A.D.) 1   Congressional District (C.D.) 1

Always include your A.D. and C.D. when writing your legislator.

My { Congressman is John X
Address: WASHINGTON, D. C.
Assemblyman is Harry X
Address: ALBANY, N. Y.

KEEP THIS CARD WITH YOU AT ALL TIMES
10

TWU members demonstrate for the 40-hour work week, 1951

retail workers, and strongly backed rent control. The CIO had a representative on New York City's Rent Guidelines Board and ran a housing clinic for its members.

Nationally, however, things did not go as well, in part because of feuding between the UAW and the Steelworkers following the death of Phillip Murray in 1952. To keep the national organization from fracturing, its leaders, in effect, decided to kill it off through a merger with the AFL, consummated at a December 1955 convention held at the 71st Regiment Armory at Park Avenue and 34th Street. In New York the CIO had a ghostly afterlife because, as a result of various disagreements, the local AFL and CIO central bodies did not merge until 1959.

The New York CIO left behind a strong legacy. Most important, during its two decades of operation, it organized hundreds of thousands of New Yorkers into unions. Unionism transformed their lives, bringing higher wages, decreased working hours, benefits such as paid holidays and vacations, medical insurance, and pensions, and increased security and equity on the job. Through alliances with liberal and left-wing groups, the CIO helped promote a social democratic polity in New York with extensive public services, such as public housing, public hospitals, and a public university, anti-discrimination laws, and legislation and administrative agencies promoting worker rights. The broad vision of unionism embraced by the CIO carried over into the AFL-CIO New York City Central Labor Council under its first leader, Harry Van Arsdale Jr., who came from the AFL International Brotherhood of Electrical Workers but shared much of the sensibility of the CIO. To the extent that New York City, to this day, remains the foremost urban center of unionism in the United States, some of the credit has to go to the tumultuous two decades when the CIO made its mark.

Puerto Rican Workers and the Struggle for Decent Lives in New York City: 1910s–1970s

P eople from Puerto Rico have been part of New York City since the late 19th century, when commerce linked the United States to the Caribbean and political exile brought pro-independence leaders to the city.

Migration expanded after the United States invaded Puerto Rico in 1898 as part of its imperial expansion and kept it as an unincorporated colonial territory. United States rule brought the island into imperial administrative, commercial, and financial networks based on the Eastern seaboard. Between 1898 and 1917 migration to New York was mostly a trickle of middle-class merchants and white-collar workers involved in the growing commercial connections between the economies of the United States and the island, supplemented by a very small number of cigar makers, ship workers, and stowaways. However, the granting of US citizenship to Puerto Ricans in 1917 and the United States' entry into World War I facilitated and encouraged migration to New York by workers from the island's cities and provincial towns. Demand for workers during World War I's wartime production brought direct recruit-

Jesus Colon speaking at a Puerto Rican worker's meeting and benefit, 1940

Leftist writer and organizer Jesus Colon (1901-1974) was a fixture of New York's Puerto Rican labor movement from 1918 until his death. Here he addresses a Spanish-language chapter of the Communist-affiliated International Labor Organization (ILO).

ment to the island and created interest among Puerto Ricans looking to migrate for work or better wages.

After the US Army recruited 12,000 Puerto Rican men to work in the American South in 1918, many did not return home, but migrated to Brooklyn, where a small community was developing between the docks of Red Hook (where steamers arrived from the island) and the Navy Yard. From there they dispersed to the Spanish-speaking areas of Harlem, the Lower East Side, and Chelsea.

Changes in the Puerto Rico–United States relationship influenced migration during the next decades. Neither the federal government nor local authorities could directly control the flow of people from the island, but they could regulate labor contracting. After World War II boosted migration, the Puerto Rican government more closely regulated labor contracting and established a program to contract seasonal farm workers on mainland farms. Puerto Ricans migrated for noneconomic reasons as well, to seek education, to join the military, or because of family conflicts.

Adjustment, Discrimination, Integration

Puerto Rican migrants were US citizens, but they initially experienced migration as a radical cultural change. They came from a colonial territory with its own language and culture and a strong awareness of its colonial history.

Most migrants did not speak English well, and they struggled to gain recognition and rights when faced with the inevitable questioning of their legal status and nativist rejections and exclusions. However, they were not deportable, and their legal status did provide the basis for claiming rights, organizing politically (despite discriminatory literacy tests for voting), and participating in movements or organizations that other immigrant groups did not or could not develop. Many Puerto Rican migrants eventually learned to claim varying sorts of dual identities based on identification with both the United States and the island.

New York City's working-class neighborhoods and workplaces were rife with diverse (and frequently conflicted) religious, linguistic, ethnic, immigrant, and racial identities and, to some extent, this fragmentation facilitated the integration of Puerto Rican migrants as one more ethnic group subject to the city's intense interethnic conflicts.

Puerto Rican traditions of racial mixture, complex racial identification, and forms of racial solidarity shaped the community's interaction with New York's racial politics. Black-identified or dark-skinned Puerto Ricans faced additional obstacles, especially before state and federal antidiscrimination efforts. Many connected with the worlds of black (and English-speaking West Indian) Harlem or black Cubans in the Bronx. Most experienced racist discrimination when seeking housing or work. White-skinned or white-identified Puerto Ricans found that their search for work, housing, or services was easier. Some distanced themselves from neighborhoods identified with darker-skinned Puerto Ricans and sought to be accepted (or pass) as white. Continued anti-black racism (including within the Puerto Rican community) has kept this issue alive today. Other factors, such as the ability to speak English with less of an accent or the knowledge of local customs and slang,

along with the ability to claim a New York identity also affected how Puerto Ricans were able to survive as workers.

Puerto Ricans who migrated in the 1910s and 1920s joined a small community of immigrants from Spain and Cuba, but they also shared neighborhoods and work with English Caribbean, eastern European Jewish, and Italian immigrants. By the 1950s Puerto Rican settlement patterns had become more complex; Puerto Ricans were as likely to live concentrated in majority Spanish-speaking neighborhoods (that were often described as slums or ghettos) as they were to live dispersed in proximity to African-American or white ethnic New Yorkers.

Beginning in the 1910s most Puerto Ricans partook in a larger Pan-Hispanic world that shared institutions and cultural, commercial, and political spaces. These spaces, created initially by Spaniards and Cubans, were enhanced significantly during the 1920s when Puerto Ricans arrived in larger numbers. This often Spanish-dominant world included political clubs, newspapers, dance halls, and restaurants and provided a bicultural comfort zone that facilitated a sort of dual integration into the city's life. Its most successful expression in the 1930s and 1940s centered around the leftist politics of the popular front associated with the Communist Party, the Workers Alliance of America (WAA), and the International Workers Order (IWO). Anti-fascist solidarity with the Spanish Republic during the Spanish Civil War encouraged these alliances and helped create a robust Hispanic working-class-led Left—a Hispanic popular front—that functioned in close cooperation with Anglo leftist and working-class leaders. The community, centered around west, south, and east Harlem, elected its first progressive pro-worker representative to the State Assembly, Republican Oscar García Rivera, in 1937. Soon after, Puerto Rican working-class radical politics congealed around the American Labor Party (ALP) and leftist congressman Vito Marcantonio in East Harlem.

Once mass migration began, stimulated by the United States' entry into World War II and wartime labor recruitment on the island, the work and community lives of Puerto Ricans became more diverse. Between 1944 and 1960 about 400,000 islanders settled permanently in New York City (the preferred destination for migrants) and a similar number visited. This helped to bring the total Puerto Rican–identified population to 817,000 in 1970, excluding third-generation descendants not counted by the census. In 1948 Puerto Rico's Labor Department opened an office in New York City known as the Migration Division. The office was opened in response not only to the needs of the massive migrant population, but also to attacks on migrants that appeared in the nativ-

ist and right-wing press and political circles. The office helped migrants find work and challenged the attacks and discriminatory practices. Directed by former Socialist Party executive secretary Clarence Senior and New York–born social worker Joseph Monserrat, the office worked to pressure unions in the 1950s to pay attention to their growing Spanish-speaking memberships. They translated, solved conflicts, and met with union officials to facilitate Puerto Rican support for union drives.

Vito Marcantonio American Labor Party campaign button, 1949

Work Patterns and Unionization

Many of the first men to migrate found work in trades that linked New York City to the Caribbean, including jobs on ships and docks in the Brooklyn Navy Yard and work in Brooklyn's sugar refineries. Women often came on their own, contracted to work by garment and food-processing factories before they migrated. They also migrated to join relatives who

had already earned enough money to pay for their travel and help them find work.

In the 1910s and 1920s, migrating to New York often meant working as a cigar maker. US companies controlled most of the tobacco exports from Puerto Rico and some of the cigar manufacturing on the island. Many men who migrated were already cigar makers. Cigar making in the United States was significantly unionized by one of the strongest unions in the American Federation of Labor (AFL), the Cigar Makers' International Union (CMIU). The union had established affiliations with locals in Puerto Rico and, when workers migrated, their union card helped them find work. As in many other sectors in these years, cigar workers were engaged in intense socialist and anarchist politics. Some Puerto Rican workers were involved in the creation of rival, more radical unions. But the ability of Puerto Rican migrants to earn a decent wage in this industry proved short-lived, as mechanization and de-skilling took their toll. Employer response to the massive general strike of New York cigar makers in 1919 and the start of the Great Depression in 1929 brought near-total collapse of wages and employment in cigar making. After the decline of cigar manufacturing, Puerto Rican men diversified their employment, entering service jobs in restaurants, cafeterias, and hotels.

The city's massive role as a global center of clothing design and manufacture was especially important to Puerto Rican women (and many men). By the 1950s the garment industry employed hundreds of thousands of women. Puerto Rican women entered this world as soon as they started migrating. Within it, they tended to occupy the lower rungs of employment, skill, and pay. But, as wages rose starting in the late 1930s, most managed to earn a decent living, with wages that often surpassed those of their male partners.

Critical to Puerto Rican workers, especially women, was the expansion of the International Ladies' Garment Workers' Union (ILGWU). In the 1930s garment workers fought to organize factories and for better wages in unions led by members of communist and socialist movements. Spanish-speaking workers (most of whom were Puerto Rican) were a growing minority within the ranks and became central to political disputes between Communists, Catholics, and other factions that fought for control of particular locals of the ILGWU. This tension resulted in appeals to Spanish speakers, in their own language, for their vote in union elections, and began what would later become more common in union newspapers: the inclusion of articles in Spanish and coverage of the Latino community.

Because of the openness of most ILGWU locals to Spanish-speaking workers and the slow but significant incorporation of Puerto Rican floor leaders, organizers, and business agents, the ILGWU became an important site for Puerto Rican engagement with unions. The ILGWU refused to allow Spanish-speaking locals—specifically, its Puerto Rican members (a process complicated by political factional fights between communists and others within the union)—but it did move to provide Spanish-language services for the growing number of Hispanic workers. Local 22, in particular, led by Charles (Sasha) Zimmerman, organized dressmakers in hundreds of factories. By the 1950s the local had become an important social and political center that brought Puerto Rican and other Hispanic women into contact with a culture of class solidarity based on the recognition of the multicultural origins of its membership. Local 22 and, eventually, other locals and unions provided improved benefits, English-language courses, leadership training, and a rich culture of dances and social events.

Sasha Zimmerman with members of Local 22 of the ILGWU, 1936

Charles "Sasha" Zimmerman (back row, center) poses with Latino, African-American, and white members of the ILGWU's Local 22 at Unity House, the union's camp in the Poconos.

This helped overcome shop-floor tensions between "old-timers" and "newcomers" that were often perceived or expressed in racial terms. Overcoming these tensions was critical to the success of the ILGWU's 1958 general strike, which included a major organizing drive in the mostly Hispanic parts of the Bronx.

Within the central offices of the national union, President David Dubinsky controlled the rigid hierarchies of the ILGWU and defended "old-timer" control of union positions. This kept Puerto Ricans from rising more quickly to the higher ranks of union leadership. It also limited the rank-and-file impulse for more forceful organizing drives and militant negotiating—a source of significant conflict during the early 1960s. Starting in the late 1960s Puerto Ricans made stronger headway within the ILGWU, but by then, the garment industry was in decline.

Except during economic crises, Puerto Rican migrants, and especially their children, did not have much trouble finding work. Migration from the island was, after all, very sensitive to changes in the availability of work in New York City. Puerto Ricans provided a significant part of the city's manual labor in a vast diversity of industries. They could be found on docks, in garment factories, hotels, laundries, and food processing plants; and working in food services, building services, chemical, pharmaceutical, metal work, printing, leather making, medical services, and electrical assembly industries. During the 1960s the city was the biggest industrial center in the United States, with tens of thousands of small and medium factories and an immense need for both skilled and unskilled workers. During this period about half of Puerto

ILGWU Local 105 "Equality for All" poster in English and Spanish, c. 1965

EQUALITY FOR ALL

...our union practices it!

Our union believes in equal opportunity and fair play for all. We oppose discrimination of any kind. We hope you will, too.

IT'S THE TRUE AMERICAN WAY.

LOCAL 105 · ILGWU

Nuestra unión cree en iguales oportunidades para todos. Es la verdadera forma de vida americana.

Members of IGLWU Local 23–25 march in New York's Labor Day parade, c. 1985

Photograph by George Colon

Latino workers—both Puerto Rican and immigrant—were an important presence in ILGWU Local 23-25 by the late 20th century.

Ricans in New York City worked in manufacturing, especially as machine operators. They were the most industrially concentrated immigrant/ethnic group in the city. Because of these opportunities, Puerto Ricans avoided domestic work almost completely.

In times of economic crisis (such as the 1930s, or the 1970s and early 1980s), when joblessness, lower wages, deindustrialization, budget cuts, or fiscal crisis struck the city, Puerto Ricans were highly vulnerable to the loss of work, especially quality jobs and year-round work. They had limited choices—other than to return to the island—and few resources, such as unemployment benefits or welfare services, to back them up. During these crises a significant part of the community became poorer, as much as 40 percent during the 1980s, even as it continued to have a solid core

of better-paid and middle-class workers. Escape from poverty depended as much on the cycles of the economy as on worker efforts to improve English-language skills, technical skills, or education, but membership in unions and collective efforts against discrimination were also critical parts of Puerto Rican struggles for well-being.

Men who served in the military or the Merchant Marine found advantages for job advancement, training, and education. Service in World War I, World War II, and the Korean War, as well as during peacetime, provided English-language training and benefits, and made island residents more familiar with the mainland United States. The Servicemen's Readjustment Act of 1944, also known as the GI Bill (which applied to World War II and Korean War veterans), provided benefits to tens of thousands of islanders along

with a few thousand New York City Puerto Ricans. Military service could be the fastest way out of low-wage jobs and was seen by both recruits and the military as a mechanism for social mobility.

For Puerto Ricans, work abounded, but conditions and wages varied wildly. These were the core issues that mobilized Puerto Rican workers, both individually and collectively, to support unions and build broader political and civil rights–based alliances in their efforts. Bringing a shop into a union could provide consistent wage increases and some protection against the myriad small injuries and abuses (and some large ones, including wage theft and sexual abuse) that workers could be subjected to by employers and supervisors. Often motivated by the realities of factory life, Puerto Ricans participated in work within unions and workplaces to gain access to skills and better jobs, including in management and supervision. Discrimination and problems with the English language

were obstacles for many darker-skinned migrants; whiter-skinned and second-generation Puerto Ricans fared better at securing better-paid or white-collar work and moving through the hierarchies.

Many Puerto Rican migrants became unionists when they took a job at an already-unionized shop, but they also partook in and invited organizing efforts on their own terms. This meant that, starting in the 1930s, unions had to recruit Spanish-speaking agents and factory representatives, translate contracts and union literature, and work with Spanish-speaking neighborhoods and organizations. Initially, incorporation brought some conflicts. Linguistic, cultural, gender, and political barriers had to be overcome, along with the outright nativism and racism of many workers. Unions developed ways of managing, if not celebrating, diversity, while building a culture based on working-class solidarity and militancy.

By the 1950s union membership and union struggles were critical to

Members of New York's ILGWU Local 32 celebrate the end of a strike in support of striking garment workers in Puerto Rico, 1974

Local 1199 protest at Mt. Sinai Hospital, 1959

Maria Cruz and her children picket outside Mt. Sinai Hospital during Local 1199's hospital strike in 1959.

the fate of Puerto Rican migrants and their children, with about half of all economically active Puerto Ricans members of unions. Puerto Ricans could be found in practically all the unions in large numbers, except some of the craft-based and construction unions. At work, Puerto Ricans encountered a double-sided struggle with bosses and coworkers for their rights and inclusion (especially if they had to rely on older workers for training). Frequently the arrival of Puerto Ricans in growing numbers led to some resistance against the newcomers, while employers sought every means to keep good wages and knowledge from the new migrants, who were eager to find work. As their numbers grew and they pushed back, these strategies became less effective. Once the majority of workers at a workplace were Spanish-speaking, the struggles lessened, and Puerto Ricans had to be promoted to foremen or supervisors.

Puerto Ricans also struggled within the unions themselves. The surge of union organizing in the late 1930s and the years following World War II was especially important to Puerto Rican workers, who were at the bottom of the pay and skill scales. Unions were critical to keeping the minimum wage at a living wage and, later, were able to fight for additional improvements, such as pensions, paid holidays, health services, and vacation leave. Within unions, Puerto Ricans participated in rank-and-file and workplace struggles. They also supported the anti-discrimination work to which many industrial and service unions were committed (especially those led by leftist leaders). Sometimes these efforts were at odds with those of white members who did not care much for minority rights. But union

leaders—such as David Livingston of the Retail, Wholesale, and Department Store Union (RWDSU), better known as District 65; Harry Van Arsdale Jr. of the International Brotherhood of Electrical Workers (IBEW); and Michael Obermeier of the Hotel and Restaurant Workers Local 6— pushed to open doors to black and Puerto Rican workers.

One important example of this transition took place in the mid-1950s. Puerto Ricans and other Spanish-speaking workers were at the center of a firestorm, promoted by the Association of Catholic Trade Unionists (ACTU), over exploitative conditions, low wages, and racketeer-controlled unions in dozens of small factories throughout the city. The fight against "exploitation" reactivated a Cold War-damaged labor movement and triggered an organizing drive for the lowest-paid and mob-exploited workers that united liberals, radicals, and Puerto Rican labor activists. They managed to mobilize support from the central office of the AFL-CIO, as well as from Mayor Robert F. Wagner Jr., and helped gain new unions and contracts for thousands of workers.

The first union leaders of Puerto Rican origin were trained by the more militant unions led by socialists and communists, especially the National Maritime Union (NMU), the United Electrical, Radio and Machine Workers of America (UE), the hotel workers, the ILGWU, the retail workers, the restaurant workers, the laundry workers, and the fur workers. By the late 1940s a cadre of workers of Puerto Rican descent, many of them second generation, came out of these unions and were in place when island migration surged. By the late 1950s, they had formed Spanish-speaking clubs or sections

within many unions, and were playing a critical role in advancing union goals among Puerto Ricans. These leaders—including Gilberto Gerena Valentín, Mario Abreu, Eddie Gonzalez, Evelina Antonetty, Joe Salguero, and Paul Sanchez—also played a critical role in the community in struggles related to housing, culture, and civil rights. By the 1960s, Puerto Rican union activists were demanding inclusion in the important New York City Central Labor Council (NYCCLC) as a distinct advisory body of the council, a goal they achieved, with significant effort, in 1969.

Charity Dance organized by District 65's Spanish Affairs and Negro Affairs Committees, 1956

Civil Rights

Unions encouraged members to fight for improvements beyond the workplace: in public housing, government minimum wages, civil rights, and electoral politics. During the late 1930s and 1940s, and again in the late 1960s, when the Left and progressive movements were strong, these larger political efforts intersected with more radical ideologies that were driven by militant solidarity from rank-and-file workers. The struggle intensified during the early 1960s, when younger, second-generation Puerto Ricans found that many job categories were closed to them, especially high-skill, high-pay work in construction, civil service, and the insurance and financial industries. Puerto Rican labor and civil rights leaders made demands on the unions, the city government, and employers to open doors for training and inclusion. Puerto Ricans converged with African Americans in developing civil rights and minority-based strategies that were both legal and militant. Their principal demand was that unions open doors to apprenticeships and create job-training opportunities. These efforts met with some successes, especially those supported by the IBEW. Under the leadership of Van Arsdale, who was also president of the NYCCLC, Puerto Ricans and blacks were trained to become electricians in large numbers while other apprenticeships were opened to minority youth.

The massive support campaign for striking hospital workers in 1961, led by Local 1199, also provided an opportunity for Puerto Rican and black collaboration with the larger labor movement. Black labor leader A. Philip Randolph led support for the movement together with Joe Monserrat, director of the Migration Division, in large public protests and strike-fund drives. Puerto Ricans found that the struggle for civil rights was in close dialogue with extending labor rights—both centered on a better life for workers and their communities.

Downturn

Despite the efforts of the labor, civil rights, and anti-poverty movements of the 1960s to improve the lives of the poorest working-class New Yorkers, the 1970s and 1980s brought significant setbacks for working-class Puerto Ricans. Many Puerto Ricans, African Americans, and other working-class people, with limited options of exit to higher-paying jobs elsewhere in the country, found a city that was collapsing around them. They faced the massive loss of industrial jobs (90 percent between the 1950s and the early 1980s), a fiscal crisis, budget cuts, and the shrinkage of the public sector. Those years of urban crisis led to the devastation of neighborhoods through arson and abandonment, the escalation of street crime, police abuse, drug use, and declining opportunities for the working poor. Because of these trends, the Puerto Rican community bifurcated sharply into a growing impoverished sector and a more stable, better-paid sector. New migrants from the island during the recession of the early 1980s (which hit the island very hard and generated another large wave of migrants) found that the devastated postindustrial cities of the Northeast provided jobs with low wages and no unions.

A partial recovery in the 1990s cut Puerto Rican poverty in New York City in half, but in the absence of a collective, working-class solution for low-wage workers and the poor in a resurgent city, paths for improvement remained limited to those with higher levels of education. For those with some level of college or technical training, opportunities (especially for women in the administration of health care) and resurgent public and service unions, helped boost wages and benefits. In the 1990s Puerto Ricans played important roles in rebuilding unions in these sectors. Many Puerto Ricans—such as Dennis Rivera of Local 1199, representing health-care workers, and Héctor Figueroa of 32 BJ, representing building workers (both part of the Service Employees International Union (SEIU))—emerged as leaders of these unions, as the unions, themselves, continued to reflect the city's changing racial and ethnic diversity.

Members of District 65 at New York City's Puerto Rican Day Parade, 1988
Photograph by Fran Vogel

Labor and the Fight for Racial Equality

In the United States organized labor's approach to racial questions has mattered enormously to the extraordinary power of unions to affect social relations and individual livelihoods.

Unions have used their power to promote equal rights and racial inclusion, and they have used their power to promote jobs and benefits for whites only. From the very beginnings of organized labor in the United States, unions have been on both sides. They have fought for and against color bars, and for and against immigrant exclusion. This paradoxical history explains why James Baldwin and Martin Luther King Jr. could arrive at starkly different views of the potential of unions to be allies. Baldwin told *Esquire* magazine that "the labor movement in this country has always been based precisely on the division of Black and white labor…Labor unions along with the bosses created the Negro as a kind of threat to the white worker. There's never been any coalition between Black and white. It's been prevented by the government and the industries and the unions." Yet, King wrote, "As I have said many times, and believe with all my heart, the coalition that can have the greatest impact in the struggle for human dignity here in America is

A. Philip Randolph (seated at left) with other officials of the Brotherhoood of Sleeping Car Porters in New York City's Labor Day Parade, 1939
Photograph by Joseph Schwartz

that of the Negro and the forces of labor, because their fortunes are so closely intertwined."

In the mid-20th century, at the height of the Great Migration of Black southerners to northern and western cities, unions acquired considerable influence over the allocation and compensation of work. And in many cities and states, especially New York City, unions also acquired significant social and political clout, influencing public policy on a range of issues. As a result, fighting for a progressive labor movement, and against discriminatory unions, became a central focus of the modern Civil Rights Movement. As union membership became linked to economic security and social benefits, and as unions became key to the political direction of the nation, the stakes of this struggle were high. In the long Civil Rights Movement in New York City, from the 1930s through the 1970s, several unions became strong advocates

for racial justice and fought to open their membership and workplaces to Black workers. But many others remained staunch defenders of the racial status quo, resisting activist pressure and defying new antidiscrimination laws. One visible indicator of a union's approach to race was the profile of its leaders and members. Were they all or mostly white men? Were they diverse by race and gender? Unions with larger memberships of Black and Latino workers and/or a history of left-wing leadership have typically been more progressive on social justice issues and more likely advocates of racial inclusion.

This chapter focuses on two of the most important contributions of organized labor to Black communities in postwar New York: first, creating a path to the middle class for tens of thousands of workers without college degrees—largely, but not exclusively, through organizing in the public sector; and, second, creating institutional space for a new type of Black leadership to emerge and exert influence over union and Black freedom struggles. On the first point, racially inclusive unions such as the Transport Workers Union of America (TWU); Local 1199 of the Drug, Hospital, and Health Care Employees Union; District Council 37 of the American Federation of State, County, and Municipal Employees (AFSCME); and District 65 of the Retail, Wholesale, and Department Store Union (RWDSU), enabled working-class Black New Yorkers to acquire job security, regular pay increases, pensions, and paid sick days. As it turns out, a union contract was a better way to ensure upward mobility than a barely enforced civil rights law. Before and alongside the important role that affirmative action in college admissions would play in expanding employment opportunities for African Americans, organized labor enabled some workers to escape the confines of menial, low-wage, and exploitative work, and build stable families and thriving communities. Local 1199 organized tens of thousands of Black and Latinx hospital workers across the city. The TWU's left-wing roots and early commitment to anti-discrimination made it a relatively welcoming union for Black workers across many decades.

Unfortunately, many other unions continued to practice unlawful race and sex discrimination, preventing a greater number of Black workers and their families from gaining their fair share of the good jobs in the metropolitan economy. The building trades were notorious in this regard, but areas of public sector employment, such as the police and fire departments, were also disproportionately white. For instance, by the early 1960s, when more than a million Black people resided in New York City, no Black person or Puerto Rican was among the 4,000 members of Pipefitters Local 638, and of the more than 4,000 members of the Metallic Lathers and Reinforcing Ironworkers Local 46, two were Black.

The second major contribution of organized labor to Black life in New York City was its role in facilitating a new kind of "race leadership" outside of the usual network of civil rights professionals and clergymen. Access to leadership positions in organized labor generated a working-class conscious Black leadership, one that developed innovative ideas and leadership for both the labor movement and the Civil Rights Movement. The Second Great Migration of the 1940s and 1950s gave New York City the largest urban Black population in the world, and the fight for good jobs became a top priority. Before the McCarthy-era purges of Communists, alleged Communists, and communist sympathizers from the labor movement, many left-led unions played a leading role in organizing Black workers, promoting their leadership and advocating for anti-racist causes and positions. The Congress of Industrial Organizations (CIO), itself, especially the CIO's New York City Central Labor Council, was a strong advocate for civil rights, and, in turn, many Black leaders and community activists became staunch supporters of unions and the right to organize. In 1945 a Black newspaper columnist advised Mayor William O'Dwyer that "Negro leaders in the trade unions are the most genuine ones in Harlem. In fact, Harlem voters listen to the shop stewards today more than to their preachers."

The Second Great Migration and Black Worker Mobilization

Who were these popular and influential trade unionists? A. Philip Randolph was the most renowned Black labor leader of the era. He bridged the tumultuous labor organizing of the early 20th century with the Black freedom struggle of the post–World War II Era. As a leader of the all-Black Brotherhood of Sleeping Car

Porters (BSCP), Randolph championed the momentous and successful fight for federal fair employment guarantees during World War II, and, in 1945, he and other labor leaders helped win an historic victory when New York became the first state in the country to enact a state-level fair employment law. Known as the Ives-Quinn Law, it outlawed discrimination in employment and union membership on the basis of race, religion, or national origin and established an enforcement commission. This achievement underscored the labor-focus of the city's civil rights struggle. The city's left-led unions produced a cohort of innovative Black unionists. Ewart Guinier, born to Jamaican parents in the Panama Canal Zone, rose to become the international secretary treasurer of the United Public Workers of America (UPWA). Guinier used his union leadership to advocate for the rights of Black workers—not only to good jobs, but also to modern housing,

good schools, equal city services, and a role in local government. Guinier, himself, ran for Manhattan Borough President as the nominee of the long-forgotten, but once vital, American Labor Party (ALP). The ALP helped to fuse labor with the rising civil rights advocacy of the 1940s, injecting class politics with greater attention to race and racism, but soon fell victim to the Red Scare.

UPWA efforts to organize African Americans and women of all backgrounds foreshadowed the importance of public sector employment and public sector unions to Black livelihoods in the coming decades. The UPWA was one of the most integrated unions by race and sex in the CIO and fought hard for a federal fair employment law. The union did not always win, but its intersectional analysis, willingness to build coalitions with Black community leaders and organizations, and fighting spirit modeled a compelling style of unionism. The UPWA orga-

nized a broad labor-Black community campaign in 1946 to save the jobs of 2,000 Black female employees of the Internal Revenue Service (IRS) in the Bronx. Strikingly, the IRS adopted the logic of proportional representation to argue that it employed too many Black women at the plant! The IRS administrator argued that since only one in 15 New Yorkers was Black, he would fire Black workers to match that proportion at the plant.

The mobilization succeeded in forcing the government to disavow this policy—and an African-American union representative testified in Washington, DC, on the need for a formal fair employment policy for federal employment. Yet, unfortunately for the workers, the plant relocated to Missouri not long after. A union leader called this "the worst case of discrimination our union has ever met," while others blamed "the spoils system," since both President Harry S. Truman and Secretary of the Treasury John W. Snyder, were Missourians. The UPWA also

boasted the first African-American woman to head a union local in New York. Eleanor Goding's local represented workers in the Department of Welfare. Goding fought against the practice of referring Black women welfare recipients for jobs as domestics or "menials." She also tried to promote solidarity between caseworkers and their clients.

Ferdinand Smith, the secretary of the National Maritime Union (NMU), was the highest-ranking Black official in the CIO. Like Guinier, Smith was an immigrant who used his union leadership position to put the cause of Black workers at the center of the northern civil rights struggle. The NMU advocated for federal civil rights laws, including anti-poll tax and anti-lynching legislation, and made it a policy to send out mixed-race crews on ships. Smith had lobbied during the war to win the appointment of the first Black captain, Hugh Mulzac, in the United States Merchant Marine. Mulzac, a proud NMU member and

Members of the National Maritime Union protest in New York, 1939

The NMU was known for its interracial membership and its fight to racially integrate maritime crews.

civil rights activist, became a famous symbol of integration in the 1940s. His multiracial crew made 22 transatlantic round-trips, transported 18,000 troops, shot down two enemy aircraft and did not sustain a single accident or loss of life.

This generation of Black left-unionists developed innovative analyses and approaches that derived from their personal understanding of how race operated in the workplace. They formulated prescient arguments in favor of affirmative action for unions whose long history of whites-only hiring meant that such seemingly race-neutral practices as seniority rights worked to entrench and solidify white racial advantage. Affirmative action, or modifying hiring procedures to ensure the hiring and promotion of Black workers, has working-class roots. Black labor leaders, especially those on the left, understood that the current distribution of jobs and resources was not "fair" and that true inclusion would require race-conscious measures to ensure racially inclusive outcomes. The CIO entertained debates on "adjusted seniority" based on race, but ultimately rejected it as divisive. Only one major union embraced the strategy of affirmative action in postwar hiring: the left-led United Electrical, Radio and Machine Workers of America (UE). The UE fought to save the wartime job gains of Black workers at Sperry Gyroscope Company, a Brooklyn defense contractor, by arguing for the appropriateness of a race-conscious, rather than strict seniority, approach to reconversion layoffs. In the end, management balked and laid off workers on the basis of strict seniority. As anticipated, this led to an almost complete end of Black employment at the plant.

Some advocates for Black women introduced a gender analysis as well. Black women workers in New York City were determined not to return to domestic service after the war. The National Council of Negro Women in Washington, DC, along with two left-wing civil rights formations in New York—the National Negro Congress (NNC) and the Negro Labor Victory Committee (NLVC)—tried to push this issue into policy circles and the larger labor movement. They argued for "special and particular attention" to "Negro women war workers" to prevent them from being "forced to return to service and domestic positions." These ideas were controversial when first introduced by leftists in the 1940s and remained so in the "house of labor," even while gaining greater mainstream acceptance in the 1960s and beyond.

Red Scare Setbacks

Some of the crucial figures in forging a role for labor in the fight for racial equality unfortunately fell victim to the post–World War II Red Scare, losing their jobs and positions in the labor movement. The anti-communist crusade undercut the radical-labor thrust of the postwar African-American freedom struggle. New York City Welfare Commissioner Raymond M. Hilliard fired Eleanor Goding and penalized or dismissed 175 staff members, 172 of whom were Black or Jewish. After the purge, Negro History Week programs in welfare centers across the city were cancelled. The UE and UPWA were both purged from the

organization called the National Negro Labor Council (NNLC). The NNLC survived until the mid-1950s in several major cities, including New York. Since Black workers were typically the last hired and first fired, and since labor market discrimination consigned them disproportionately to unskilled positions in various industries, they were first to experience the impact of automation. The NNLC brought attention to this issue, as well as to the emerging phenomenon of plant flight as employers sought cheaper labor in nonunionized regions. The NNLC organized pickets and boycotts against job discrimination by large companies and attracted considerable support from younger workers, in spite of being labeled by the government as a subversive organization.

Strong advocacy for racial justice in the workplace and in society did not end with this wave of repression, even as many individuals suffered and innovative ideas were marginalized. District 65, the warehouse and department store union, survived the Red Scare, and continued to fight against racism in the labor movement and across society. Black organizer and District 65 leader Cleveland Robinson became a major civil rights activist as the movement revived in the 1960s and 1970s. Robinson later played a pivotal role in pushing the labor movement to back the anti-apartheid struggle in South Africa. Intergenerational connections and inspirations proved important for the reinvigoration of Black labor activists. When future labor activist and writer Bill Fletcher Jr. was finishing college at Harvard, he asked his mentor, Ewart Guinier, for advice. Guinier urged him to go to District 65's headquarters in New York and look up Cleveland

Cleveland Robinson at the National Headquarters of the March on Washington in Harlem, 1963
Photograph by Orlando Fernandez

District 65's Cleveland Robinson was a key organizer of the 1963 March on Washington and other civil rights demonstrations.

CIO. Ewart Guinier later worked for the Queens Urban League and helped build the Afro-American Studies Department at Harvard University in the late 1960s. Ferdinand Smith was ousted from the NMU and deported to his native Jamaica, where he continued to organize workers. Hugh Mulzac was part of a generation of labor activists who were blacklisted from the waterfront, 50 to 70 percent of whom were either foreign-born or Black. But, as he had done all his life, Mulzac fought back. He sued the government, shipowners, and the NMU, ultimately prevailing in federal court.

After the CIO purges, leading Black labor leftists organized a relatively short-lived, but dynamic,

Robinson. District 65 and Local 1199, the hospital workers union—famously Martin Luther King Jr.'s favorite union—were the major sources of racial justice advocacy in organized labor in New York City in the 1960s and beyond. The municipal employee union District Council 37 joined them as a major site of Black worker incorporation into organized labor.

A. Philip Randolph continued his career as a leader in the more socially conservative AFL-CIO of the late 1950s and early 1960s. In many ways, Randolph's stature later in life as both a revered figurehead and occasional punching bag for AFL-CIO President George Meany illuminates the diminished stature of Black workers in the labor movement in the aftermath of the purges and consolidation of the AFL and CIO in 1955. Although Black membership in organized labor was growing, reaching more than one million members by the late 1950s, racial discrimination and segregation were still rife in workplaces and unions. While Randolph endorsed the anti-communist ouster of Black labor leftists in the late 1940s, a decade later he joined a critique by Black unionists of racism within the AFL-CIO. He was rebuked and sidelined as a result. His mostly unsuccessful efforts to make the labor federation adhere to antidiscrimination policies illustrates the meager gains of Cold War liberalism for the Black working class in New York City.

View of a group of African-American men standing behind a police barricade on 14th St. and Seventh Avenue during a protest of the hiring practices of the Longshoremen's Union, May 1970
Photograph by David Bernstein, Aesthetic Realism Photographer

As the city lost industrial and port jobs, and the Black Civil Rights Movement grew more militant, confrontations over hiring discrimination by unions grew more intense.

Civil Rights, Northern Style

Tellingly, the most robust support from New York City unions for civil rights during the 1960s was for the southern Civil Rights Movement rather than desegregation movements closer to home. The International Ladies' Garment Workers' Union (ILGWU) funded In Friendship, an important New York–based organization that funneled money and other support to the Montgomery bus boycott and other flash points in the southern civil rights struggle. At the same time, the ILGWU became notorious for its low-wage, predominantly female membership, including large numbers of African Americans and Puerto Rican women, and white, male leadership. The National Association for the Advancement of Colored People (NAACP) would later bring formal charges of discrimination against the union. There was a huge outpouring of support for the 1963 March on Washington, and many unions sent busloads or trainloads of members to participate in the historic rally for jobs and freedom.

Sit-down protest against discriminatory hiring practices at the construction site of SUNY Downstate hospital, 1963
Photograph by Bob Adelman

But, when hundreds of thousands of public school students boycotted classes in February 1964 demanding integrated schools in New York, unions stood on the sidelines. The United Federation of Teachers (UFT) did not formally support this nonviolent mass protest although many teachers helped boycott organizers set up alternative educational sites. By the end of the decade, after the continuing failure by New York City to integrate its schools, many in the Black community embraced the idea of "community control" of schools. UFT leaders bitterly opposed community control for its potential to grant local administrators the power to hire and fire teachers. Tragically, a series of teacher strikes against community control polarized labor and civil rights advocates and ended in rancor, lasting mistrust, and contributed to a revived conservatism in the city.

Another striking illustration of the failure of organized labor to support even modest and compelling civil rights goals unraveled in Brooklyn in 1963. The construction of the new Downstate Medical Center, part of the State University of New York, brought white control of the city's 119 building trades unions, and, as a result, virtually all of the well-paid construction jobs in New York City, into glaring public view. A clergy-led direct action campaign brought thousands of protesters out on the streets, dramatic confrontations, and, eventually, statements of support for antidiscrimination laws by city leaders—but very little action. One would think that a campaign by African Americans for a fair share of jobs in a very diverse borough on a publicly funded project would be easy for New Yorkers to rally around and elites to embrace. And,

certainly, many did. Like the school boycotts, the Downstate protests showed a well-organized, highly mobilized Black community, with many allies, willing to put their bodies on the line for equality and inclusion. At the same time, these protests revealed that Democratic Party liberalism in New York City (of which labor was a mainstay) could accommodate racial segregation and inequality. Calling it "de facto" segregation or attributing it to supposedly race-neutral union

contracts seems to have allowed many to wash their hands of any responsibility for a genuine engagement with civil rights enforcement.

As historian Joshua B. Freeman has shown, organized labor helped build an exceptional and flourishing social democratic state and society in postwar New York. If African Americans were disproportionately denied the better jobs and housing of the era, they were able to benefit from many of the municipal services and programs that were at its heart.

A housing project in Queens illustrates some of the contradictions of labor and race in working-class New York. The United Housing Foundation (UHF), an organization rooted in the early 20th-century anarchist wing of the Jewish labor movement, developed affordable cooperative housing for thousands of working-class families in New York City. In the early 1960s UHF built Rochdale Village, an enormous cooperative housing project of 5,860 apartments located in the predominantly Black

ADA B. JACKSON
for Borough President

EDMUND H.H. CADDY
for District Attorney

LEWIS S. FLAGG, JR.
r Judge 2nd Municip. Court

AMERICAN LA

ROW C

UNITED A

THOSE RESPONSIBLE

POLIC

BRUTALIT

VOTE ROW C... MARCANTONIO F

American Labor Party campaign poster, 1949

neighborhood of South Jamaica, Queens. The UHF promoted the development as an integrated community—a rarity in urban housing markets where the segregationist profit strategy had typically won the day. Sadly, many unions had already internalized the same segregationist logic. The UHF usually relied on investments from union pension funds to build cooperative housing, but, in this case, union leaders deemed integration to be too risky an investment. Even though thousands of whites eventually lived there—in its early years the complex was even majority white—these labor leaders expressed doubts that whites would ever move to South Jamaica. Fortu-

nately, New York State stepped in as a lender, ensuring the completion of the project.

The labor movement's retreat on race doomed the dream of genuine working-class solidarity that had grown out of periods of working-class militancy in the United States. Especially in the 1980s and beyond, this retreat made particular unions and many white workers ripe for courting by the Republican Party. The consequences of not fully integrating union leadership and not infusing unions with a genuine commitment to racial justice have had negative consequences in many aspects of urban life, but perhaps most glaringly, in the practice of

PARTY

INST

MAYOR

policing. After enduring many cases of police brutality and murder, Black leaders in the era of the Second Great Migration fought for criminal justice reform and civilian review of police conduct. Various struggles produced tepid reform and weak police-dominated review boards. Finally, after a couple of summers of Black uprisings over police violence nationwide, including in New York City, began to tear at the fabric of urban peace, Mayor John V. Lindsay appointed four civilians to the formerly police-controlled Civilian Complaint Review Board (CCRB), established in 1953 to investigate civilian complaints of police misconduct. The New York City Patrolmen's Benevolent Association (PBA), the city's police union, immediately mobilized to undermine the new CCRB and led a successful ballot referendum to return the CCRB to police control in 1966. Thus, in the middle of a decade of massive urban unrest sparked in almost every US city by a police shooting of an unarmed Black person or other alleged police brutality or misconduct—a phenomenon soon to be corroborated by the 1968 Kerner Commission Report—New York voters repealed civilian oversight of police misconduct. The police union's long history of racial animus undergirded and shaped its campaign against the civilian-led CCRB and brought into sharp relief the Police Department's fractured relationship with Black and brown communities in New York. In our own era of escalating police use of force and video after video of police shootings or killings of unarmed Black people, the legacy of that 1966 defeat is palpable.

The history of African Americans and unions in New York City has been marked by incredible highs and devastating lows. This makes it hard to draw generalizations, apart from the fact that unions matter. As this history illuminates, they matter in all sorts of ways—from a family's livelihood to the city's public policy. As deindustrialization has escalated in recent years, the significance of public sector employment and public sector unions to Black job security has loomed large. Because of past and present racial discrimination in the private sector, Black workers have been disproportionately employed in the public sector and at the forefront of building public sector unions, which have become the bedrock of the Black middle class in many cities, including New York.

Public Workers

Public workers began self-organizing in New York City in the late 19th and early 20th centuries, coinciding with an increase in governmental services and the advent of civil service reform.

Various associations of federal, state, and local government workers formed along occupational (postal, sanitation, and clerical workers; teachers, police, and firefighters) and departmental lines, or according to civil service status. An early, important goal of many employee associations was enforcement of civil service rules, a goal shared by government-reform groups to end political patronage-based decision-making.

Organizational strength varied. Interunion rivalries and factional disputes, as well as political and strategic differences, permeate much of the city's public-sector labor history. Among the most unified have been occupation-specific organizations. Over time, the racial, ethnic, and gender composition of the city workforce has substantially changed as well, with the uniformed services requiring litigation to compel a diverse and integrated workforce.

One thing has not changed: the persistent stereotype of government workers as a privileged class with job security, pensions, and alleged immunity from hard work. The stereotype is more than a century old. It was used in a May 1911 speech by President William Howard Taft to justify placing conditions on public workers "that should not be and ought not be imposed upon those who serve private employers." It remains a rhetorical tool used to create divisions between public- and private-sector workers, and to attack collective bargaining, job security protections, and pensions.

Some early New York public employee organizations affiliated with the labor movement, which had long sought to make government a "model employer" as a means of persuading private employers to follow suit, particularly in efforts to win the eight-hour workday.

In the late 19th century postal and sanitation workers joined the Knights of Labor. Later the American Federation of Labor (AFL) chartered public-sector organizations and advocated for laws to improve working conditions in government, even when it eschewed legislative solutions for industrial workers. The

New York City Teachers Union affiliated with the AFL in 1916. Two years later, the Uniform Fireman's Association (UFA) joined as well. Other employee organizations remained nonaligned, priding themselves on being protective associations of civil servants, rather than defining themselves as unions bent on collective bargaining. Resistance to unionization came from another employee group—those holding white-collar government jobs who viewed unionization as undermining their professional status. And some had no choice: the Patrolmen's Benevolent Association was prohibited by municipal law from affiliating with the labor movement, even after the AFL had lifted its two-decade ban on chartering police unions. (The lifting of the ban led to Boston's dramatic 1919 police strike after officers were fired because their union accepted an AFL charter.)

Traditional Means of Collective Advocacy: Lobbying and Political Action

The fact that they worked for the government caused public-sector workers to rely on strategies and tactics different from their private-sector counterparts. State power necessitates public-sector unions to develop and maintain good working relationships with public officials. The government has the power to grant or deny labor rights to its workers and to create and enforce laws concerning public employment. A prime example of the exercise of that power is the exclusion of government workers from the right to unionize and engage in collective bargaining guaranteed by the 1935 National Labor Relations Act (NLRA), the 1937 New York State Labor Relations Act, and the 1938 New York State Constitution.

Without collective bargaining, public employee organizations lobbied and engaged in political action

Strikebreakers "Breaking Garbage Strike at $5 a day," 1911

to improve working conditions. Most public-worker organizations limited their focus to bread-and-butter issues: wages, hours, pensions, and job security. The latter was what attracted many workers, including African Americans, women, and ethnic minorities, to public service. Early legislative victories brought elements of industrial democracy to New York's public sector by giving employees a voice in the workplace through due process disciplinary procedures, a salary classification system, equal pay for women teachers, and platoon systems for firefighters and police.

A prominent practitioner of maintaining close working relationships with elected officials, party leaders, and candidates was an organization of workers in city departments known as the Civil Service Forum, long led by onetime Deputy Comptroller Frank J. Prial who owned the civil service newspaper, *The Chief.* The Civil Service Forum closely aligned itself with politicians and it opposed collective bargaining and strikes. The organization's close collaboration and entanglement with partisan political forces undermined its organizational independence.

The effectiveness of lobbying and informal negotiations was limited. Public officials had no legal obligation to meet or confer with subordinates or their representatives. The civil liberties of government workers were suppressed, and workers were retaliated against, based on political or union activities. Presidential gag orders had prohibited federal workers from lobbying Congress concerning working conditions. The New York City Charter once banned police officers, firefighters, and teachers from joining or supporting organizations that lobbied, and teachers were subject to loyalty oaths.

During the first half of the 20th century, legislation made gradual inroads. The federal Lloyd-La Follette Act of 1912 was the first important law to protect the civil liberties of public workers. The law overturned the presidential gag order, granted postal workers the right to form a union, and codified tenure protections for many federal workers.

Another important civil liberties development was the 1920 Civil Rights Law provision signed by New York Governor Alfred E. Smith protecting the right of public workers to petition government officials. Extending that individual right into a collective right to file departmental grievances with union representation became a priority for many organizations, but such procedures did not get codified until the 1950s and 1960s. Even today, most workplace-related speech and petitions by individual public employees remain unprotected by the First Amendment.

Early Examples of Militant Public Unionism in New York City

Lobbying and political action were never the sole means adopted by municipal workers. From the beginning there was a more militant strain. Early examples include periodic strikes by sanitation workers over wages, hours, and workloads, including an April

1911 strike that was defeated with strikebreakers.

In the 1930s militancy grew among other groups of city workers. Bricklayers and other building trades workers struck over wages on projects funded by the federal Works Progress Administration (WPA). Many of the more militant public-sector unions were Communist led. A union of city relief workers, the Association of Workers in Public Relief Agencies (AWPRA), demanded the right to bargain collectively, led demonstrations and sit-ins, challenged civil service exams as having an adverse impact on African Americans, and protested anti-union retaliation. Informal negotiations between the AWPRA and agency officials resulted in a 1935 departmental disciplinary procedure that included union representation, a review of the discipline by a neutral board, and a ban on discrimination based on race, creed, or union activity.

Social unionism, which links workplace issues with broader social justice causes, grew as well during the Depression Era. The AWPRA opposed race discrimination and police brutality and aligned itself with others in advocating for the unemployed. The New York City Teachers Union worked with community groups to improve public schools by supporting increases in funding, the hiring of African-American and Puerto Rican teachers, the introduction of African-American history and culture into the curriculum, and a ban on racist and anti-Semitic textbooks.

In 1936 the AWPRA joined the American Federation of State, County and Municipal Employees (AFSCME), an AFL affiliate. The AFSCME's primary mission at its founding was to expand and enforce the civil service system. New York AWPRA leaders VVW Flaxer and William Gaulden became AFSCME vice presidents, making Gaulden one of the highest-ranking African Americans nationally in union leadership.

Following the creation of the Committee for Industrial Organization (CIO), the AWPRA and its members formed the nucleus of a competing CIO public-sector union, the State, County and Municipal

Abram Flaxer, 1937
Photograph by Harris and Ewing

Abram Flaxer, a leader of public relief workers, became an important figure in the city's emerging CIO union politics during the 1930s.

Workers of America (SCMWA). African Americans and women, including Ewart Guinier, Mary Luciel McGorkey, and Eleanor Goding, were among the SCMWA's leaders. It took decades before other public-sector organizations had integrated leadership.

The SCMWA's founding principles focused on bargaining, legislation, education, and antidiscrimination. Strikes and picketing were prohibited. The union's moderate tactics were remarkably different from the CIO-led industrial sit-down strikes. The initial rejection of strikes stemmed from the CIO's alliance with President Franklin D. Roosevelt, who opposed militancy by government workers, but recognized the legitimacy of public employee self-organization. The SCMWA's position on strikes fluctuated throughout the 1940s. The union was successful in negotiating collective bargaining agreements in the late 1930s and 1940s with public employers in other states including New Jersey, Michigan, and West Virginia.

City Worker Unionization in the 1940s and 1950s

For the next decade the SCMWA, the AFSCME, the Civil Service Forum, and other organizations competed to represent city workers, department by department. This competitive form of plural representation required each organization to have a presence in the workplace, and regular personal contact with department workers. The SCMWA's strongest base of support was among welfare and hospital workers.

In 1941 New York City Department of Sanitation workers quit the Civil Service Forum and joined the AFSCME. The move took place in the face of an organizing campaign by the CIO's Sanitation Workers Organizing Committee led by the SCMWA's Flaxer. Mayor Fiorello La Guardia and Sanitation Commissioner William F. Carey thwarted the CIO campaign to organize the 10,000 workers by granting the AFSCME exclusive representation rights in the department. Collective bargaining rights for city workers and political favoritism in the Sanitation Department were issues raised in William O'Dwyer's unsuccessful campaign in 1941 to deny La Guardia a third term.

The SCMWA also organized state workers in the city, creating locals in state departments in competition with the Civil Service Employees Association (CSEA). The SCMWA successfully lobbied Governor Herbert H. Lehman in 1939 to issue a memorandum directing state agency grievance procedures with a right to representation. But a bill supported by the SCMWA to require each city department to create a similar grievance procedure and to grant city workers the right to a join a union died in the City Council.

Collective bargaining in New York's public sector was slow in coming. The delay can be attributed to three factors: lack of support from civil service organizations, legal impediments, and opposition from politicians, including Mayor La Guardia, who objected to negotiating limitations on his authority. Indeed, La Guardia opposed SCMWA-supported collective bargaining legislation. He also refused to negotiate with the CIO's Transport Workers Union of

Members of the New York City Teachers Union protest Board of Education interrogations and firings of alleged communists, 1950

America (TWU) after two bankrupt private subway lines were unified with a municipal line to create an extensive public system, although he did agree to a grievance procedure with union representation.

The tide began to turn in the O'Dwyer administration. After succeeding La Guardia in 1946, William O'Dwyer aligned himself with the TWU and its president, Michael J. Quill, to support negotiations for transit workers. O'Dwyer rewarded the SCMWA by ending the AFSCME's exclusive representational role in the sanitation department. Later that year, the CIO merged the SCMWA with another of its public-sector unions to form the United Public Workers of America (UPWA).

But tensions remained high. Public workers in New York State were part of the nationwide strike wave that followed World War II. Upstate strikes and threatened strikes by the TWU resulted in a strong political backlash in Albany. A teachers' strike in Buffalo for higher wages precipitated the legislature to pass the Condon-Wadlin Act in 1947 with draconian anti-strike penalties for public workers.

The passage of the Condon-Wadlin Act coincided with the beginning of the Cold War, a dark and repressive period in public employment. The UPWA tried to remain vigilant, leading demonstrations at Welfare Department offices concerning staffing levels and relief payment increases, and bargaining contracts at The New School (a Manhattan University) and trade schools. The UPWA and its activists were subject to city and federal investigations, targeted by city officials, and purged from the CIO in 1950, claiming the organization was dominated by Communists.

Meanwhile, public school teachers active in the New York City Teachers Union, a UPWA affiliate, were investigated and fired under the Feinberg Law. (This 1949 civil service law amendment prohibited the employment of teachers and others in public schools and colleges who advocated or taught "the doctrine that the government of the United States or of any state or of any political subdivision thereof should be overthrown or overturned by force, violence or any unlawful means.")

The attacks on the UPWA and its activists by the CIO and government officials led to the union's demise. The UPWA's destruction did not end worker militancy or efforts to attain legal protections for self-organization and collective bargaining. Instead, it opened space for expanded organizing by rival labor organizations, some of which hired former UPWA activists such as Jack Bigel, who, years later, became a key labor advisor during negotiations that helped the city avoid bankruptcy during the mid-1970s fiscal crisis.

In the early 1950s, leadership and tactical disputes resulted in the AFSCME losing more than two-thirds of its city membership. The biggest loss came in 1951 when the United Sanitationmen's Association (USA), under the leadership of John J. DeLury, affiliated with the International Brotherhood of Teamsters. The following year, Henry Feinstein received a charter to form Teamsters Local 237 with hundreds of former members of AFSCME District Council 37 (DC 37), who were auto-engine men and a small group of hospital workers. Feinstein's departure provided the AFSCME's Jerry Wurf with an opportunity to rebuild DC 37 using trade union strategies and tactics.

The Beginning of Collective Bargaining for City Workers

The dawn of public-sector collective bargaining in New York came with the 1953 election of Mayor Robert F. Wagner Jr., who received support from the labor movement. Following his inauguration, Wagner gave a green light for the holding of representation elections and collective bargaining for transit workers, leading to the first formal public-sector agreements in New York. He also issued an interim order in 1954 that recognized the right of city workers to join a union without retaliation and to have representation under agency grievance procedures. Governor Thomas E. Dewey issued a similar executive order a few years earlier, at the urging of the CSEA, for state workers.

DC 37 put the interim order to use and campaigned to organize 5,000 New York City Department of Parks employees. Following a well-publicized battle with Parks Department Commissioner Robert Moses, and City Hall intervention, DC 37 won the right to represent park workers after an election.

Another turning point came in 1957, when the city implemented nonexclusive dues deduction check-off for all city unions. Dues checkoff was a goal of many unions, because it is a more efficient alternative to collecting dues directly from members in the workplace and after work. Dues checkoff had been part of deals reached a decade earlier between the TWU and transit officials, and between the UPWA and the City of Yonkers, to avoid threatened strikes.

Finally, after years of study, in March 1958, Wagner issued Executive Order 49 (EO 49), referred to as the "Little Wagner Act," which created the largest public-sector collective bargaining program in the country. Yet EO 49 had its limitations: it created a representation system dominated by Wagner and his appointees, with a cumbersome array of citywide and departmental units based on occupational classifications; it also lacked a neutral impasse procedure. Still, it introduced public-sector collective bargaining in New York.

The UFA was the first union certified as the exclusive representative for a bargaining unit, which included officers of all ranks within the fire department, except the chief and deputy chiefs. The USA was the second, and the first to negotiate a contract with the city, covering 10,000 sanitation department workers.

From then on, collective bargaining between unions and the city grew rapidly, and so did strikes. A short teachers strike for recognition in 1960 led to a representation election won by the United Federation of Teachers (UFT) over other teacher unions. In 1962 the UFT and the Board of Education negotiated a first contract for a unit of more than 35,000 teachers, but only after another one-day strike. During this period, there were other short strikes by sanitation

workers, city motor vehicle drivers, and others.

Wagner, in 1963, lifted the original exclusion of police from coverage under EO 49 (although in lifting the ban, he disqualified any union that admitted employees other than police force members or advocated in favor of strikes). His extension of collective bargaining to the police department resulted in five bargaining units based on rank and represented by separate unions, with police officers being represented by the PBA.

AFSCME leaders welcome Lilllian Roberts (second from right) after her release from jail, 1968

DC 37's Lillian Roberts was jailed under the Taylor Act for leading a strike by workers in New York State mental hospitals. A judge released her after she served 14 days of a 30-day sentence.

Civil Rights, Collective Bargaining, and Strikes

Even as they fought for bargaining rights, a number of municipal unions also pursued broader social goals. DC 37, the UFT, and other city unions supported the growing Civil Rights Movement and provided it with financial support. Thousands of their members participated in the 1963 March on Washington for Jobs and Freedom.

In 1965, the Welfare Department and the Department of Hospitals, two former strongholds of the UPWA, became the focus of increased

Anti-Mike Quill button, 1966

The 1966 transit strike sparked a backlash of commuter resentment.

TWU President Mike Quill tears up a temporary strike-barring injunction issued by State Supreme Court Justice George Tilzer, December 31, 1965

Photograph by Paul DeMaria

militancy and organizing. Eight thousand Welfare Department workers represented by the Social Service Employees Union (SSEU) and DC 37 participated in a month long strike that was settled after the city accepted a fact-finding panel's recommendations for substantial wage and health-benefit increases, workload limitations, and increased staffing. Mayor Wagner also agreed to appoint a panel to recommend changes to the city's collective bargaining program composed of labor representatives led by DC 37's Victor Gotbaum, city officials, and neutral public members.

Later that year, DC 37 scored a major victory over Teamsters Local 237 in an election to represent 20,000 hospital workers after a decade of interunion rivalry. Two African Americans, Local 237's Bill Lewis and DC 37's Lillian Roberts, played leading roles in the bitter campaign. Subsequent DC 37 victories in departmental elections resulted in the union gaining majority support and the right to negotiate on a citywide basis for a unit of all clerical workers and a unit of employees under the Career and Salary Plan, a city classification system of mostly white-collar titles and occupational groups. Additional election victories by DC 37 made it the largest and most powerful municipal union in the city.

But DC 37 was not the only militant union. After decades of strike threats, on January 1, 1966, the

TWU Local 100 members on strike, 1966
Photograph by Paul Slade

TWU pulled the trigger with a strike of 35,000 members that shut down the transit system for 12 days. The strike began the same day a new mayor, Republican John V. Lindsay, was sworn into office, a harbinger of labor conflicts to come during his first term. Virtually all the municipal unions had endorsed Lindsay's opponent, Democrat Abraham Beame, in the 1965 campaign, and they remained suspicious of Lindsay's aloofness and his labor agenda.

Union Rights Granted to All New York Public Workers and Strike Penalties Increased

The 1966 transit strike led to new calls for replacing the Condon-Wadlin Act, which had proven ineffective in deterring the strike. Governor Nelson Rockefeller appointed a committee of experts, headed by George Taylor, a professor at the Wharton School of Business, to propose legal changes to improve labor relations and avoid strikes. The Taylor Committee's March 1966 report broke new ground by recommending collective bargaining rights for all state and local government workers, along with new penalties and procedures for strikes. In the same month, the tripartite panel appointed by Wagner issued a report with its own recommendations for improving city-labor relations. Those recommendations, which were opposed by the SSEU and other unions, formed the basis for the New York City Collective Bargaining Law (NYCCBL).

Opposition to the proposed Taylor Law substantially delayed its passage in Albany and the enactment of the NYCCBL by the city council. Municipal unions vehemently opposed the Taylor Law's anti-strike provisions and held a May 1967 rally at Madison Square Garden to condemn them. Local governments opposed the expansion of collective bargaining rights to employees of counties, cities, towns, and villages beyond the five boroughs. On the other hand, the CSEA strongly supported the law because it would expand collective bargaining geographically and continue the ban on public-sector strikes.

On September 1, 1967, the Taylor Law and the NYCCBL became effective. Besides extending collective bargaining rights throughout New York State and increasing strike penalties, the Taylor Law codified dues deduction checkoff, established bargaining-impasse procedures, permitted card-check certification, and banned unions that discriminated based on race, creed, color, or religion. The NYCCBL created a new

city collective bargaining program consistent with the Taylor Law, replacing EO 49. A neutral tripartite municipal agency, the Office of Collective Bargaining (OCB), was formed to determine representation issues, consolidate the unwieldy system of bargaining units, and administer procedures to resolve contract grievances and bargaining impasses.

The Taylor Law's new strike penalties did not deter the UFT, led by Al Shanker. The UFT organized a three-week strike of 45,000 teachers shortly after the law became effective. The strike concerned wages, class size, and the power of classroom teachers to remove disruptive students.

In 1968, there were major and divisive strikes by sanitation workers as well as teachers. The sanitation

Day three of the sanitation workers strike, 1968

workers walked off the job after rejecting an agreement with the city negotiated by their leader, John J. DeLury. The strike angered many city residents as thousands of tons of garbage remained uncollected for nine days.

At the beginning of the 1968–69 school year, the UFT led a series of strikes over community control of the schools and tenure rights in Ocean Hill–Brownsville, shutting down the school system for months. The strike created a major wedge between the city's labor movement and Civil Rights Movement, and between elements of the African-American and Jewish communities. The Ocean Hill–Brownsville conflict pitted the UFT, which had a large Jewish membership with tenure and other contract rights, against African-American leaders and parents who insisted that their communities should control the hiring, firing, curriculum, and administration of schools in their neighborhoods.

In the same year, after two years of negotiations, DC 37 and the city reached a first citywide contract for a unit of 120,000 workers. The agreement enhanced the employee pension plan and made further changes, concerning hours, overtime, and other working conditions. In February 1969, the city signed contracts with DC 37 for more than 40,000 clerical and hospital workers, resulting in substantial wage increases and a minimum salary of $6,000.

By the end of Lindsay's first term, New York City's new system of collective bargaining had begun to work. There were newly negotiated contracts, a decline in strikes and contract impasses, the consolidation of bargaining units, fewer interunion rivalries, and a greater voice for city workers in workplace policies. Outside the city, there was a massive wave of organizing by numerous unions seeking to represent state and local government workers with bargaining rights under the Taylor Law. The organizing led to a proliferation of new collective bargaining relationships, contracts, impasses, and a large increase in strikes, which did not dissipate until the late 1970s.

Victor Gotbaum, executive director of DC 37 at a press conference during a strike of workers responsible for the operation of drawbridges, 1971

City labor negotiations were sometimes long and contentious, but the fruit of the process was a substantial improvement in the economic well-being of municipal workers and their families, along with greater uniformity in city departmental policies. Internal union bureaucracies were established to negotiate and pursue issues through the grievance process. Lindsay took a leading role in advocating for legal changes to require nonmembers to pay an agency fee for union representation to help ensure labor peace. Satisfaction with the improvement in city labor relations led DC 37, the USA, and the TWU to support Lindsay's reelection in 1969.

This did not mean that all was harmonious in Gotham. Firefighters and police participated in sick-outs and slowdowns in the early 1970s. DC 37 and Teamsters Local 237 led a disastrous two-day June 1971 job action of 8,000 drawbridge and sewer operators to protest the failure of the state to approve further enhancements to the pension plan that had been negotiated with the city. The strike resulted in major traffic jams as thousands of motorists were unable to cross drawbridges and millions of tons of untreated sewage was dumped into the city's waterways.

The 1971 strike was the antithesis of social unionism. Rather than trying to build community support, the strike had consequences that angered the public, politicians, and the press, feeding a growing dissatisfaction with the city's trajectory. Taxpayers, fueled in part by white backlash, were resentful over the salaries and benefits for an increasingly African-American and Latino municipal workforce. Financial analysts questioned the city's reliance on short-term debt to finance budget deficits emanating from a shrinking tax base caused by deindustrialization and suburbanization, in addition to the growing cost of expanded municipal services and collective bargaining agreements.

The Aftermath of the Fiscal Crisis and Public-Sector Unionization Today

Those dark clouds foreshadowed the mid-1970s fiscal crisis, which upended, but did not destroy, collective bargaining. The shock of the fiscal crisis opened the door for a new age of austerity that included external controls over negotiated contracts, layoffs, and less militancy among city workers and their unions. The concept of government as the model employer to be emulated by the private sector disappeared from labor-advocacy and public-policy discussions.

The relative weakness of city unions at the bargaining table, growing out of the fiscal crisis, led them to develop more sophisticated political-action programs, primarily as a rearguard measure to preserve and enhance benefits and protections. Unions developed get-out-the-vote initiatives, such as phone banking and door-to-door canvassing, in support of union-endorsed candidates in primary and general elections.

Union density today among all government workers in the New York City metropolitan area is 69 percent. Constructive relationships between the city and its unions continue to form the necessary bedrock for positive labor relations. But the increased prioritization of political action and the centralization of authority in union bureaucracies throughout the decades caused membership mobilization about workplace issues to atrophy. Militancy still exists, but only within occupational pockets, including the unlikely pair of police and faculty unions that have led street demonstrations and other forms of protest in support of their respective bargaining demands.

Public-sector unions face new threats, including the 2018 Supreme Court decision striking down the agency shop as unconstitutional, thereby mandating the "right to work" in public employment. These developments have made public-sector collective labor rights more vulnerable and has required government workers and their unions to begin to relearn the important organizing lessons of the past.

Members of the Uniformed Firefighters Association Local 94 during a brief (five-and-a-half-hour) strike, 1973
Photograph by Harry Harris

CRISIS &
TRANSFO

RMATION

2018

Crisis & Transformation: 1975–2018

T he 1970s were a watershed moment for New York City. The economic and political structures built up over the previous century proved unsustainable in the face of a deep national recession and a drain of jobs and people out of the city. The most dramatic manifestation of the resulting crisis was the near bankruptcy of the city government in 1975, which led to massive cuts in city services and the removal of power from local elected officials. However, the effects of hard times could be felt almost everywhere, as life for most New Yorkers grew increasingly harsh. Unions, especially the municipal unions, saw their power checked, as the state and federal governments as well as large banks and businesses took command over steering the municipality.

When the city recovered in the 1980s, it depended much more on finance, office jobs, tourism, and the service industries than in the past, and much less on blue-collar work, especially manufacturing. Once again, large-scale immigration, now more from Latin America and Asia than Europe, rejuvenated the city, with foreign-born workers filling the ever-growing number of low-wage jobs in domestic service, restaurants, health care, and other industries, in a city increasingly marked by income inequality.

In the face of economic changes and political leaders promoting a pro-business agenda, organized labor saw its membership and bargaining power diminish, even as it remained exceptionally strong by national standards. Over time, though, new groups of workers began to mobilize, sometimes through traditional unions and, in other cases, through new types of organizations. In the first decades of the 21st century, though labor movements no longer had the clout they once did, they still helped set the agenda for the city and contested for power on behalf of working people.

Economic and Fiscal Crisis

From 1790 to 1960, every 10 years the federal census reported that the population of New York City had grown. The 1960s saw a small drop, concentrated in Manhattan. Then the floor dropped out: during the 1970s the city's population shrank by more than 823,000, a loss of more than 10 percent. People moved out of the city for all kinds of reasons, including a desire for affordable, single-family homes that could be found in the suburbs, fear of racial change in their neighborhoods, rising crime, and the draw of other parts of the country, with warmer weather and new opportunities. However, many left— and fewer came—because of changes in the city's economy.

Manufacturers had been moving out of New York for many years, seeking more space, lower energy and labor costs, an escape from powerful unions, or to be closer to their markets; but after World War II new businesses no longer grew fast enough to counter the outflow. Employment on the waterfront also declined, the result of containerization and a shift of shipping to the New Jersey side of the harbor. At the same time, white-collar employment grew, as New York strengthened its role as a center for corporate headquarters, business services, and international finance and trade. The national recession that began in 1973 hit New York especially hard, accelerating the decline in manufacturing and leading to a net loss of more than 600,000 jobs between 1969 and 1977, 16 percent of the total. In 1975 the unemployment rate peaked at 12 percent, the highest level since the Great Depression.

The deep economic downturn exacerbated a municipal fiscal crunch that had been developing since the mid-1960s. The city government in New York, with its extensive social services, unionized municipal workforce, growing population of poor newcomers, and loss of tax-paying residents and businesses, kept going only by borrowing ever larger sums. In 1975 the large commercial banks refused to continue underwriting city bonds, raising the possibility of municipal bankruptcy. In a dizzying sequence of events, the state government intervened, setting up new, unelected bodies that effectively could force the city to act as they insisted. Under pressure, the city undertook massive layoffs of municipal employees and huge service cuts, including in core areas such as education and policing, which led to a rapid deterioration in the quality of city life. With people streaming out of New York, housing abandonment and arson became epidemic.

Unions were both targets during the fiscal crisis and part of its solution, as public workers were forced to give up wage increases and

Minimum wage workers and supporters rally for higher minimum wage, 2013
Photograph by Richard B. Levine

labor on, under deteriorating conditions, while their organizations agreed to use public employee pension funds to help bail out the city. The ineffectiveness of strikes that sought to check cutbacks was a measure of labor's declining power. Unions did keep in place collective bargaining and most of their contractual gains, while popular mobilizations succeeded in slowing, if not stopping, some austerity measures. Overall, however, the fiscal crisis left labor movements on the defensive, while business and financial interests gained more say in the day-to-day workings of New York.

Gotham Transformed

New York City's economy began to recover in 1977, but the city's historic role as a center of goods production and distribution continued to shrivel. Over the next dozen years, employment in manufacturing, wholesale trade, and goods transportation fell, with almost all new jobs coming from financial and business services; entertainment, tourism, and culture; health and social services; and government. The boom sectors were highly stratified, with Wall Street, corporate law, insurance, advertising, and accounting executives receiving extremely high wages, while jobs servicing the wealthy—driving cars, cleaning homes, working in restaurants, providing security, taking care of children, doing laundry—were poorly paid, with few, if any, benefits. The result was a growth of economic inequality in a city that often prided itself on its liberalism, but had a greater economic gulf between the rich and the poor than many cities that did not claim any special concern for social equity. As jobs disappeared in traditionally unionized sectors and grew in largely nonunionized ones, the overall size of organized labor fell: in 2000, 24.8 percent of workers in the greater metropolitan region belonged to a union, down from 34.4 percent in 1986, with almost all the loss in the private sector.

Renewed immigration made possible the revival of the city. Between 1980 and 2005 the city's population would have continued to fall, if not for the arrival of 1.3 million immigrants. The 1965 Immigration and Nationality Act, also known as the Hart-Celler Act, which ended the racist immigration quota system in place since the 1920s, led to both an overall increase in movement to the United States and a shift in the population's countries of origin. In New York, the largest post-1965 immigrant groups came from the Dominican Republic, China, Jamaica, Mexico, Guyana, and Haiti, with other Caribbean, South American, and Asian countries heavily represented as well. More immigrants than in the past were middle class, but most were of modest means, taking low-paid jobs in manufacturing, construction, health care, restaurants and hotels, and domestic service. Some depended on casual employment, "shaping up" (waiting to be hired by the day, in parking lots and on street corners) for jobs in demolition, construction, and landscaping. Without their labor, the city—especially the lifestyles of the well-off—would have ground to a halt.

The 21st Century

The September 11, 2001, terrorist attack on the World Trade Center was the deadliest catastrophe the city ever faced. It sent the local economy into a temporary tailspin, with permanent damage to the remaining pockets of blue-collar work in lower Manhattan. In the short term, the attack and the city's response to it highlighted the continuing centrality of ordinary working people to the functioning of New York's economy, both in the deaths of so many maintenance, restaurant, clerical, and security workers and in the heroism and sacrifice of the first responders. (Six hundred and thirty-six union members died during the attacks on September 11.) Yet labor movements had very little say in the massive investment of public funds in the rebuilding of lower Manhattan as an internationally oriented high-end corporate zone.

The city's economy soon recovered from the disaster, as New York entered a period of prolonged growth. Between 2000 and 2015, the city gained more than half a million residents. In 2018 its population exceeded 8.5 million, more than double the size of Los Angeles, the next-largest city in the country. A wealth of service jobs at the low end and finance and business service jobs at the high end continued to draw people from around the country and around the world. A sheen of wealth covered more and more of the city, spreading from the traditionally wealthy parts of Manhattan to other Manhattan neighborhoods, more and more of Brooklyn, and parts of Queens. However, for those without high incomes, life became increasingly difficult. Affordable housing grew ever harder to find, public housing deteriorated, public schools were among the most racially segregated in the country, and transportation became increasingly unreliable.

Faced with growing inequality and daily challenges of living, city labor movements began a revival, at first largely out of public view. New types of labor groups, such as worker centers, began addressing the problems of domestic and service workers, along with the growing legion of freelance and nominally self-employed workers who had little actual control over their work situations. Meanwhile, after a long decline, traditional unions in New York began to increase membership after 2012. A few unions, such as the health-care group Local 1199 and the building service union, 32BJ, both affiliated with the Service Employees International Union (SEIU), grew into New York–based regional giants.

The issue of economic inequality burst into public discourse with the Occupy Wall Street demonstrations in September 2011, which sparked widespread debate in the city and across the country; they also set the stage for the election of Mayor Bill de Blasio as an advocate of greater economic equality. In the years that followed, brief strikes by fast-food workers demanding living wages and pressure from labor groups led New York State to pass a $15-an-hour minimum wage and a law mandating paid family leave. Meanwhile, New York City enacted an ordinance requiring many employers to offer paid sick leave for the first time. Once again, labor movements—some representing groups such as domestic workers who had rarely had much say in city politics—made New York a leading force nationally in promoting an agenda to improve the condition of working people. New York remained a city of workers, a city of struggle.

The Fiscal Crisis and Union Decline

O n Wednesday, June 4, 1975, the narrow blocks of lower Manhattan were overwhelmed by a political demonstration, as 10,000 public-sector union members gathered to protest what they feared was the growing control of their city by banks.

Protest against city budget cuts, 1975

They listened to their leaders criticize the city's government for planning to lay off thousands of public employees in response to an emerging fiscal crisis. The unions promised to withdraw their money from the banks that they insisted bore primary responsibility for the city's fiscal woes, and to encourage their members to do the same, saying that the city's budget should not be balanced "on the backs" of city workers.

As it turned out, public-sector unions soon dropped their militant stance toward the city's financial elite, even as the city shrank its public workforce by tens of thousands.

Indeed, public-sector unions joined the ranks of the city's major creditors, loaning it money that helped New York avoid bankruptcy. In retrospect, the 1975 Wall Street protest is notable less for the actual impact it had on the city than for its symbolic resonance: it was one of the relatively few times in recent New York history when the long-standing institutions of the working class openly challenged the political power of finance. However, the uneasy resolution to the city's fiscal crisis also suggests something about the limits of labor's power in contemporary New York.

The Transformation of the Public Sector

The city's public-sector unions were transformed by the fiscal crisis of 1975. In the years leading up to the crisis, a recession, job loss, and an outflow of the city's population to its suburbs (all aided by state and federal policies that favored capital mobility and middle-class flight) had severely hampered the city's ability to pay for the generous array of social services it provided, including a network of municipal hospitals and health clinics and free tuition at the City University of New York (CUNY), as well as a substantial proportion of the bill for the federal assistance programs Medicaid and Aid to Families with Dependent Children (AFDC). At the same time, demand for these services was high and rising, given the deepening poverty of the city and the politics of the time. A changing climate for banks made them less willing to, and less interested in continuing to, extend money to the city, and the market of investors for city debt contracted, as news about the city's unstable finances became more widely known. In the spring of 1975, following the default of the Urban Development Corporation (a state agency), the banks that marketed New York City's debt to the country refused to do so any longer. For most of the rest of the year it appeared highly likely that the city would go bankrupt.

When the crisis began, the city's public-sector labor movement appeared to be surging, its signal victories still fresh. The 1965 strike of welfare workers that marked the beginning of the rapid expansion of District Council 37 (DC 37)—part of the American Federation of State,

County and Municipal Employees (AFSCME)—as the bargaining agent for city employees in a wide variety of occupations was still a recent memory. While city workers had been able to organize and collectively bargain since 1958, the Taylor Law (which recognized the right to collective bargaining in New York State, but penalized municipal workers for striking) had only been passed in 1967. The public-sector labor movement in New York City—as across the United States—built on the success and energy of the Civil Rights and Black Power Movements, organizing workers who were often people of color who labored in low-wage and low-status occupations. It also galvanized a generation of white ethnic workers who recognized the benefits that unions had attained for industrial workers, and wanted to bring those to the public sector.

The fiscal crisis came as a profound blow to this mobilization. Even

"Welcome to Fear City" pamphlet, 1975

A coalition of unions protested layoffs by presenting the fiscally challenged city as a dangerous place for visitors.

WELCOME TO FEAR CITY

A Survival Guide for Visitors to the City of New Yo

DAILY ☕ NEWS

FINAL ★★★★

NEW YORK'S PICTURE NEWSPAPER®

15¢

Vol. 57. No. 109 — New York, N.Y. 10017, Thursday, October 30, 1975 — Sunny, cool, 47-55. Details p. 135

FORD TO CITY: DROP DEAD

Vows He'll Veto Any Bail-Out

Abe, Carey Rip Stand

Stocks Skid, Dow Down 12

Three pages of stories
begin on page 3: full text
of Ford's speech on page 36

During the fiscal crisis,
the *Daily News* ran
arguably the most
notorious headline in
the city's history.

though the city's fiscal problems were primarily caused by the recession and the deindustrialization that was changing New York's economic base (as well as by changes in municipal bond markets that left the city prone to fiscal crisis), the city's labor movement was widely blamed for bringing it about. In addition, for most commentators across the political spectrum, the only possible answer to the crisis was retrenchment: layoffs of city workers, downsizing of city functions, and wage freezes or cuts for public employees. (In truth, wages and salaries for New York City's public-sector employees were not notably out of step with those in other cities; the stereotype of overpaid union workers bankrupting the city did not have merit, although it was true that New York

Victor Gotbaum, chairman of the New York City Municipal Labor Committee, 1975

DC 37's Victor Gotbaum became a key player in the decision by public-sector unions to invest in the city's debt to help avert municipal bankruptcy.

City's government was more ambitious than most other cities, and thus hired more workers altogether.)

At first many of the city's labor leaders were unsure that the city was, in fact, in actual danger of bankruptcy. They emphasized (as in the Wall Street rally) the political nature of the crisis, arguing that, surely, there were other options for New York. But Victor Gotbaum and the leadership of DC 37 increasingly became persuaded that the city might well declare bankruptcy, which would place the fate of the unions and their members in the hands of a single judge. DC 37 agreed to a program of wage deferrals for union members, and, in the fall of 1975, it was one of a number of city unions that agreed to its their pension fund money to purchase city debt—effectively giving the unions a fiduciary stake in the city's project of retrenchment.

Not all unions got on board so quickly, and the crisis revealed profound divisions in the city's labor movement. When police layoffs were announced in June 1975, a coalition of police unions produced the infamous "Welcome to Fear City" pamphlet, which purported to warn international tourists of a dangerous, violent city (the plan was to hand it out at Kennedy Airport), telling them to stay off the subways and likening the South Bronx to "Fort Apache." Laid-off police officers rampaged across the Brooklyn Bridge in early July, snarling traffic and threatening motorists. In September the city's public schoolteachers engaged in a one-week strike, protesting the conditions of schools after layoffs pushed class size up to 45 or 50 children per class. The city nearly defaulted when the United Federation of Teachers (UFT) briefly reneged on a promise to purchase $150 million of the near-bankrupt city's debt with pension funds (a decision that was reversed, under intense pressure, within a day). By October there were rumors of a general strike of city workers.

In the end, the city's municipal unions largely acquiesced to the project of shrinking the city's workforce by about 69,000 during the five years that followed the crisis. By and large, the unions chose layoffs and the accompanying decline in city services as a substitute for cuts to wages and benefits for members. (There was some effort to stanch the impact on city services by encouraging the use of federal Comprehensive Employment and Training Act funds to hire workers to make up for the losses to the city's payroll.)

For municipal unions, the formal expression of this changed relationship to the city came with the creation of the Municipal Unions/Financial Leaders Group (an organization known by the acronym MUFL, or "muffle"). This group was established in 1977 with the intention of facilitating communication between bankers and presidents of municipal unions, which had become among the city's largest creditors. Meeting regularly during the late 1970s, MUFL pushed for federal investment to replace the West Side Highway with an enormously expensive underground road, to improve the city's "business climate," and to encourage the federal government to assume a larger share of the city's welfare pro-grams in order to limit their impact on the city's budget. As important as the specific proposals, though, was the way in which MUFL helped to give institutional form to the new relationship between union leaders and the city's financial elite, which, in turn, limited the city's labor leaders' ability to protest the austerity of the era more vigorously.

In April 1980 labor gave its most dramatic test of the city's post-fiscal-crisis politics when the Transport Workers Union of America (TWU) went on strike. Members' wages had not increased since the crisis began, and their incomes were being seriously eroded by the era's high inflation. Mayor Edward I. Koch, elected in 1977 on a program of bringing the city's budget into balance and its unions to heel, took an adversarial stance toward the strike from the start. During the walkout he made a point of going to the Brooklyn Bridge from his office in City Hall to greet commuters who were walking to work and cheer them on. In the press the TWU was vilified for its selfishness and for breaking the law

Mayor Ed Koch joins commuters on the Brooklyn Bridge during the transit strike, 1980
Photograph by Willie Anderson

Mayor Koch's defiance of city employees' unions helped establish a new urban politics much less friendly to organized labor than in the past.

that barred them from striking. After 11 days, the strikers returned to work. While workers did, in fact, win wage increases of about eight to nine percent per year (much smaller than what they had sought), Koch insisted on the enforcement of the Taylor Law, collecting fines to penalize the strikers. What was more, the Metropolitan Transportation Authority (MTA) raised subway and bus fares in the wake of the strike. Public hostility toward the strike showed that municipal unions could no longer count on liberal support: instead, the city's Democratic establishment now felt that it had no obligation to appear to support organized labor. On the contrary, Koch's actions during the strike demonstrated that municipal unions could be treated as a narrow and selfish special interest, rather than as organizations that defended services in the interest of all New Yorkers or as groups that were capable of helping to create a more economically just city.

Although city payrolls grew again in the late 1980s, the mayors who followed Koch continued to make political capital out of taking a tough stance toward municipal unions. Facing renewed fiscal difficulties during the recession of the early 1990s, Mayor David Dinkins—generally thought of as quite liberal—engaged in another round of layoffs, failing, as historian Joshua B. Freeman put it, "to depart in any serious way from the post-fiscal cri-

sis consensus that city government best served the populace by creating a pro-business climate through tax breaks, zoning and spending priorities." Mayor Rudolph Giuliani took a belligerent public stance toward the city's organized workforce. Even though he ultimately pursued more concessionary policies toward municipal unions, his negative tone helped to set the framework for the city as a whole. Mayor Michael Bloomberg came into office promising a more tempered position, but, in fact, allowed many union contracts to expire and took years to negotiate new ones. At one point during his administration, every one of the city's 152 union contracts had expired, leaving the entire municipal workforce effectively working without a contract.

Meanwhile, some of the most important municipal unions (most notably DC 37) were divided by corruption scandals, including various pilfered funds, in the late 1990s. One scandal, in particular, involved rigging a contract ratification vote during the Giuliani years. While it might be too simple to say that the internal political climate of the union had been atrophied by the way that it developed following the fiscal crisis, the choice that union leaders made to stay away from articulating, fighting, and organizing for a different vision for city labor may have helped to create the culture that made the corruption possible.

Private-Sector Struggles

Although unions in the private sector were not directly affected by the fiscal crisis, the belt-tightening atmosphere in the city in the years that followed—and the way that

the crisis generally shifted the city's politics toward business—affected them as well. Chase Manhattan Bank executive David Rockefeller and Harry Van Arsdale, a buildings trade union leader and of the New York City Central Labor Council (NYCCLC), gathered union leaders from the private sector to create the Business/Labor Working Group in the late 1970s, similar to MUFL. The group brought top union leaders together with various corporate executives, with the goal of providing a forum for conversation and, ultimately, developing a common agenda to press in Albany and Washington, DC, and at the city level. Most of the group's goals were narrowly focused on finding ways to stimulate "job generation" by developing a business-friendly public agenda. The group advocated for lowering the city's personal income tax, reducing business taxes to stimulate real estate development, granting tax abatements (similar to the one that was famously awarded to Donald Trump and the Hyatt Organization to build the Grand Hyatt in Midtown), and extending tax credits to businesses to persuade them to come to New York.

None of this was particularly helpful in developing an independent agenda to improve the conditions of workers in New York. Poverty rates in the city rose from around 14 percent in the late 1960s to more than 20 percent in the early 1980s, hovering around there through the second decade of the 21st century—with a slight drop in 2018.

For some private-sector unions, the problem had to do with corrupt leadership. By the late 1990s, locals representing one-quarter of the city's union membership (about 300,000 people) had recently been in, or still were, under trusteeship from their national unions. The problems were especially serious in many of the construction unions: the carpenters, the plumbers, and the mason tenders. Aggressive efforts

to root out corrupt leaders did have some success. For example, Local 32B-32J of the Service Employees International Union (SEIU), which represents building service workers including doormen and maintenance workers, had been rife with corruption during the 1980s and 1990s. The leader of 32B-32J, Gus Bevona, was known for his annual salary of about $400,000 and his cushy penthouse apartment. In 1996, after Andrew Stern came in as president of the SEIU, Bevona was kicked out. The union's new leaders were more committed to organizing, and 32B-32J grew again—not just in New York City, but also in other northeastern states and Washington, DC.

Yet the very power of such large locals (and, perhaps, the residual effects of the history of corruption) may have had the effect of making it more difficult for city unions to develop a common agenda. SEIU locals, such as 32B-32J—and 1199SEIU, which has expanded far beyond New York City to represent health care workers in upstate New York, Massachusetts, New Jersey, Florida, and Maryland—count hundreds of thousands of workers as members, more than some national unions. These locals do not need to rely on institutions such as the NYCCLC, which once sought to coordinate mutual support between different unions in the city. By and large, they are able to set their own path in the city without relying on other unions for support. As a result, the city's unions are powerful, but also fragmented, dividing their support between different candidates in mayoral races and rarely staking out common political ground. No single union leader in the city holds a prominent place in the public imagination today.

Rally in support of striking employees of the *Daily News*, 1990

Photograph by Ron Frehm

Connected to this lack of public visibility, there have been very few major strikes in the city over the past few decades. In 1990 striking workers at the daily tabloid the *Daily News* were able to push back union-busting efforts by the Tribune Company (the paper's parent company) in what appeared, at the time, to be a victory that might resonate through the newspaper industry. This triumph was far less secure than it initially appeared to be, and it was hardly followed by notable private-sector successes. Late in the Bloomberg administration, a strike by the city's 8,800 school bus drivers (led by a local that historically had been influenced by organized crime) ended in defeat. More recently, 1,800 members of the International Brotherhood of Electrical Workers (IBEW) employed by Time Warner Cable engaged in a protracted strike after the company was purchased

by Charter Communications in 2016; the new company sought to replace the contract with one that offered less-generous health and retirement benefits. Despite some statements of support from the mayor and the governor, the company faced little real political pressure to settle.

One result of this low public profile and the relative independence and autonomy of particularly powerful locals has been the real difficulty of developing a working-class agenda for the city as a whole. This is evident in their relatively slow efforts to organize new groups of workers. As the city's economy recovered in the 1980s, and as immigration to New York surged, especially from Asian, African, and Latin American countries, a new working class took shape in the city, increasingly based in services and retail as opposed to manufacturing—jobs that have tended to be low wage, without much security. Throughout the 1980s and 1990s, there were sporadic organizing efforts among immigrant workers and low-wage service workers, both by established unions (such as the International Ladies' Garment Workers' Union [ILGWU], which led a major strike in Chinatown in 1982) and by immigrant "worker centers" outside of the traditional labor movement. In certain cases, unions followed the cues of worker centers, both competing with and emulating them. In the mid-1990s, for instance, an affiliate of the Laborers Union successfully unionized asbestos-removal workers, mostly undocumented Latin American immigrants; the Union of Needletrades, Industrial and Textile Employees (UNITE) sought to organize Mexican immigrants employed in food service; and the United Food and Commercial Workers International Union (UFCW) tried to organize African food-delivery workers.

In the years that followed the fiscal crisis, there were also some important victories in organizing white-collar workers—often professionals, artists, writers, and others, who found their craft and profession threatened by dynamics of the "new economy." Local 2110 of the United Automobile Workers (UAW) organized clerical staff at Columbia University in the early 1980s, curators at the Museum of Modern Art in the 1990s, and adjunct faculty at New York University (NYU) and The New School in the early 2000s. Local 2110 won the first contract for graduate-student teaching assistants and research assistants at a private university at NYU in 2001. Often, cultural and educational institutions fought unionization bitterly; Columbia, for example, appealed a National Labor Relations Board decision granting graduate employees the

right to organize, despite an election in 2016 that went 70 to 30 percent in favor of the union. These organizing campaigns involved many female workers, as well as professionals in academia and at cultural institutions who had never before been active participants in labor struggles. Even journalists at online publications have been drawn to unions (sometimes facing intransigent opposition—several Internet magazines simply shut down when their workers requested union representation). Ninety percent of the staff of *The New Yorker* magazine signed cards in support of unionization with the NewsGuild in the summer of 2018, citing concerns about the pressures that the magazine was coming under from parent company Condé Nast. "We believe that the ability to collectively bargain is the best way to secure a fairer workplace and to insure that the people who produce *The New Yorker* can continue to do so far into the future," they wrote in a letter asking for voluntary recognition.

These white-collar workers may be drawn to unionize because the city has progressively become a more difficult place to live for middle-class, as well as working-class, New Yorkers. Median income in the city is lower than that for the country as a whole (about $55,000, compared to $59,000, including Manhattan, the wealthiest borough). In the Bronx, median income is about $38,000. Despite some important gains under Mayor Bill de Blasio—most notably, legislation guaranteeing workers the right to take sick leave without retaliation from their employers and the expansion of the right to public education to three- and four-year-old children—spiraling rents, fraught schools, rising tuition at CUNY, and fare hikes and declin-

MoMA's union members march in the Labor Day Parade, hours after a 135-day strike ended in victory, 2000

Photograph by Thomas Griesel

ing service from the MTA have created serious problems for poor and middle-class people alike. Many of the 60,000 people who sleep in the city's homeless shelters are, in fact, employed, suggesting the extent to which homelessness is really a crisis of the working class.

The Paradox of New York Labor

Early in the 21st century, unions remained much stronger in New York City than in the rest of the country, a testament to the remarkable working-class mobilizations that transformed New York throughout the 20th century. In 2016 they represented nearly one-quarter of the city's workers (compared to 10 percent nationally). Even private-sector union density was higher in New York than elsewhere: 17.2 percent of the city's private-sector workers were in unions, as compared to only 6.4 percent nationally. This has meant substantial and sustained material benefits for those who belong to unions. Union members earn higher wages, receive better benefits, and have more job stability than people in similar jobs. To a great and under-recognized extent, New York City's unions are responsible for the continued presence of a diverse middle class in the city.

Yet there is a paradox: despite their continued importance, labor unions in New York are far less visible and influential than they once were, and, in particular, they seem less capable of shaping the city's broader politics. They have not played

CRISIS & TRANSFORMATION: 1975–2018

Héctor Figueroa, president of 32BJ SEIU attends a rally for higher wages, 2014
Photograph by Luiz Rampelotto

With over 163,000 members in the northeast, New York-based 32BJ SEIU is the nation's largest property service workers union, representing office cleaners, maintenance workers, doormen, and others.

the central role one might have imagined in public debates about the most pressing issues that confront contemporary New York: rising rents, homelessness, transit, and economic inequality—all issues of great importance to working-class people. This might lead to the question: Have unions in New York effectively accepted a subordinate position in the city's political life, perhaps (whether this is a conscious calculation or not) trading a more confrontational and disruptive role in its politics for relative stability?

The continued strength of the city's labor movement indicates the sheer scale of human work that is required to power New York, to reproduce life here on a daily basis. It can help us to think about the continued importance of working-class culture and politics in a city that appears a "capital of capital" for the world. Yet the city has not been immune to the transformations that have swept through the United States has a whole, and the problems facing workers in New York today closely resemble those in the rest of the country—indeed, there may be even more similarities today than there were in the past.

Health-care Workers and Union Power

The emergence of unions in the nation's expanding health-care industry was not supposed to happen.

Local 1199 strike against Mt. Sinai Hospital, 1959

Congressman Adam Clayton Powell Jr. (center left, with clerical collar), Local 1199 president Leon Davis (to the left of Powell), and NAACP New York chairman Joseph Overton (to the left of Davis) join striking members of Local 1199.

The low status of service and maintenance workers in hospitals and their lack of legal bargaining rights, as well as the special status that society accorded their employers (notably, the moral sanction against work stoppages that would leave patients helpless), combined to forestall union interest in organizing hospitals. However, starting in the late 1950s,

Local 1199, Retail Drug Employees, a 6,000-member union of pharmacists and drugstore employees rooted in left-wing industrial unionism of the 1930s, began a concerted effort to organize workers in New York City's voluntary (nonprofit) hospitals. To head the campaign, Leon J. Davis, the president of 1199 almost from the union's beginnings, recruited

71

Elliott Godoff, who had led numerous earlier, but mostly unsuccessful, efforts to unionize hospital workers in New York.

Having long-standing contacts at Montefiore Hospital in the Bronx, Godoff chose that institution as the initial target for 1199's campaign. Working alongside Theodore Mitchell, a former drugstore porter and the drug union's first African-American officer, Godoff launched an organizing drive in 1957 that lasted for about nine months. Ultimately, on the eve of a December 8, 1958, strike deadline, Montefiore agreed to recognize Local 1199 as "the sole collective bargaining agent pending a certification election and negotiate an agreement dealing with all issues." In a pattern that still characterizes labor-management relations in the health-care industry in New York, the agreement was tied to an increase in the reimbursement rate that the city paid to voluntary hospitals to take care of ward patients. By March 1959, a contract had been signed between 1199 and Montefiore, and a hospital workers' union was finally a reality.

Shortly after its prolonged campaign at Montefiore ended in victory, 1199 began organizing workers in other hospitals across the city. On May 8, 1959, some 3,500 workers at seven New York City hospitals took part in an unprecedented strike that lasted for 46 days. This time, 1199 was confronted by a more determined opposition, and the strike ended in a stalemate. Denied formal recognition, 1199 agreed to a Statement of Policy that established a quasi-public agency, the Permanent Administrative Committee (PAC), to conduct annual wage and job-grading reviews. In its first report, in 1960, the PAC announced that 1199's demand for union recognition and collective bargaining lay outside its jurisdiction. Within two years, hospital workers were again out on strike throughout the city. When public and political pressure to end the strike was applied, New York Governor Nelson Rockefeller decided to intervene. A settlement was reached after the governor pledged his support for legislation that would grant hospital workers collective bargaining rights.

In negotiations in 1968, 1199 demanded that its members receive a "$100-a-week" minimum salary, declaring its position to be "not arbitrable, not negotiable, it's irreducible." To represent their side, 15 New York City hospitals formed the League of Voluntary Hospitals and Homes of New York (LVHH) in March 1968. Despite its public stance that any strike was illegal, the league settled with the union one hour after a strike had begun and agreed to the $100-a-week minimum. Even so, this "breakthrough" meant that voluntary hospital workers would only now be earning a weekly salary that was above that established for a family of four to qualify for welfare in New York City.

DC 37 Enters the Fray

By the mid-1960s, 1199 was no longer the only union organizing workers in the health-care industry in New York City. In 1965 District Council 37 (DC 37) of the American Federation of State, County and Municipal Employees (AFSCME) entered the field. Founded in the

Midwest in 1936, AFSCME organized unions among public employees. Initially weak in New York City, AFSCME issued a charter to DC 37 in 1944. Three years later, Jerry Wurf, a young socialist and labor advocate, was chosen to lead the New York union. Charged with breaking a municipal labor-relations pattern that he termed "collective begging," Wurf turned DC 37 into a powerful union that, in 1956, won a 40-hour workweek for the city's public hospital and park workers, with voluntary dues checkoff to begin the following year. In 1964, Wurf left DC 37 to take over the national leadership of AFSCME.

Wurf chose Brooklyn native Victor Gotbaum as his successor at DC 37. During the previous decade, Gotbaum had been AFSCME's chief organizer in the Chicago–Cook County area. The nonprofessional workers in most of the region's hospitals labored under deplorable working conditions. To assist him in his campaign, Gotbaum called on Lillian Roberts, who, at age 18, had become Chicago's first African-American nurse's aide, to join the union's staff. A union member since 1948, Roberts had been elected to represent her fellow workers as a shop steward.

In New York and fresh off a union victory for social workers in the city's Welfare Department (now the Human Resources Administration), Gotbaum found DC 37 already in a battle with Teamsters Local 237 for the right to represent the city's more than 16,000 nonprofessional

Local 1199 flyer in Spanish and English encouraging workers to "Vote Yes" to unionize, 1959

 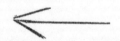   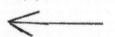

VOTE YES FOR LOCAL 1199

YES ⊠ ⟵ NO ☐

TUESDAY, DECEMBER 30th
from 7:00 A.M.
to 6:00 P.M.

The election will be held in the LOUNGE near the Employees Cafeteria.

Voting is secret. Local 1199 representatives will be present as watchers.

All full time and regular part time employees in the following categories MUST VOTE:
Nutrition Department, Laundry and Linen, Building Service Porters, Maids, Laboratory helpers, Animal Men, Nurses Aids, Attendants, Orderlies. Engineering Department. Including maintenance. Pharmacists, Messengers, Elevator Operators, store room employees. Technicians (X-Ray, Lab. etc.) HIP employees, Guards, watchmen, Switchboard operators, Clerical employees except Accounting Department.

ALL FULL TIME AND REGULAR PART TIME EMPLOYEES IN THE ABOVE CATEGORIES.

Even if you are off that day, be sure to come in and vote.

REMEMBER, THE BIGGER THE YES VOTE FOR LOCAL 1199....
THE BETTER THE CONTRACT.

The election for PN's has been set aside for the present.
12/58

VOTAR SI EN FAVOR DE LA LOCAL 1199

SI ⊠ ⟵ NO ☐

MARTES, 30 de DICIEMBRE DESDE LAS 7 POR LA MAÑANA HASTA LAS 7 DE LA TARDE.

La elecciones se celebraran en el salon social (loun serca de la cafeteria de los empleados.

El voto es secreto. Los representantes de la Local 1199 estaran presentes para observar. Todos los empleado que trabajan todo el tiempo y aquellos que trabajan solamente parte del tiempo las de siguientes categorias DEVEN VOTAR:

Departamento de nutricion, empleados de lavanderia, empleados de servicio del edificio, porteros, doncellas de servicio, (maids), ayudantes de laboratorio, cuidadores de animales, ayudantes de enfermeras y enfermeros, asistente departamento de ingenieria, farmaceuticos, mensajeros, ascensoristas, empleados del almacen. Tecnicos, (de laboratorio de rayos X etc), empleados del HIP, guardias, vigilantes, operadoras de telefono, empleados de oficina, exceptuando los del departamento de contabilidad.

TODOS LOS EMPLEADOS QUE TRABAJAN TODO EL TIEMPO Y LO EMPLEADOS QUE TRABAJAN SOLAMENTE PARTE DEL TIEMPO EN LAS CATEGORIAS ARRIBAS INDICADAS.

NO importa que si Usted tenga el dia libre, asegurase de venir a votar.

...RECUERDE, CUANTO MAS VOTOS EN FAVOR DE LA LOCAL 1199, MEJOR SERA EL CONTRATO.

Las elecciones para los PN'S se ha pospuesto al presente.

hospital workers, the mostly Puerto Rican and African-American aides, cooks, cleaners, and other support personnel who suffered from low pay, dreadful working conditions, and little respect from supervisors. Local 237 was led by Bill Lewis, a former hospital worker and, at the time, one of the highest-ranking African Americans in the New York labor movement. Gotbaum knew that Lewis was about to petition for representative elections, which, given DC 37's late start, made the union a decided underdog. Once again, Gotbaum's response was to turn to Roberts, who he brought to New York to lead DC 37's hospital campaign. Roberts promised workers that the union would win higher wages, improved working conditions, and more dignity on the job; in addition, she pledged to develop a career-training program that would help workers to move out of dead-end jobs.

For DC 37, as had been true for 1199 during its negotiations, political considerations were key to the union's eventual victory. Critically, Gotbaum won the support of veteran black leaders, including Bayard Rustin and A. Philip Randolph. Their endorsement and support from the city's other labor leaders helped convince Mayor Robert F. Wagner Jr. to agree to delay the union vote until the end of 1965, a tactic that clearly benefited DC 37. When the vote did finally take place, DC 37 won the largest unit, the hospital aides, with a narrow margin of just more than 800 votes, and also carried the messengers and clerks, leaving Local 237 with only the cooks. In the contract negotiations that followed, the city agreed to provide each worker with a cash raise of $900 and an annual $60 welfare-fund contribu-

DC 37's Victor Gotbaum (left) and Lillian Roberts (center, with microphone), 1979–1980

tion, which was increased to $85 the following year.

Of particular significance to nurse's aides in the city's hospitals was that Roberts made good on her promise to develop a training-and-upgrading program. In 1968, 422 aides graduated from an intense 14-month course; 96 percent of them received state licenses and became licensed practical nurses (LPNs). Looking back, Roberts recalls, "The union gave those Aides an opportunity I never had, and they responded with not one dropout."

In establishing their unions in New York's voluntary and public hospitals, 1199 and DC 37 benefited from the expansion of health services in the 1960s. Both unions confronted a more competitive and combative environment in the following decade. By 1980, more than 30 unions were actively organizing in health care. Because of legal maneuvers by hospital management, even an apparent victory, the passage in 1974 of amendments to federal labor law, which ended the exemption of voluntary hospitals from the 1935 National Labor Relations Act (NLRA), proved to be a mixed blessing. As an antidote to 1199's languishing fortunes due to the growing opposition from hospital management and from rival unions, Leon Davis proposed to the 1979 National Union convention that 1199 merge with the Service Employees International Union (SEIU).

Despite the convention's approval of Davis's resolution, the merger did not move forward. Unbridgeable divisions within 1199 soon developed that would tear the union apart a decade later.

Caring for the Nurses

The problem of competing unions would become particularly acute when, in the mid-1970s, 1199 sought to organize registered nurses. The union's interest in organizing registered nurses is hardly surprising. In New York City's hospitals, while total full-time equivalent personnel had fallen by 6.5 percent between 1975 and 1980, the number of registered nurses had risen by twice that number. In 1977, 1199 established the League of Registered Nurses as a new union division. At the same time, the American Federation of Teachers (AFT) opened its rolls to nonteaching professions, including registered nurses. In addition to the new players, long-established professional groups, such as the American Nurses Association (ANA), assumed trade union functions. For example, in 1977, the New York State Nurses Association (NYSNA) voted to drop its long-standing no-strike policy and to accept work stoppages as a valid collective-bargaining tool.

The first state nursing association in the United States, the NYSNA had been founded in 1901 "to promote the interests of registered nurses and exert its influence to improve the healthcare system." In its first initiative, the NYSNA supported passage of the 1902 Nurse Practice Act (NPA), which permitted registration of qualified nurses and created the title "registered nurse" (RN). But into the mid-1950s, the NYSNA resisted members' attempts to have the association become the collective-bargaining agent for registered nurses. In 1957 such a resolution was passed unanimously in the NYSNA's House of Delegates. The association's appeal among registered nurses undercut 1199's efforts to build its league division. By the early 1960s, the NYSNA would become the largest union for registered nurses in the country, representing nearly 30,000 RNs.

In 1978, and again a year later, the New York City Health and Hospitals Corporation (HHC) conducted elections to determine whether the NYSNA, 1199, or the AFT would

Mayor John Lindsay greets members of the New York State Nurses Association, 1968
Photograph by Anthony Calvacca

Members of the New York State Nurses Association were protesting a lack of progress in contract negotiations with the city.

represent RNs in the city's hospitals. Both times, 1199 lost the run-off election to the NYSNA. In addition, although 1199 had, in 1980, successfully organized the registered nurses at Lenox Hill Hospital, within a few years, its staff nurses were disillusioned with the union's representation. After considering affiliating with other unions, Lenox Hill's RNs chose instead to be represented by a union of their own making. Thus, in 1984, 1199 was decertified, and

the New York Professional Nurses Union (NYPNU) was born. Initially, the union represented current or retired RNs, nurse practitioners, and case managers. The NYPNU was the first nurses' union in the nation to set specific nurse-patient ratios in their collective-bargaining agreements. Soon after the NYPNU was established at Lenox Hill, the union was chosen to be the collective-bargaining agent at a number of other New York City hospitals.

Save Our Union

Leon Davis suffered a severe stroke in 1979. He formally stepped down as 1199's president three years later. Among the union's longtime leaders, two stood out as possible successors: Doris Turner, who, after serving as a rank-and-file organizer at New York's Lenox Hill Hospital, had, by the 1970s, risen up through union ranks to become vice president of 1199's Hospital Division; and Henry Nicholas, a former nursing attendant at Mount Sinai Hospital in the city, but whose union career was largely in Philadelphia, where he developed 1199's second-most powerful local. A succession crisis quickly developed and was exacerbated by the ongoing merger discussions that Davis had begun with the SEIU. A compromise gave Turner command of District 1199 (New York, New Jersey, and Connecticut) and Nicholas, the national union, but this arrangement only made matters worse. In 1985, an insurgent group called Save Our Union (SOU) challenged Turner in New York. SOU ran Georgianna Johnson against Turner for union president. Johnson, an African American like Turner and Nicholas,

was a former social-work assistant who had been an active union delegate. The next year, in the largest voter turnout in the union's history, Johnson was elected union president by an almost 3,000-vote plurality.

Leon Davis, leader of Local 1199, being interviewed at a rally, 1971
Photograph by San Reiss

Local 1199 delegate training session, c. 1980

Yet Johnson's election did not end the crisis. Looking to reassure members that they had a say in union policy, the SOU slate sought to enact a series of constitutional reforms that would restrain the power of the union president. Over Johnson's opposition, 1199's members ratified the amendments in a close vote. Union elections and negotiations for a new contract were both still a year off when SOU leaders, hoping to promote unity and to restore 1199's activist image as a champion of social justice for the powerless, launched a campaign to organize and upgrade the standing of the overwhelmingly female and multiethnic home care workers.

Caring at Home

In the mid-1980s, 1199 was one of three unions that represented home care workers. About 20,000 belonged to 1199's Hospital Division, 6,000 were represented by District Council 1707 of AFSCME (DC 1707), and some 24,000 were members of Locals 32B and 32J of the SEIU. Even as the number of patients receiving home care doubled and expenditures grew fourfold in the 1980s, the yearly income of most home care workers was well below the poverty line for a family of four in New York City. Classified by the city as "independent contractors," they were hired either by non-profit home health agencies or by for-profit agencies. In 1987, DC 1707, under its executive director, Robert McEnroe, and its home care director, Josephine LeBeau, united with 1199 (the SEIU refused to join them) to form the New York Labor Union Coalition for Home Care Workers. To generate a grassroots political campaign to achieve its ends, the coalition launched the "Campaign for Justice for Home Care Workers."

The Campaign for Justice reflected the dedication of both DC 1707 and 1199 to what the political scientist Immanuel Ness has called social movement unionism, "where union leaders use the militancy of members as a bargaining chip to influence public regulation and legislation in the effort to reach favorable bargaining agreements." As 1199 and DC 37 had during their early years, the coalition reached out to sympathetic public figures, such as John Cardinal O'Connor and presidential candidate Reverend Jesse Jackson. Prompted by the campaign, David Dinkins, the Manhattan borough president, agreed to hold a public hearing on the plight of the home care worker, during which many home care workers testified. In the fall of 1987 the campaign sponsored speak-outs at which home care workers, along with representatives from the community and religious groups, described the workers' plight before panels of local elected officials. Advertisements highlighting the sacrifices that these caregivers made and the compassion that they showed to their patients were run in *The New York Times*. The Home Care Council of New York City (HCC), which represented 60 nonprofit vendors, joined in the campaign. As the hospitals had during their negotiations with their workers' unions, the employer council pressed for greater state funding to help meet the demands of home care workers.

On March 31, 1988, unprecedented

negotiations with New York Governor Mario Cuomo resulted in the allocation by the state of the highest level of funding support ever given to home health care workers. The workers received a 53 percent wage increase, health insurance, prescription drug coverage, and guaranteed days off. Basil Paterson, an African-American political leader in New York who was also an attorney for 1199, likened the home care contract to the breakthroughs of the 1950s and 1960s, which had brought "an underpaid army of predominately black and Latin hospital workers out of the shadows of poverty." In 1988, 1199 established its Home Health Care Division; some 20 years later, it would have more than 75,000 members.

Labor-Management Cooperation

Dennis Rivera, an active member of the SOU coalition, led 1199's participation in the Campaign for Justice. Rivera had been a political activist in his native Aibonito, Puerto Rico, before coming to New York in 1976 and being hired as an 1199 organizer. He moved up quickly through the union ranks and, in 1989, was elected president of 1199. He immediately faced the union's latest round of contract negotiations with the LVHH. Believing that 1199 was still weakened by its internal struggles, the league took a hard line. However, with Cardinal O'Connor's blessing, on July 7, 1989, four Catholic hospitals held intensive informal negotiations with the union that led to a contract. League unity finally broke following a ten-to-one vote by union members in September in favor of going out on strike on October 4. One of the city's largest voluntary institutions, Presbyterian Hospital, reached an agreement with 1199 on October 2. Four days later the rest of the league gave way and agreed to a contract.

New York's voluntary hospitals appear to have drawn a practical lesson from being outmaneuvered

New York Governor Pataki shakes hands with Dennis Rivera, head of Local 1199SEIU, 2002
Photograph by Jim McKnight

Members of Local 1199SEIU were in Albany to lobby for the Health Care Reform Act.

in 1989. Kenneth Raske, president of the Greater New York Hospital Association (GNYHA), announced that he was "very happy" that a strike had been avoided and told the city's newspapers that he and "Mr. Rivera agreed to work together to see if we can make our case known in both Albany and Washington to deal with a health care crisis that transcends even the cost of this contract." Perhaps it is more accurate to say that, in 1989, the GNYHA had "relearned" an important lesson regarding labor relations in the health-care industry. As both the Montefiore and home care workers settlements had shown, more could be gained by collaboration between the hospitals and the union than from open warfare. Public funding was crucial, and input from the political system had clearly been necessary for getting that money and achieving the outcomes sought by both the hospitals and the union.

Shortly after becoming 1199's president, Rivera turned to reviving Davis's long-held dream of building "one big union of all health care workers." Rivera reached out to SEIU president John Sweeney, but, despite some early progress, those discussions fell apart. Ten years later, after Sweeney became president

of the AFL-CIO in 1995 and Andrew Stern was elected SEIU president the following year, merger negotiations finally succeeded. As a result, Rivera declared, "we will have more money for politics, more money for organizing, more money for collective bargaining." Members voting in both unions overwhelmingly endorsed the merger, and Local 1199 was renamed 1199SEIU United Healthcare Workers East.

Under Rivera, 1199 took a more collaborative than confrontational approach to employer-employee relations. The "understanding" established by Raske and Rivera in 1989 was formalized a decade later when the Healthcare Education Project (HEP) was launched. Since 1999, under the HEP, the union and the hospital association have jointly conducted dramatic public campaigns intended to "educate public officials and community members on healthcare issues [and] work to protect healthcare funding."

Unstated, but clearly as important, has been the goal of protecting hospital workers' jobs and standard of living. The HEP has protested potential cuts in health-care coverage and promoted new programs, such as Family Health Plus, enacted by New York State in 1999 to provide additional funding for the uninsured. Its public campaign in 2000 in support of the Health Care Reform Act, which extended health-care insurance to more than one million uninsured New Yorkers, included frequent 30-second television ads and was part of a lobbying effort that was said to have cost $13.3 million. In 2005 the HEP succeeded in convincing Governor George Pataki not to carry out his previously announced extensive health-care budget cuts.

Departing president of 1199SEIU Dennis Rivera (right) with George Gresham, his successor, 2007
Photograph by Don Hogan Charles

By the time George Gresham succeeded Dennis Rivera at the helm of 1199SEIU in 2007, the organization was New York City's largest labor union, representing 300,000 health care workers.

Militant Pragmatism

Roughly 60 percent of hospital revenue derives from Medicare and Medicaid funds, and 1199's alliance with the GNYHA in the HEP represents a practical understanding by both labor and management of the importance of public funding to their shared interests. Throughout the union's history, 1199 has not been averse to forming alliances with those who serve the union's interests. In 1962, after Governor Nelson Rockefeller had intervened in support of a law enabling collective bargaining in New York City hospitals, Leon Davis backed him for reelection. And in 2002 Rivera invoked Davis's endorsement of Rockefeller as he announced 1199SEIU's support for the reelection of New York's anti-welfare Republican Governor Pataki. Their alliance had been forged that year after the governor had, in response to a HEP-led campaign, guaranteed hospital workers raises and job security over a three-year period.

Rivera stepped down as president of 1199SEIU in 2007, and George Gresham, the union's secretary-treasurer, replaced him. Gresham has kept alive 1199SEIU's tradition of militant pragmatism, a combination, on the one hand, of left-wing unionism and, on the other, of "no-nonsense unionism." In 2011 Gresham was among the city's labor leaders who endorsed Occupy Wall Street (OWS), the radical encampment in Zuccotti Park in downtown Manhattan. Vowing 1199SEIU's help "in whatever ways possible," Gresham convened a series of meetings with other New York labor leaders to work with OWS. Gresham has also looked to tie 1199SEIU's efforts on behalf of home care workers to the "Fight for $15," the nationwide campaign to win a $15-an-hour minimum wage and union rights, particularly for workers in the fast-food industry. In this effort, Gresham became an enthusiastic supporter of New York Governor Andrew Cuomo. Nevertheless, 1199SEIU joined in an ultimately successful HEP-led "shock-and-awe" campaign in 2018 to convince Cuomo to support increased spending on health care. Tactics included a $6 million media blitz, public rallies in Albany, and continuous meetings with state legislators. Today, even as anti-union forces gain authority nationally, it seems likely that, at least in the health-care industry in New York City, a more collaborative approach will live on.

1199SEIU Placards, 2018

These placards are from an 1199SEIU picket line outside New York City's Terence Cardinal Cooke Health Center.

Chinatown, the Garment and Restaurant Industries, and Labor

Manhattan's Chinatown has been the primary gateway for working-class Chinese immigrants arriving in the United States for nearly a century—an ethnic enclave where wave after wave of men and women have found affordable housing and work in hand laundries, restaurants, garment shops, construction trades, and the tourist industry.

Chinatowns originally formed in the United States as safe havens, or ethnic islands; locations for protecting against racial hostility and violence, as well as for mobilizing financial and social capital from other Chinese immigrants. Manhattan's Chinatown has often been viewed as the quintessential example of an ethnic enclave, described as a place where immigrants of a particular immigrant group live and find work in locally owned ethnic enterprises.

Central to the theoretical formulation of the ethnic enclave, these areas are assumed to allow new arrivals to build on bonds of ethnic solidarity to mobilize social capital and achieve successes within the enclave that are unattainable in the primary economy. But the experience of Chinese labor is far more complex. While the Chinatown ethnic enclave can serve as a springboard for higher wages and improved social mobility that are unavailable to immigrant workers in the primary US economy, for many vulnerable, low-skilled, and even undocumented immigrants it is a trap where they are exploited by co-ethnics operating under the guise of ethnic solidarity.

Despite historical immigration restrictions, notably the Chinese Exclusion Act of 1882–1943, recent decades have seen unprecedented demographic growth as the total Chinese population in New York City has expanded exponentially from 32,831 in 1960 to 522,619 by 2012. As with much of the contemporary US immigrant population, the Immigration and Nationality Act (also known as the Hart-Celler Act) of 1965 opened the door to increasing Chinese immigration over the past 50 years. Economic opportunities rooted in Chinatown's ethnic enclave have provided the pull.

Prior to 1965 the vast majority of Chinese in the United States traced their origins to a few counties in the Taishan region of China's southern Guangdong (Canton) province.

After 1965 US reforms created legal migration opportunities for new immigrants from Hong Kong, Taiwan, Malaysia, Singapore, Cambodia, and Vietnam who arrived in increasing numbers. Five to seven thousand arrived in New York City each year through 1970 and the numbers increased dramatically after that. After normalization of relations between the United States and China in 1979, waves of immigrants from mainland China also began to arrive in New York, most notably from the Fuzhou area of southeast China. Post-1965 immigration also transformed the gender dynamics of Chinatown. Previous exclusion laws had created what has often been considered a bachelor society in which as many as 90 percent of Chinatown residents were men. Expanding immigration rapidly increased Chinatown's population of women, children, and families.

Chinatown and the Global City

The growth of Manhattan's Chinatown has relied not only on an influx of new immigrants, but also on new patterns of decentralization and mobility in the emerging global economy. Prior to 1965, Chinatown

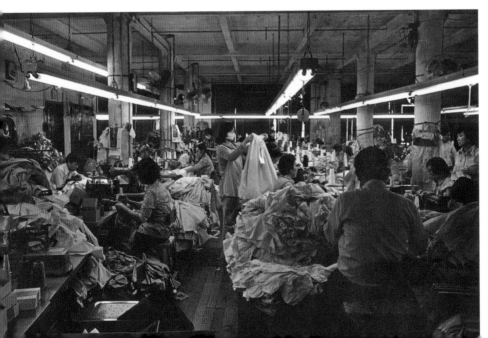

Workers in a Chinatown garment factory, 1979–1984
Photograph by Bud Glick

functioned as a small business enclave. Local entrepreneurs relied on the community's cheap labor, including family labor, to operate restaurants, hand laundries, produce markets, fish and meat stalls, and general grocery stores. Bakeries, jewelry shops, herbal stores, and cigar makers provided opportunities for both small-scale investment and small-scale employment. After 1965, however, Chinatown shifted from a small-business-oriented enclave to a working-class neighborhood and manufacturing center. The Chinatown garment industry expanded, even as overall garment manufacturing in New York City declined. The Chinese restaurant industry rose in tandem with it. While clothing companies increasingly began to "offshore" their garment production, they turned to Chinatown as a kind of unregulated export-processing zone. It was a place where subcontractors could work with garment-shop owners to access a plentiful supply of immigrant women who would work long hours at low wages in a community where labor, health, and safety standards largely went unenforced, even in unionized shops.

While the ethnic economy provides avenues to survival and upward mobility for many immigrant workers who are able to accumulate modest social and financial capital to move up the economic ladder, the physical and emotional toll in the garment and restaurant industries is intense, and, for many, the promised results do not materialize. In fact, the success of some within the system requires the exploitation of their co-ethnics. This was true in the garment industry that emerged in Chinatown in the 1960s, and it continues to be true in the restaurant industry, two economic sectors that have relied on cheap, vulnerable, and plentiful low-wage labor.

Garment Work and the Ethnic Enclave

ILGWU Local 23–25 Registration Drive, Mott Street, 1976
Photograph by Emile Bocian

In 1965 there were 35 Chinese-owned unionized garment shops. By 1969, 23 percent of Chinatown residents were working in the garment industry. By 1979, 85 percent of the Chinese women working in the ethnic economy were in the garment industry. The proportion of workers kept growing in tandem with increasing Chinese immigration to the United States, as there were few other options for Chinese women. Chinese factory owners easily recruited their co-ethnics via word of mouth, and, in turn, women were very willing to take these jobs. Moreover, women who recruited others to work in garment shops were often trained in factory work, and willing to teach a sister, a

cousin, or an aunt the new skill of sewing garments in a factory. In many of these factories women were only paid for the number of garments they completed.

Chinese women saw these jobs not only as a means to earn an income, but also as a way to get health insurance, paid vacation and sick leave, and other benefits for themselves and their families via the International Ladies' Garment Workers' Union (ILGWU). Since garment factories paid with checks, garment workers learned how to handle finances and American banking. Women's income records, bank and checking accounts, and other financial statements became the documents that were the backbone of applications to sponsor their relatives coming to

the United States. Moreover, these financial records also allowed many Chinese women to get mortgage credit to buy their first homes. Connections to banking provided an important way for new immigrants to forge connections with American institutions that would assist in their upward mobility.

From the 1960s through the 1990s, Chinese membership in the ILGWU grew despite declines in other union locals in New York City. By 1971 Local 23-25, with membership that was mostly Chinese, became the largest affiliate of the ILGWU and remained that way through 1995, when the ILGWU and the Amalgamated Clothing and Textile Workers Union (ACTWU) joined together to become the Union of

Striking members of ILGWU Local 23–25, 1982

Members of Local 23-25 displayed leaflets publicizing a mass rally to prepare for their July 15 strike

ILGWU Local 23–25 strike, 1982

The July 15, 1982 garment strike brought over 20,000 protesting workers onto Chinatown's streets.

Needletrades, Industrial and Textile Employees (UNITE). (In 2004, UNITE merged with the Hotel Employees and Restaurant Employees Union to become UNITE HERE.)

Throughout the 1970s and 1980s the garment industry in Chinatown remained robust. The city attracted prominent design houses because New York had the communication and financial connections that facilitated the marketing of fashion products both globally and locally. In addition, New York City had a sizable local population willing to buy such products and plenty of immigrants who could produce them. During the 1980s Donna Karan, Liz Claiborne, Anne Klein, Eileen Fisher, and many other notable designers and manufacturers made their headquarters in New York.

Garment shops in lower Manhattan were in close proximity to Chinatown, close enough that immigrant Chinese women could walk to work. The number of garment shops expanded along Canal Street and Broadway, reaching into Little Italy along Mulberry and Elizabeth Streets, and extending into the Lower East Side along East Broadway and Allen Street. From the late 1960s to the 1980s, Chinese contractors could purchase a factory of 25 sewing machines for as little as $25,000 by making a down payment of about $6,000 to $7,000. As a result, the Chinatown garment industry grew rapidly. From 1965 to 1975, the number of garment shops increased from 35 to 247; by the 1980s the number had peaked at more than 450. In 1983, Chinese garment workers were paid an estimated $125 million in wages, which meant that Chinatown was one of the city's largest manufacturing neighborhoods.

The Garment Industry and the 1982 Strike

The 1982 garment strike initiated by Chinese women was a landmark in labor history, similar to the New York City shirtwaist strike of 1909–10, known as the Uprising of the 20,000. Chinese women took to the streets to protest working conditions, including long hours, low wages, and employers who threatened them and withheld wages. When their union contract was up for renewal, female Chinatown workers feared that co-ethnic garment-shop owners would not sign it, depriving them of medical coverage, pensions, and other benefits that came with union membership. During the last few months of contract negotiations, workers were mobilized and threw their support behind the union instead of Chinese shop owners. As workers continued to join the union's side, small contractors signed the new contract. However, it wasn't until more than 20,000 workers held a one-day strike on July 15, 1982, that all garment-shop owners signed the contract. It was the largest labor strike in Chinatown's history.

The 1982 strike changed the face of the ILGWU. Even as Chinese women had come to make up an increasing share of the New York garment workforce, they had not moved into leadership roles within the ILGWU. But, to the surprise of many, women who were leaders of the 1982 strike were offered positions in the union. A few rose through the ranks. This was meaningful in that the union started explicitly to recognize the needs of Chinese workers and their families. Nevertheless, Chinese women continued to be excluded from the top leadership positions of Local 23-25, even though they made up the majority of its members.

The Decline of the Chinatown Garment Industry

Even though US garment production fell during the 1990s in general, in New York City the Chinese garment industry kept producing a substantial portion of all women's moderate and high-end apparel sold in the United States. Three hundred and fifty unionized shops and nearly 17,000 workers in Chinatown were still earning money in the 1990s. With improved computer tracking and project-management software, New York City filled the "quick-time" niche. Once a high-selling garment was identified using software tracking, orders to replenish the item were placed in New York garment shops. Chinese women, often working overtime and on weekends, turned around smaller runs of garments that then would be trucked to any US destination. Overseas production, by contrast, was cumbersome.

Following the September 11, 2001, terror attacks on the World Trade Center, at least a quarter of Chinatown's workforce became unemployed, mostly female garment workers. Chinatown and its garment industry were located just 10 blocks (about half a mile) from the World Trade Center site. After the attacks, no work, not even quick-time work, could be completed for at least three months. Many factories went out of business as a result. The women who lost their jobs were strongly connected to the community, and when disaster and recession hit Chinatown, they had few friends outside of Chinatown who could help them get other work.

After 2001 the garment industry deteriorated at an increasingly fast pace. The 2008 recession dealt another blow to the remaining shops in Chinatown. Today there are few shops left.

Quilt depicting garment work, 1989
Designed by Debbie Lee; sewn by garment workers Ng Mui Leung, Sheung Ngor Leung, Cecilia Lo, Yan Chai Mak, So Fong Lee Ng, Sun Ng, and Heng Yu Yan

This quilt was created by Chinese garment workers for the exhibition *Both Sides of the Cloth* presented at the Museum of Chinese in America in 1989

Chinatown's Restaurant Industry

The earliest Chinese "kitchen" in New York City emerged in a boardinghouse on lower Mott Street in Manhattan in the mid-1800s, serving the few dozen Chinese longshoremen and sailors working

along the East River on docks and in the shipping industry. Later, New York residents were also attracted to mysterious "Chinatown" and its exotic food. Chinese restaurants grew to meet this additional customer base, though the food, cooked by immigrants not trained as chefs, drew on local American foodstuffs and developed a distinctly American flavor. Chow mein and egg foo yung, two dishes that became American Chinese food standards, had no parallels in mainland Chinese cuisine.

The Chinatown restaurant industry, often perceived today as tourist-based, developed rapidly in the 1960s and 1970s to serve an extensive local Chinese clientele. As Chinatown's garment industry expanded during that period, more and more women were incorporated into the restaurant workforce. This development, coupled with increasing immigration, fueled the growth of Chinatown's restaurant industry to provide convenient and inexpensive food for the local Chinese

population. By the mid-1980s, more than 450 restaurants employed 15,000 people, mostly men.

These restaurants were only the most visible indication of a more comprehensive Chinese restaurant industry. A vertically integrated network of Chinese suppliers emerged to serve all aspects of the Chinese ethnic restaurant economy. Vegetable wholesalers purchased

Wireless portable payphone provided by Verizon in response to service disruption, September 23, 2001
Photograph by Lia Chang

Following the September 11, 2001 attack on the World Trade Center, telephone service was disrupted throughout Chinatown. The attack hurt the neighborhood's working people economically.

Program for the eighth annual Chinatown Labor Fair, printed in English and Chinese, 1991

The Chinatown Labor Fair was sponsored by the Chinese Staff and Worker's Association and 318 Restaurant Workers Union, among others.

produce from Chinese-owned farms in New Jersey, Long Island, and Florida; import/export firms brought canned mushrooms, bamboo shoots, and lychees from China; and restaurant-supply shops sold kitchen equipment, chopsticks, teacups, soy-sauce packets, Chinese zodiac placemats, and neon signs for shop windows. New York warehouses and noodle factories shipped rice noodles and dumplings across the United States. Print shops produced menus for Chinese restaurants across the country. Today the network of restaurant-ori-ented businesses includes a cluster of Fuzhounese-operated computer stores that design and support the dual-language software programs (written by programmers in Fuzhou, China) and supply the computer hardware for the point-of-sale systems used by restaurant cashiers and waiters to enter orders and process credit-card payments. The extensive local network of restaurant suppliers concentrated in Chinatown's ethnic enclave has made starting a restaurant much easier and opportunities for business investment more accessible and viable.

Fuzhounese Ethnic Restaurant Economy

New York's Chinese community has been transformed over the past 35 years by the arrival of more than 300,000 Fuzhounese immigrants from coastal southeast China. Spurred by the lack of opportunities at home, promises of jobs in New York and beyond, and easy access to a vast human trafficking network, today these mostly rural Fuzhounese have supplanted the Cantonese as Chinatown's largest ethnic Chinese community, vying for leadership in the area's economics, politics, social life, and even language use.

With the collapse of Chinatown's garment industry after 2001, the surge of new Fuzhounese immigrants and rapidly accumulating capital were channeled almost exclusively into the expansion of Chinatown's successful restaurant industry. After quickly saturating the surrounding New York tristate area market, the Chinatown restaurant industry and related business network have expanded to encompass a far-flung, yet highly integrated, national ethnic Fuzhounese restaurant economy. Across the United States a vast array of all-you-can-eat buffets and small take-out restaurants have opened in strip malls and remodeled restaurant buildings, largely run by Fuzhounese immigrants. As a result, there are 40,000 Chinese restaurants in the United States today, more than the number of McDonald's, Wendy's, and Burger King locations combined. Fuzhounese have also been establishing Thai, Vietnamese, Japanese, and Pan-Asian restaurants as a slightly more upscale market niche in which American customers are willing to pay higher prices. This far-flung national ethnic economy of Chinese restaurants relies heavily on Chinatown's dense assemblage of employment agencies, long-distance bus networks, restaurant supplies, know-how, capital, and labor. What is centralized is the business model developed and replicated through the Fuzhounese community and the New York–based infrastructure that supports it.

Employment agencies clustered

along East Broadway in Manhattan's Chinatown, and in Flushing, Queens, and Sunset Park, Brooklyn, are at the heart of the Fuzhounese ethnic restaurant economy. These agencies facilitate the circulation of an esti- mated 50,000 workers at any given time among far-flung restaurants. Long-distance Chinatown buses deliver workers along interstate high- ways to Maine, Wisconsin, Arkansas, and Florida. Yet, Fuzhounese restaurant entrepreneurs rely on New York's Chinatown hub for more than access to cheap, vulnerable labor. Chinatown is also the primary location for mobilizing capital to open a new restaurant, renovate an existing establishment, or trade up to a bigger operation. Fuzhounese en- trepreneurs rely heavily on informal

credit networks and revolving-loan funds maintained among kinship, hometown, and religious networks. Modest start-up capital, sometimes as little as $50,000, enables first-time entrepreneurs to launch a small take- out restaurant or buffet in an urban strip mall or small rural town.

The success of the Chinese restaurant industry model is built upon clear patterns of co-ethnic ex- ploitation. In particular, the illegality structured into the US immigration system drives down labor costs, as vulnerable, undocumented Chinese restaurant workers fear challenging the unfair labor practices of their co-ethnic employers. Since the 1986 Immigration Reform and Control Act, employer sanctions have pro- vided the primary mechanism for

Protesters carry a Chinese Staff and Workers' Associa- tion banner during the Campaign for Economic Justice, Foley Square, 1992

enforcing immigration law within US borders. But most Fuzhounese restaurant workers are paid off the books. Random labor inspections are rarely conducted. In addition, worker-initiated complaints run the risk of closing the ethnic enterprise that employs them and putting fellow workers at risk of deportation. Thus, the presence of large numbers of undocumented workers built into the Chinese ethnic economy leaves workers doubly vulnerable to unfair labor practices, even within their own ethnic community.

Organizing Chinese Restaurant Labor

The isolation of Chinatown from the US primary economy, the vulnerability of new immigrants with minimal English-language skills (particularly undocumented workers), and Chinatown's intense internal stratification have made labor organizing a difficult project. The dispersion of the Chinese restaurant economy across the country has made it more so. Despite this, labor organizations, such as the Chinese Staff and Workers' Association (CSWA), the independent 318 Restaurant Workers Union, and National Mobilization Against Sweatshops (NMASS) have had some notable and strategic successes.

In 1980, with the support of the CSWA, workers at Silver Palace restaurant became the first in Chinatown to establish an independent union after successfully striking to protest unfair working conditions, including tip skimming by management. But in 1994 the owners of Silver Palace fired all their unionized workers, claiming their wages were "too high," and attempted to undercut wages across Chinatown and the entire restaurant industry. Workers picketed for seven months before winning their jobs back in a settlement with the owners.

In 1995 workers at Jing Fong restaurant, Chinatown's largest, went on strike and picketed to protest

$1 hourly wages, no overtime pay, and the confiscation of 40 percent of waiter tips. Large-scale demonstrations, supported by the CSWA, were met with threats and harassment by Chinatown's restaurant owners, many of whom had direct ties to Chinatown's organized crime networks. The loft directly above the CSWA office was set on fire in what the New York City Fire Department called an act of arson. Eventually, the New York State Attorney General filed charges against Jing Fong for allegedly cheating workers out of $1.5 million. A parallel lawsuit led by the Asian American Legal Defense and Education Fund (AALDEF) resulted in a settlement in the workers' favor.

In 2007 the owners of Saigon

Demonstrators picketing outside of the Silver Palace during a lockout, 1993
Photograph by John Sotomayor

Deliverymen picketing Saigon Grill, Amsterdam Avenue and 90th Street, 2007

Photograph by Ruth Fremson

Grill, located outside Chinatown on Manhattan's Upper West Side, fired deliverymen and waiters who complained about their pay of less than $2 an hour, no overtime, workweeks as long as 80 hours, and a system of fines that forced workers to kick back wages if they were perceived to be breaking restaurant rules, such as failing to log in deliveries or letting the door slam too loudly. Two years of strikes, pickets, boycotts, and rallies, supported by the CSWA, the 318 Restaurant Workers Union, and the "Justice Will Be Served" campaign, led to a $4.6 million settlement for 36 employees, all immigrants from Fuzhou, China. The owner was charged with 400 counts of violating labor laws, including falsifying documents, and eventually jailed. Protests reignited in 2010 when new owners fired several older workers and refused to complete payment of previous settlement obligations. Saigon Grill eventually closed in 2013.

While not directly targeting the majority of Chinese-owned restaurants, these legal victories against unscrupulous owners and their exploitative practices sent a message throughout the restaurant industry and the Chinatown business establishment that workers can organize—and win. As a result, they have had a positive impact on wages and working conditions throughout the industry.

Conclusion

While most US Chinatowns have succumbed to the forces of urban renewal, development, and gentrification over the past 20 years to become, primarily, tourist destinations, expanding immigration and entrepreneurial economic activity, particularly in the restaurant trades, have provided the foundation for the continuation of New York City's Chinatown as a working-class job incubator. At the same time, the spatially unbound ethnic enclave has also extended patterns of inequality, stratification, and co-ethnic exploitation into the national ethnic restaurant economy. The continuous circulation of workers with extremely limited employment options creates a labor pool from which co-ethnic business owners can extract surplus value to enhance their profits. While opportunities for social mobility exist for some workers, for others, promises of ethnic solidarity are often fulfilled with wages of marginalization and co-ethnic exploitation.

Passerby argues with workers celebrating the closing of Saigon Grill, 2013
Photograph by Robert Caplin

Domestic Workers

Domestic workers have been a part of the landscape of New York City's labor force since the earliest European settlement.

Often referred to as "invisible workers," they are anything but invisible at their jobs. The nannies, cleaners, cooks, eldercare workers, and others who do the work of social reproduction—cleaning, cooking, and caring—that takes place in the home are intimately involved with family life. Unlike manufacturing workers, who are often employed in distant locations and whose labor is generally indiscernible in the finished product, the labor of domestic workers is, in most cases, carried out in full view of the employer-consumer. Moreover, it is, as the 21st century advocacy organization Domestic Workers United (DWU) put it, "the work that makes all other work possible."

Despite the importance of domestic work to sustaining family life and reproducing the workforce, both of which are essential to capitalism, the occupation has rarely been accounted for in mainstream labor history, union organizing, or in scholarship. In fact, domestic workers have a long history of organizing and resistance. In New York City, household workers began to mobilize most visibly during the Great Depression and continued to do so in periodic intervals up to the present. Through this organizing, they expanded the notion of work to include paid labor in the domestic sphere and forged innovative strategies that lend insight into organizing a precarious workforce.

The Great Depression

The Great Depression exposed the vulnerability of private household workers in an unstable labor market and fueled an incipient movement for reform. As difficult as the economic collapse of 1929 was for many Americans, the situation for domestic workers was dire. With 25 percent of the nation unemployed, work was especially hard for them to come by and, for those lucky enough to find a job, exploitation was rampant. As family incomes dwindled, employers fired domestic workers, reduced rates of pay, or simply squeezed more work out of their employees.

Although in New York City 60 percent of private household workers in 1930 were white (many of them immigrants), black workers captured the public's attention and became the most lauded organizers.

In 1935 two African-American women, investigative journalist Marvel Cooke and activist Ella Baker, coauthored a widely circulated article about what they called the "slave markets" of domestic labor— evoking both the legacy of slavery that had confined African-American women to paid housework and the bodily control that characterized the occupation. The article, published in the NAACP's magazine, *The Crisis*, cast light on an estimated 200 informal markets in New York City— essentially street corners—where African-American women waited in hopes of being hired for the day by white employers. "Rain or shine, cold or hot, you will find them there—Negro women, old and young—sometimes bedraggled, sometimes neatly dressed...waiting expectantly for Bronx housewives to buy their strength and energy." Cooke and Baker highlighted the exploitation of these workers, who had few occupational options: "Often, her day's slavery is rewarded with a single dollar bill or whatever her unscrupulous employer pleases to pay. More often, the clock is set back for an hour or more. Too often she is sent away without any pay at all."

Although domestic workers labored in isolation in the ostensibly private domestic sphere and were unable to form unions to leverage employers (since each employer usually had only a single employee), they nevertheless organized collectively. The Domestic Workers Union (DWU) was established in 1934 and led by Dora Jones, an African-Amer-

ican domestic worker from Sunnyside, Queens. The DWU was part of a constellation of domestic-worker organizations around the country in the 1930s. With bases in several New York City neighborhoods, it had an estimated 1,000 African-American and Finnish members, but soon became almost entirely black. Its activists recruited in public parks, apartment buildings, and in the "slave markets" to encourage workers to set a base wage below which they would refuse to work. The DWU organized mass meetings, advocated for individual workers, established a hiring hall, and campaigned for minimum wage and workers' compensation legislation.

According to historian Vanessa May, organizing was an opportunity for household workers to speak for

Domestic worker identified as "Mrs. Ackermann's Maid," c. 1914
Photograph by Wurts Brothers

Domestic service was one of the few work opportunities open to New York's African-American women.

Make a Wish (Bronx Slave Market, 170th Street, New York), 1938
Photograph by Robert H. McNeill

During the Great Depression, African Americans stood on specific Bronx streetcorners, waiting to be offered domestic work by white apartment dwellers.

themselves, and union members created a "community of shared experience and suffering." Participation seemed to have a tangible effect on those women who joined. In her 1940s master's thesis on domestic-worker organizing, veteran activist Esther Cooper Jackson recounted the views of one union member: "Before I belonged, I quit two jobs 'cause I couldn't stand it, and then spent a month on the 'slave market' working by the day for 25c an hour. ... I ain't never been sorry that I'm a Union member and I'll fight for the Union all I can."

In 1936 the DWU affiliated with the Building Service Employees International Union (BSEIU), a member of the American Federation of Labor (AFL). Under the slogan "Every domestic worker a union worker,"

the DWU required workers who came to the hiring hall to join the union, and insisted that employers sign contracts with its members. The union built alliances with labor and civil rights groups and the Women's Trade Union League (WTUL) to lobby for protective labor legislation in the state. Although hampered by a shortage of funds, opposition from white housewives, and a competitive labor market, which posed challenges for enforcing collective standards, the DWU continued to operate until at least 1950, after which there is little information about its activities.

Despite widespread and persistent exploitation, household workers were excluded from nearly all New Deal labor laws in the 1930s. As labor rights and economic security expanded for other working people, domestic workers were denied minimum wage, unemployment compensation, Social Security, and the right to organize and bargain collectively. Southern congressmen demanded, and northern Democrats acquiesced to, the exclusion of both domestic and agricultural workers for fear that extending rights to these workers would upset the racial order of the South. Even mainstream union members, who viewed some forms of labor as more worthy than others, failed to fight for legal protection for household workers.

Street-corner markets became a graphic example of the pervasiveness of racism in the labor force. The image of poor African-American women being subjected to a mod-ern-day "slave market" and mistreated with impunity by white employers fueled organizing and a commitment to reform. In the wake of the outcry, New York Mayor Fiorello La Guardia established the Committee on Street Corner Markets, which outlawed the hiring of women off the street, and opened two city-run employment offices to combat exploitative practices. This piecemeal reform, in a context of almost no protective labor legislation, failed to adequately address the problem of informality and exploitation in the occupation. Marvel Cooke continued throughout the 1950s to write journalistic exposés about the plight of African-American household workers.

The Civil Rights Movement

The Civil Rights Movement helped facilitate another movement for domestic workers' rights. Household workers across the country—in Cleveland, Atlanta, Montgomery, Detroit, and New York—who had been organizing locally came together in 1971 and formed the first nationwide organization of domestic work-ers, the Household Technicians of America (HTA), a title that denoted what they believed was the skilled nature of their labor. With the help of middle-class employers in the National Committee for Household Employment (NCHE), they sought to overturn the culture of servitude that characterized domestic work,

Carolyn Reed, undated

Domestic worker and activist Carolyn Reed became the National Committee on Household Employment's executive director in 1979.

Geraldine Miller, undated

Geraldine Miller founded the Bronx Household Technicians and the New York State Household Technicians during the 1970s.

the women with the worst-scarred knees were hired first because they looked like they worked the hardest." The stories were transformative for Miller: "This is just one of the things that kind of woke me up." As she immersed herself in the movement, the stories of the Bronx slave market became part of her organizing toolbox. She shared the anecdotes with other household workers to mobilize them to establish a common set of standards. By circulating these stories, Miller suggested that no household worker should ever have to scrub floors on their hands and knees. Her approach is indicative of how storytelling became invaluable in the formation of a collective political identity for domestic workers.

Miller formed the Bronx Household Technicians and the New York State Household Technicians, eventually becoming a leader in the national HTA. Joining hundreds of other workers at the first national gathering of the HTA in 1971 thrilled her. It was unlike anything she had ever seen before: "Over 500 black women who were household workers, who looked like they was Miss Ann herself—not Miss Ann's maids, but Miss Ann."

Reed had worked full time as a domestic worker since the age of 16. She organized locally and eventually became the executive director of the HTA. Reed was especially attuned to the way that employers used the trope of "one of the family" to extract labor from and deny rights to household workers. She unequivocally rejected any presumption that household workers were part of the family. As she put it: "I don't need a family. I only want a job."

While employed in a wealthy household in Scarsdale, New York,

aimed to professionalize the occupation through training programs, and lobbied for and won federal minimum wage after nearly 40 years of exclusion.

Geraldine Miller and Carolyn Reed were two prominent household-worker leaders in New York City. Born in Kansas, Miller began doing domestic work with her mother at the age of six. She moved to New York City in 1954, finding an apartment on Morris Avenue in the Bronx, a short distance from some of the most notorious "slave markets" of the Great Depression. She recounted hearing stories from women who stood on Burnside Avenue a generation earlier, waiting to be selected for cleaning jobs. "Sometimes they'd ask to see your knees and

Reed was welcomed as "one of the family." This meant working from seven in the morning until midnight. In five years, she never got a raise, received Social Security, or had a vacation. "Then one night," according to Reed, "the woman of the house—who had been having an affair and was very, very nervous—began to scream at me for not having done something she thought I should have done. ... As she screamed I realized I wasn't real to her. I mean, I wasn't a person to her. ... She had no respect for me, for what I did. ...I was a servant to her, maybe even a slave. I remember while she was screaming I began saying 'I don't work for you anymore.' ... And that was it. I packed my bags in the middle of the night; my husband, who was then my boyfriend, came and got me, and we took off." This incident exemplified for Reed the way emotional demands, intimacy, and bodily control were coupled with invisibility. She concluded: "Household workers have not been selling their services; they have been selling their souls."

Reed's aim was to ensure that household work was respected like all other forms of work and believed that organizing was the key. "Labor has to recognize us as a force. And how do you do that? Maybe it's developing a union of our own."

To this end, she painstakingly built a political base by reaching out to private household workers in public venues—bus stops, service entrances, laundry rooms, and neighborhood gourmet shops—since the workplace was off-limits. Shopkeepers and doormen on Lexington Avenue, where she lived and worked, regularly sent household workers her way.

Household Technicians of America poster, 1965–1980

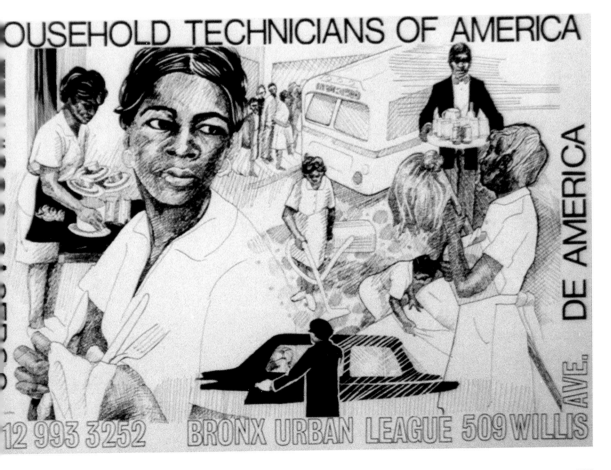

The *Village Voice* called her a "natural organizer at large." Reed firmly believed that household workers had power, which could take the form of a strike with the support of other service workers. One reporter explained Reed's position this way: "The idea of striking entire residential streets of Manhattan with delivery and repairmen honoring the picket lines doesn't faze Reed in the least." Her sense of the potential to strike came from her view of the indispensable labor power of household workers: "The houses could not be run. You could never know how helpless people can be—especially wealthy people—until you've worked in their homes. Just one day of true hardship or true inconvenience and they'd want to bargain." Only through this kind of collective power, she argued, could wages be raised and working conditions improved. For Reed, "Housekeepers, mostly black women, are the last frontier of labor organizing."

Workers in the 1960s and 1970s received little support from mainstream unions and maintained their autonomy from traditional labor leaders. However, they did garner support from employers, women's activists, and politicians in their push for amendments to the federal Fair Labor Standards Act (FLSA) that would assure them federal minimum wage. Congresswoman

Shirley Chisholm, an unwavering advocate, repeatedly championed bills to expand protections for domestic workers. Activist Gloria Steinem was a staunch supporter who organized a campaign to ensure enforcement of the minimum wage law. Although domestic workers strategically allied with middle-class feminists around the shared idea of upgrading housework, there was a vast gulf between the two. Middle-class feminists depended upon hiring and, in many cases, exploiting, the labor of domestic workers to realize their feminist dreams of professional success—a conflict that would ultimately prove difficult to surmount.

The passage of the 1974 FLSA Amendments was a milestone. It is important, however, to note that home health-care aides, who the Supreme Court defined as "companions," were exempted from the legislation, leaving a growing sector of household workers outside the purview of the FLSA. Moreover, as immigrants—now a more diverse group because of the 1965 Hart-Celler Act—continued to find their way to the city, many ended up as domestic workers. These workers were vulnerable because of limited English proficiency or knowledge of American law, or were undocumented, making the enforcement of the rights to which they were entitled less likely.

Contemporary Organizing

In 2000 Domestic Workers United (DWU) (no relationship to the Domestic Workers Union of the Great Depression), a citywide multiracial coalition of local organizations, came together to address patterns of exploitation and egregious instances of abuse. This coalition included Haitian Women for Haitian Refugees (HWHR), the Committee Against Anti-Asian Violence (CAAAV), Damayan Migrant Workers Association (a Filipina organization), Adhikaar (a Nepali organization), and Andolan

Ai-jen Poo during a panel discussion on domestic work in the United States at The Ford Foundation, 2012
Photograph by Donald Bowers

(which organized South Asian workers). These neighborhood-based ethnic organizations had taken up the issue of worker organizing, sometimes through the formation of worker centers. The diversity of these organizations reflects the changing character of domestic work and the city's workforce.

The DWU adopted the slogan, "Tell Dem Slavery Done," drawing parallels, as earlier organizers did, to the racialized nature of domestic work and the near-total control employers wielded. Organizers recruited at playgrounds, where workers mingled as their charges played. Erline Brown, a nanny and one of those early organizers, was born in Barbados and raised in England. She explained that neither race nor nationality served as a barrier to organizing because of their common experiences. "Wherever you go the story is the same. Once you are doing this work, you just do not get respected. You get very little pay. You get abused." The DWU's multiracial base was evident in its mass meetings, which brought together young and old, men and women, and people of different national, ethnic, and linguistic backgrounds. Meetings were conducted with interpretation in multiple languages and decision-making was often collective.

The DWU advocated on behalf of individual workers who experienced wage theft, exploitation, or abuse. One case involved the household worker of a family that owned an Italian restaurant. The worker, a Colombian immigrant, slept in a sewage-filled basement and labored 72 hours a week, cleaning, cooking, and caring for a disabled boy, for which she was paid less than two dollars an hour. When she was fired without notice and told to leave the next day, she had nowhere to go and turned to the DWU. By organizing public protests, a picket of the employers' home, and a boycott of the restaurant, along with employing legal strategies, the DWU won a settlement for the worker in 2009 after a four-year battle.

In addition to advocacy work, the DWU's first legislative victory was a New York City law passed in 2003, which mandated that employment agencies provide a written contract to employers and employees—a document that outlines workers' rights and benefits. With the help of employer allies, the DWU also lobbied for and, in 2010, won passage of a statewide Domestic Workers' Bill of Rights, the first in the country. The Bill of Rights provides for overtime pay, a day off every seven days, three days of paid leave every year after one year of employment, and protection from racial or gender harassment.

Domestic workers have scaled up their organizing with the formation of the National Domestic Workers Alliance (NDWA) in 2007. Ai-jen Poo, executive director of the DWU, eventually went on to head the NDWA. The NDWA joined a global effort under the auspices of the International Domestic Workers Federation (IDWF) to push for an International Labor Organization Convention on Domestic Work, which established international standards for the occupation in 2011. Although the conventionit needs to be ratified by individual countries, it is a step forward in the recognition of domestic workers' rights.

In addition to scaling up, household workers have scaled out, forming partnerships with other workers. Many local workers' advocacy groups, including worker centers, represent workers with different occupations: day laborers, domestic workers, taxi drivers, car washers, restaurant workers, and nail-salon workers. Workers float between these occupations or they may hold down more than one job.

Through their organizing, domestic workers from the early 20th century and into the 21st century have redefined the meaning of labor and labor organizing. They have drawn attention to work that takes place in the privacy of the home, work that previously was not recognized as "real" work. Domestic workers are the quintessential precarious workers—laboring with little job security, few wage or benefit guarantees, and minimal protected rights to organize. Their marginalization from the labor movement and exclusion from the National Labor Relations Act (NLRA), as well as the distinctiveness of their labor, have made it necessary for them to develop new and untested patterns of labor organizing. Given the imbalance of power between employer and employee, they have sometimes allied with employers and, at other times, bypassed employers to advocate state-based reforms that would protect all workers, whether they were organizational members or not. The isolated nature of their work prompt-

DWU rally for the Domestic Workers Bill of Rights, 2009
Photograph by Frances Roberts

ed them to utilize public spaces—playgrounds, city buses, and laundry rooms—as sites of organizing and to rely on storytelling to recruit workers and build a collective political identity. The contingent nature of their work encouraged them to reach out to workers of all different racial and ethnic backgrounds, including all skills levels, whether documented immigrants or not.

In some ways, domestic workers foreshadowed a strategic shift in the labor movement to meld labor organizing with social-movement strategies—what has come to be known as social-movement unionism. Domestic workers mobilized a support base of students, clergy, and employer organizations to draw attention to egregious instances of abuse and move the moral compass of ordinary people. They broke new ground in worker organization by targeting those workers deemed "unorganizable"—primarily women of color—and expanding the contours of American labor activism.

As the city's workforce continues to transform with the growth of service-sector jobs filled largely by white women and people of color, as the character of work becomes more contingent, and as the rights of workers to organize are whittled away, the lessons of domestic-worker activists might be ever-more salient as the 21st century workforce searches for new models of labor organizing.

New Forms of Struggle: The "Alt-labor" Movement in New York City

N ew York has the dubious distinction of ranking first among the nation's cities in its level of income inequality.

Home to some of the world's wealthiest people, it also relies on a vast army of low-wage workers whose labor is indispensable to its day-to-day functioning. Among them are nannies, house cleaners, day laborers, dishwashers, street vendors, taxi drivers, and food-delivery workers. These vulnerable workers are mostly foreign born, often undocumented. Immigrants make up almost half (45 percent) of the city's overall labor force and a much higher proportion of those in low-wage occupations.

Struggling to survive at pay levels close to (or sometimes below) the legal minimum wage, and without any type of job security, these workers are part of the new "precariat." That term is novel, but the conditions to which it refers are not: similar forms of labor exploitation were widespread before the New Deal reforms of the 1930s and the ac-companying upsurge of unionism. In recent years, against the background of declining union power, nearly forgotten forms of labor organizing that were commonplace in the pre–New Deal Era have resurfaced.

Starting in the 1970s new business strategies designed to shift market risks from employers to subcontractors, or directly to individual workers, stimulated rapid growth in nonstandard, precarious forms of work. A vast array of "independent contractors" appeared, many performing tasks previously done by wage and salary workers, but no longer protected by minimum-wage laws and other labor standards. In the same period, a surge of deregulation paved the way for the expansion of sweatshop labor, which had virtually disappeared in the New Deal Era. Meanwhile, rapid growth in the ranks of unauthorized immigrants, who are especially vulnerable to employer abuse and often fearful of seeking redress, provided a new labor supply, facilitating the rise of the precariat.

A concerted employer effort to weaken or, where possible, eliminate labor unions also contributed to the transformation of the employment landscape.

Fekkak Mamdouh, founder of the Restaurant Opportunities Center (ROC), 2016
Photograph by Rick Wenner

Street Vendor Project protest, 2016
Photograph by Erik McGregor

SVP organized a protest to push for city legislation lifting the cap on the number of vendor permits and licenses.

Street Vendor Project protest, 2015
Photograph by Ethel Wolvovitz

tor, unionization is much more extensive: the 2017 rates were 70 percent in New York City and 36 percent nationwide.) Yet very few members of the city's burgeoning precariat are unionized. Some are employed in jobs that have traditionally been beyond the reach of organized labor, such as domestic work and other personal services, which soaring inequality renders increasingly affordable to the affluent. Others toil in industries where unionization once flourished but has fallen sharply in recent decades, such as restaurants or residential construction. Still others are independent contractors and ineligible for unionization under US labor law.

Although largely lacking union representation, the precariat is not entirely voiceless. It is the key constituency of the "alt-labor" movement that took root at the end of the 20th century, made up of community-based "worker centers" that advocate for improvements in pay and conditions for those on the margins of the labor market and organize precarious workers to defend and expand their rights. At last count, there were 220 worker centers around the nation, 26 of which were operating in the five boroughs of New York City.

Organized labor remains a significant presence in New York City, where the private-sector unionization rate was 17 percent in 2017, far higher than the US average of just above 6 percent. (In the public sec-

Origins

The nation's very first worker center, the Chinese Staff and Workers' Association (CSWA), was founded in 1979 in New York City's Chinatown. Supported by foundation grants and, to a lesser extent, by members' dues, the CSWA set up a legal clinic for Chinese immigrants working in local garment shops and restaurants, many of whom regularly experienced nonpayment of wages and other violations of labor and employment law. The organization also prioritized leadership development and rank-and-file collective action, encouraging workers, themselves, to address the problems they confronted on the job, rather than simply relying on services from lawyers and other experts.

This pioneering effort set the template for the worker centers that suddenly sprang up by the dozens across the nation in the 1990s. Some centers, such as the CSWA, have an ethnic focus, but most aim to organize and advocate for workers in particular occupations. In New York City, examples of the latter include Domestic Workers United (DWU), the New York Taxi Workers Alliance (NYTWA), the Restaurant Opportunities Center of New York (ROC-NY), and the Street Vendor Project (SVP). A few other centers aim for a wider reach, organizing and advocating for low-wage immigrant workers, generally, such as Make the Road New York (MRNY), currently the city's largest alt-labor organization. New York is also home to a worker center for middle-strata professionals who find themselves in precarious employment, the Freelancers Union (which, despite its name, is not a traditional union).

Worker centers use a variety of tactics to organize and advocate on behalf of precarious workers. Framing their campaigns as struggles for social and economic justice, they build compelling narratives featuring the voices of workers, themselves, drawing public and media attention to the plight of the new precariat. They "name and shame" employers into making concessions. They build alliances with consumers and other community actors, including faith leaders and elected officials, to gain material and moral leverage. They actively participate in the immigrant rights movement, reflecting the fact that their constituency is largely foreign born. They conduct strategic research to identify key pressure points in the power structure. They lobby lawmakers to win legislative reforms. In addition, they initiate legal actions on behalf of aggrieved workers, filing complaints with governmental enforcement agencies and lawsuits in the courts.

Traditional unions have used many of these same tactics, either separately or in combination. Although more common before the New Deal, recent examples include

Bhairavi Desai (center), director of the Taxi Workers Alliance, 2012
Photograph by Bryan Smith

Desai cheers as New York City's Taxi & Limousine Commission approves a 17% fare increase for yellow cabs, the first since 2006.

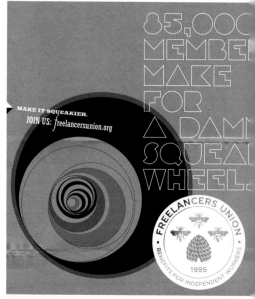

Sara Horowitz, founder of the Freelancers Union, 2014
Photograph by Angel Franco

Subway posters for Freelancers Union, 2008 and 2009 (center)
Designed by Julie Lamb and Phil Gablea

organizing by the United Farm Workers of America (UFW) in the 1960s and 1970s and the "Justice for Janitors" campaign of the Service Employees International Union

(SEIU) in the 1980s and 1990s. Yet when unions deploy such tactics, they do so with the end goal of either establishing collective bargaining or strengthening existing bargaining relationships with employers. In contrast, worker centers typically lack any presence at jobsites and, by definition, do not engage in collective bargaining. Nor do they have any means to systematically collect membership dues from their constituents, which makes it difficult for them to build durable organizations.

Worker centers are also distinctly different from traditional unions in their emphasis on popular education and leadership development to empower rank-and-file workers to act collectively on their own behalf. On the other hand, most worker centers are professionally led by advocates: lawyers or other college-educated staffers with specialized training. In that respect they resemble the settlement houses and labor reform groups of the early 20th century that organized and advocated on behalf of the era's low-wage immigrants, who had come to New York and other US cities from southern and eastern Europe. Much like today's worker centers, those Progressive-Era groups exposed sweatshops and publicized employer abuses, lobbied for protective legislation, offered educational and social services to immigrant workers, and helped them organize. Another similarity between these predecessor organizations and worker centers is that both have often relied extensively on philanthropic support. Indeed, one reason for the strength of alt-labor in New York is the city's heavy concentration of foundations and philanthropic institutions.

Today many traditional unions enthusiastically support the alt-labor movement, although that has not always been the case. When worker centers first emerged on a significant scale in the 1990s, most union leaders were deeply skeptical about their prospects. How could these small organizations, most of which had just a few paid staff members and modest budgets, effectively address the plight of the growing low-wage, precarious workforce? Indeed, unions have millions of dues-paying members and collective bargaining agreements with employers that give them long-term stability, but worker centers are fragile organizations, operating on shoestring budgets and heavily dependent on foundation funding. To traditional union leaders, the centers seemed hopelessly ill-equipped to meet the massive challenges of taming rogue employers and organizing the burgeoning precariat.

In turn, most worker center staff and leaders were highly critical of traditional unions, which they saw as bureaucratic, ossified "dinosaurs" that were inhospitable to low-wage, immigrant workers. Indeed, few New York City unions had shown much interest in recruiting the foreign-born workers who joined the city's workforce in droves in the late 20th century, and some were overtly hostile to immigrants. An important exception was the International Ladies' Garment Workers' Union (ILGWU), which had a long and storied history as an immigrant workers' union. As more and more clothing production left New York for production sites where labor was cheaper, and with immigrants in nonunion sweatshops making up a growing proportion of the garment manufacturing that remained in the city, the ILGWU faced a life-threatening crisis, which made it open to innovation. In the late 1980s, it launched a "Campaign for Justice," establishing community-based walk-in centers offering English classes, skills training, and immigration counseling to nonunion garment workers—in many ways anticipating the worker centers that would proliferate in the following decades.

In contrast, most of New York City's unionized workers were employed in place-bound sectors, such as construction, hospitality, and health care, which could not be outsourced and in which unionization was relatively stable. Organized labor did lose ground in the retail and restaurant sectors (and it is no coincidence that the unions in those sectors would later sponsor worker centers of their own), as well as in manufacturing. Still, New York City has been relatively insulated from the devastation afflicting unions in the rest of the United States. The city did not entirely escape, to be sure: in 1986 private-sector unionization in the New York metropolitan area stood at 20 percent; 30 years later it had fallen to 12 percent. Yet, in the nation as a whole, the private-sector unionization rate fell even more precipitously, from 14 percent to 6 percent during those three decades.

Organized labor had come to be widely viewed as an anachronistic bastion of privilege that no longer served the average worker. In contrast, the new alt-labor groups seized the moral high ground. Their nimble campaigns riveted the media and the larger public by calling attention to the extreme forms of exploitation suffered by the growing precariat and to flagrant viola-

tions of long-established labor and employment laws. During the 1990s, savvy media campaigns spotlighting employer abuses put worker centers in the forefront of low-wage worker advocacy, especially in New York City, which became home to more worker centers per capita than any other part of the nation. The NY-TWA emerged in the early 1990s; the Freelancers Union was founded in 1995; DWU, although officially established in 2000, built on predecessor organizations created in the 1990s; and MRNY was founded in 1997.

Unions and Alt-Labor in the 21st Century

Worker centers continued to flourish in the new century. And now that they had moved beyond the "proof of concept" stage, a few New York unions began to incubate worker centers of their own. The first was ROC-NY, launched by the Hotel Employees and Restaurant Employees (HERE) union in the immediate aftermath of 9/11. The victims of those attacks included HERE members employed by Windows on the World, a restaurant at the top of the former World Trade Center. As it name implies, HERE had once represented a substantial share of the city's massive restaurant industry, but by 2001 it had become a union almost exclusively of hotel workers, along with a few high-end restaurants. Against that background, the union decided to experiment with the alt-labor approach.

A second example is the Retail, Wholesale, and Department Store Union (RWDSU)'s Retail Action Project (RAP), launched in 2005 as a worker center for retail workers. Although union erosion was less

pronounced in retail then in restaurants, RWDSU represented a much smaller share of the sector than it had in prior decades. In partnership with MRNY, the union had already had begun experimenting with efforts to organize the growing number of immigrants employed in retail; RAP was a logical next step.

Union interest in immigrant organizing gained even more momentum after the massive immigrant rights street protests in the first half of 2006, which definitively laid to rest the once-conventional labor movement wisdom that immigrants were "unorganizable." The AFL-CIO already had shifted its official position on immigration in 2000, abandoning its previous support for restrictive policies; in the second half of 2006 it began to actively collaborate with the alt-labor movement. That November, the New York City local AFL-CIO central body, the Central Labor Council (CLC), invited the TWA to become an affiliate. This was an unprecedented move: never before had a non-union organization been welcomed into the fold. The CLC leadership also encouraged the city's unions to support the efforts of DWU, the Freelancers Union, and other worker centers. And the New York unions also lent their considerable political clout to support the worker-center-led campaigns for the Domestic Workers Bill of Rights and the New York Wage Theft Prevention Act, both of which were enacted by the state legislature in 2010.

Thanks to the alt-labor movement's high-profile legal challenges to violations of minimum wage and overtime pay laws and other bedrock employment standard, public awareness of "wage theft" grew dramatically, and alt-labor groups succeeded in bringing many targeted employers into compliance. They also campaigned successfully to win new protective legislation. Yet, as some critics of alt-labor have pointed out, in the absence of collective bargaining rights, it is virtually impossible for worker centers to win more extensive economic improvements, such as higher wages, health insurance, or job security.

Traditional unions historically did extract such concessions, but in recent decades their organizational model and the New Deal collective bargaining system on which it was predicated has become less and less viable. Although New York City unions have weathered the storm better than those in other parts of the country, they nevertheless face enormous obstacles in regard to organizing the unorganized. Almost all private-sector employers vigorously resist efforts to unionize their workers, drawing on an army of "labor consultants" who are only too happy to assist them in such efforts. Strikes to win higher wages or other economic gains have become rare events, as employers routinely hire "permanent replacements" to fill the jobs of strikers, taking advantage of a loophole in the labor law.

In the 2010s, a few of New York's traditional unions tried to overcome these challenges by entering into collaborative efforts with alt-labor groups, jointly launching unionization drives focused on the precariat. For example, RWDSU embarked on a campaign to organize car wash workers in 2012, in collaboration with MRNY and New York Communities for Change (NYCC). Following in the footsteps of a similar successful effort by the Steelworkers' union to organize carwasheros in Los Angeles a few years earlier, the New York car wash campaign organizers drew heavily on the alt-labor playbook. They conducted extensive strategic research on the industry, successfully publicized violations of the minimum wage and overtime laws as well as tip stealing, and also exposed health and safety issues affecting car wash workers. With the help of such "naming and shaming" tactics, RWDSU won union recognition and collective bargaining agreements at

Demonstration for carwash workers rights, Brooklyn, 2015
Photograph by Spencer Platt

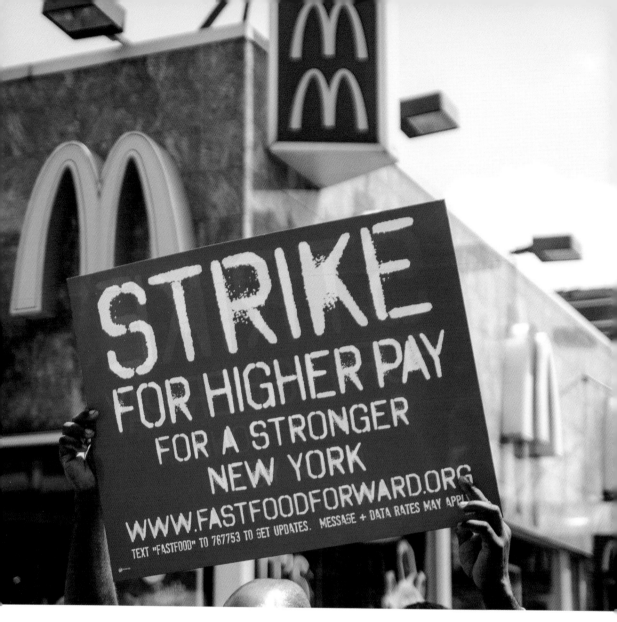

Strike for higher pay outside a Manhattan McDonald's, 2013
Photograph by Annett Bernhardt

several of the city's car washes. This campaign also won passage of the New York City Car Wash Accountability Act, which took effect at the beginning of 2018, introducing new licensing requirements and other regulations for the industry.

An even more ambitious example is "Fast Food Forward," a New York City organizing drive focused on fast food workers, launched in November 2012 by NYCC with funds from SEIU – which later took over the effort and expanded it into the nationwide "Fight for $15." Again

drawing on the alt-labor tactical playbook, this campaign staged a long series of street demonstrations and one-day strikes to capture media attention, exposing the low pay and difficult working conditions of fast food workers, as well as the fact that many were paid so little they were eligible for public assistance. The campaign's key demands were for $15 per hour and union recognition.

Although it did not succeed in winning union recognition from any of the fast food companies, nor in pressuring them to raise their minimum hourly pay to $15, the Fight for $15 did have a major impact. In New York, the first victory took place through a little-known regulatory mechanism called a wage board. Under pressure from the SEIU, New York governor Andrew Cuomo ordered the convening of a fast-food industry wage board in 2015, which then moved to raise the minimum hourly wage for fast-food workers to $15 over the next several years. The following year, New York State enacted a new minimum wage law with a series of increases bringing the legal minimum to $15 per hour in 2019 for all covered employees, not just fast-food workers (although with a lower minimum for tipped workers). The SEIU's Fight for $15 also helped generate campaigns in several other cities and states for similar laws raising the minimum wage to $15. These gains were won in the political sphere, however; the

fast food companies have remained intransigent in resisting unionization.

Another notable development in the alt-labor movement in the 21st century was the expansion of several New York City-based worker centers into national alt-labor organizations. The National Domestic Worker Alliance was formed in 2007, as a spinoff of DWU, which is now one of its local affiliates; a similar process followed when the Restaurant Opportunities Center-United was formed in 2008. In 2011, the National Taxi Workers Alliance received an official charter as an Organizing Committee affiliated with the national AFL-CIO; it now has several affiliates around the country. In 2012, the Center for Popular Democracy was launched, with MRNY as a key affiliate. These national organizations have helped to expand the reach of the worker center movement, and enhanced its visibility.

Ai-jen Poo, executive director of the National Domestic Workers Alliance (center, at podium) at a Women for Paid Sick Days rally, City Hall, New York, 2012
Photograph by Richard Drew

One result of that visibility is that alt-labor has become a target in the crosshairs of a variety of right-wing anti-union organizations. They argue that worker centers are really "unions in disguise" and therefore should be forced to abide by the rules governing unions under US labor law. If that were to occur, the ability of alt-labor groups to launch consumer boycotts would be restricted, along with some of their other activities. Thus far

Protesters demanding $15 an hour minimum wage, 2015
Photograph by Robert K. Chin

The "Fight for $15" movement drew support from both alt-labor organizations and traditional unions. In 2016 Governor Andrew Cuomo signed a $15 an hour minimum wage law covering all New York City workers by the end of 2019, and workers elsewhere in the state at later dates.

these attacks have not been successful, but they offer an ironic testimony to the success of the worker centers, both in New York and nationwide. Although organized labor is also under continual assault from the political Right, it refuses to die. As it struggles to adapt to the radically transformed conditions of the 21st century, it has increasingly embraced alt-labor as a partner and an indispensable fount of innovation.

How Labor Shaped New York and New York Shaped Labor

Walking around New York, tangible signs of the influence that labor has had on the city abound.

There are monuments and plaques, like the statue of a garment worker, hunched over his sewing machine, on Seventh Avenue in the old garment district, and the marker on the side of the building at 29 Washington Place, where 146 workers died in the 1911 Triangle Fire. There are union headquarters, past—such as the one-time Labor Lyceums at 64 East 4th Street in Manhattan and 949 Willoughby Avenue in Brooklyn—and present—such as the headquarters of District Council 37 (American Federation of State, County, and Municipal Employees) and the United Federation of Teachers, just a stone's throw away from Wall Street. Large, affordable, union-sponsored housing complexes dot the city, such as Electchester in Queens, created by the International Brotherhood of Electrical Workers Local 3, with its 2,400 apartments, union headquarters, library, union-owned savings bank, auditorium, cocktail lounge, and bowling alley. Union-run health clinics, one over a century old, serve hundreds of thousands of patients. In Yorkville and East Harlem, buildings that once housed German, Bohemian, and Hispanic worker societies remain standing, predecessors to modern worker centers now scattered around the city.

There are less tangible markers of labor influence, too. The liberal polity that characterizes New York City owes much to worker movements. The expansive vision of government that has been prevalent in New York stems, at least in part, from the influence of labor. For over eighty years, there have been union-sponsored political third parties in the city, which have pushed the mainstream parties, in which labor also has been active, to the left. A host of state and city laws provide workers with rights and benefits unusually capacious by national standards, from a minimum wage far above the federal level, to family leave and sick pay, to a bill of rights for domestic workers. New York State not only guarantees both private and public sector workers the right to collective bargaining, it has enshrined that guarantee in its constitution. With labor support, New York was a pioneer in workplace health and safety protections and in anti-discrimination legislation (though in practice racial segregation remains widespread in housing and schools).

Histories of labor often are framed by two master narratives. The first is a story of unending struggle between workers and employers, the oppressed and their oppressors. The second is a story of continual progress resulting from the collective activity of workers. The chapters of this book, looking at nearly three centuries of labor activity in New York City (and New Amsterdam before that), provide support for both these ways of understanding the past. But they also show how oversimplified they are.

The history of New York has been marked by persistent struggle over work, but the protagonists have not been the same actors, the same social formations, clashing time and time again. Today we have a dominant notion of "worker" as a person paid wages for tasks they perform. But for much of New York history, such wage workers were a minority of those who did the work of the city. Slaves, indentured servants, apprentices, and unpaid family members labored in material circumstances that might resemble those of wage workers but lived lives fundamentally different, marked above all by a lack of freedom, of full self-possession. Necessarily, the kinds of struggles such workers engaged in often differed greatly from those of wage workers and sometimes wage workers were even their masters.

Employment relationships radically changed over time. Ship captains and slave owners had total, intimate control over their workers, including the right to physical punishment. Master artisans controlled not only the work life of their apprentices but almost all aspects of their living, a situation faced by many domestic servants as well. By contrast, wage workers were at least nominally free, though often forced by necessity to accept the dictates of their employers. Labor relations could be direct and personal, as typical in small workshops, stores, and offices, or impersonal and bureaucratic, as in many large companies. Recently, technologically-mediated systems allow employers to control workers with little, if any, face-to-face contact. If struggle has been a defining feature of labor in New York, it has been between ever changing types of workers in ever changing work environments.

Labor struggle has brought progress, but in anything but a direct line. Rather, the history of labor movements has been one of waves of organization and conflict, often followed by setbacks and long periods of quiescence. A burst of worker organization in the 1830s, at both work sites and in the political realm, was followed by nearly two decades of inactivity. An upsurge of organizing drives and strikes, many in the public sector, during the 1960s and early 1970s, came to a crashing halt with the fiscal crisis in the mid-1970s. Some forms of organization and struggle have been hard for outsiders to see, operating informally with little public presence, like the networks of sex workers protecting one another. Others have been impossible to miss, like the massive strikes and demonstrations that episodically have paralyzed the city, most recently the 2005 transit strike. Yet for all the unevenness of their development, across time and types of workers, New York labor movements have had a profound, long-lasting effect, not only on their participants but in shaping the city itself.

Some commonalities emerge from the complex, multi-century history of New York labor movements, as seen in the preceding chapters, in what workers have wanted and in what they have achieved. Perhaps foremost has been the fight for greater freedom from owners, masters, employers, and family members, to break formal and informal bonds and obligations that gave others power over workers' labor and lives. Open revolts, running away, withholding labor, acting collectively in mutual defense, creating unions, pressing for new laws, and establishing workplace norms have been among the many ways workers have sought more control over their own beings. Sometimes individual and sometimes collective, these struggles have had a democratic air that has helped set the tone of the city, with their implicit or explicit demand for equal rights. The fight for better pay and working conditions, central to labor movements, in its own way also has been a demand for freedom, for time for richer, self-defined lives, and income to allow more than mere survival (or sometimes just to allow survival).

Over and over, efforts to win greater freedom and equality at the work place have spilled into other arenas, and vice versa. Organized workers have plunged into the political arena, be it Jacksonian-Era artisans forming their own political party or young Progressive-Era garment workers joining the fight for female suffrage. Female workers, empowered by workplace struggles, fought at home for less oppressive and more equal familial and marital relations. Irish immigrants, fresh from the fight for independence from Great Britain, became key organizers of the Transport Workers Union and other unions. Labor activists played central roles in the Civil Rights Movement and the struggles by Puerto Rican New Yorkers against discrimination and for better lives, movements that in many ways were themselves labor movements.

Even as workers fought for their own freedom, there were times when they sought to limit the freedom of others. From the earliest days of labor activity in New York through the modern era, there have been plenty of examples of groups of workers seeking to exclude other workers, on the other side of racial, ethnic, and gender divides, from access to favored jobs and membership in labor organizations. The boundaries of solidarity have been in flux and contested throughout the history of New York labor movements.

The push by workers for greater freedom often took on a spatial dimension, a quest for physical spaces where they might act and appear as they chose, unregulated by employers, their agents, or official forces. For sailors that might mean housing controlled by neither shipowners and their allies nor by elite philanthropists. For workers more broadly, it might mean saloons where they could drink and socialize, workers' clubs and union halls, or house party spaces. Labor movements also fought for democratic public spaces, for the right to demonstrate on public streets and in public parks, and for schools, bathhouses, playgrounds, and parks to serve working-class families living in overcrowded homes and neighborhoods.

The demand for such public facilities was part of a broad labor orientation towards looking to government for help with the everyday trials and challenges of working-class life. New York workers have long had an

expensive conception of the function of government. From a century before the New Deal all the way up to the 1970s, in hard times New York workers demanded that the government provide jobs for the unemployed. For just as long, they pushed the government to regulate the labor market and protect workers, limiting the hours of work, establishing minimum wages, protecting worker health and safety, outlawing discrimination, and requiring work-related benefits. Labor movements pressed for a broad array of government services and programs, to give working people access to decent homes and medical care, basic schooling and higher education, and cultural

Area workers take a lunch break at the Garment Worker Statue by Judith Weller, 2007 Photograph by Richard Levine

enrichment. The unusually broad range of city services and regulations in New York, from rent control and a large public housing system to an extensive public transportation network and low-cost cultural activities exist, in part, as a result of pressure from labor groups.

Finally, workers have contributed to the civility and humanity of the city through their self-organization, formal and informal. Although to outsiders New York has often seemed a city of anonymity and atomization, to the contrary, throughout its history, it has been characterized by dense mutualism, as working people have supported one another through family, friendship, ethnic and racial organizations, social clubs, athletic groups, and labor unions. Solidarity, a central tenet of organized labor, has been a critical strand of New York life, a counter to the dizzying size, complexity, and rapid change that has made New York loom large on the national and global stages. At crisis moments, like World War II and September 11, 2001, labor movements and their ethos of standing together have come to the fore, providing a moral compass for New Yorkers.

Just as labor movements have helped shape New York, in turn New York has helped shape labor movements, both locally and nationally. Many of the people who became central to American labor history came from elsewhere to New York, drawn by its position as one of the major nodes in the Atlantic world (with ties beyond) and its culture of openness and opportunity. In the city, they helped create and recreate an exceptionally robust set of labor movements, informed by ideas from around the world. The dynamism of the local economy, with its mix of small and mid-size enterprises with a few larger concerns and its strong ties to trade and communication around the country and around the world, imparted a particular character to organized labor. Rarely did any one employer or industry dominate labor relations. Unions, rather than employers, often acted as the defining agent in establishing workplace relations. With its exceptional circumstances, the city served as an incubator for labor leaders, ideologies, and organizational forms that became nationally influential.

In the Era of the Revolution, Tom Paine, the great propagandist and author of the widely-read pamphlet "Common Sense", put forth a rationalist, egalitarian, democratic vision that proved critical in winning support for the War for Independence and that informed labor activists, especially artisans, for generations to come. In the Age of Jackson, New York workers and labor reformers pioneered independent labor political activity and promoted a host of schemes for democratizing American life. In the post-Civil War Era, New York provided leaders for a host of national labor organizations. For most of its 69-year history, the American Federation of Labor (AFL) was headed by a New Yorker, first Samuel Gompers and later George Meany. The same has been true of the AFL-CIO since its formation in 1955, with first Meany and later John J. Sweeney at the helm.

While white men long dominated labor leadership, out of New York came many non-white and female leaders who gave voice to workers otherwise all but ignored. In the early 20th century, young female garment workers not only helped establish unions in New York but went on to organize and staff clothing unions nationally. New Yorker Elizabeth Gurley Flynn, one of the most electrifying labor rabble-rousers the county has seen, became a national sensation as a leader of the Industrial Workers of the World. A. Philip Randolph, operating out of New York, led the Brotherhood of Sleeping Car Porters for decades while becoming one of the most important civil rights leaders nationally. More recently, as worker centers and other new forms of labor organizations have emerged, New Yorkers have yet again been at the national forefront, like Saru Jayaraman, president of Restaurant Opportunities Centers (ROC), and Ai-jen Poo, director of the National Domestic Workers Alliance.

New York has long been a font of ideas as well as personnel for national labor movements. One common thread in the history of New York has been the strength of radical ideas and their influence on labor. In the 19th century these included Painite republicanism, which rejected great social or economic inequality, cooperativism, abolitionism, feminism, anarchism, and socialism. In the 20th century, socialists remained influential, though eclipsed in the 1930s and 1940s by Communists and their allies. New York radicals helped lead national left-wing labor groups and put forth alternative platforms in more centrist ones.

Arguably, though, the most important ideological contribution of the local labor movement was the so-called "pure and simple" trade unionism that dominated the AFL. As developed by Gompers and other New York unionists, this outlook adopted the Marxist sociology widely accepted by 19th century New York unionists that saw society divided into two dominant classes, labor and capital, inherently opposed to one another, with the work place as the central site of exploitation. But Gompers and his allies, impressed by the power of capital, rejected as unrealistic the revolutionary change socialists advocated. Instead they adopted an incrementalist strategy of seeking ever better pay, benefits, and workplace control through the tight organization of workers in strategic positions within business enterprises, mostly skilled white men, a strategy Gompers once summed up as simply seeking "more."

Between the extremes of craft unionism and radical universalism, a host of hybrid forms of labor organization emerged in New York, to be copied elsewhere. In the Progressive Era, garment workers created organizations that united skilled and unskilled workers, men and women, though a combination of craft and ethnically defined units, linked together through regional boards. This "new unionism" fused socialist ideology with bread-and-butter collective bargaining. Labor groups themselves provided their members with a range of benefits, including health care, housing, unemployment insurance, and educational, cultural, and recreational programs. This comprehensive vision of the role of unionism—"social unionism" as it was sometimes called—was later adopted by other unions, including those representing New York municipal employees. During the 1930s and 1940s New Yorkers brought the industrial union model of the Congress of Industrial Organizations (CIO) to non-manufacturing sectors, including retail, maritime, journalism, and public transportation, creating national unions in these spheres that went on to organize elsewhere. Later, New Yorkers were pathbreakers in the organization of government and health care workers and, more recently domestic, service, fast-food, and freelance workers.

New York has not been the only city that has played an outsize role in national labor movements. At various times, Philadelphia, Indianapolis, Pittsburgh, Chicago, Detroit, and, especially in recent years, Los Angeles have been key centers of labor leadership, innovation, and organizational strength. But over the whole stretch of the history of the United States, no place has come near New York in importance for the development of the labor movements that have played so large a role in American life.

Too often, New Yorkers take labor and labor movements for granted, seeing them as simply part of the landscape. But, as the chapters of this book show, the city of New York would not exist in anything like its current form without the struggles of working people over the past three centuries, struggles that, in turn, helped shape national labor movements, right up to today. New York always has been a city of workers, a city of struggle, and all signs are that it will continue to be so long into the future.

SECTION 1

WORKERS IN THE CITY OF COMMERCE, 1624–1898

Burrows, Edwin G., and Mike Wallace. *Gotham: A History of New York City to 1898*. New York: Oxford University Press, 1999.

Jackson, Kenneth T., Lisa Keller, and Nancy Flood, eds. *The Encyclopedia of New York City: Second Edition*. New Haven: Yale University Press, 2010.

Museum of the City of New York. *NY at its Core: 400 Years of New York City History*. New York: Museum of the City of New York, 2017.

CHAPTER 1

ARTISAN LABOR IN COLONIAL NEW YORK AND THE NEW REPUBLIC

Clark Smith, Barbara. *The Freedoms We Lost: Consent and Resistance in Revolutionary America*. New York: The New Press, 2010.

Foner, Eric. *Tom Paine and Revolutionary America*. Oxford: Oxford University Press, 2005.

Hartigan-O'Connor, Ellen. *The Ties That Buy: Women and Commerce in Revolutionary America*. Philadelphia: University of Pennsylvania Press, 2009.

Hill, Christopher. "Pottage for Freeborn Englishmen: Attitudes to Waged Labour." In *Change and Continuity in Seventeenth-Century England*. London: Weidenfeld and Nicolson, 1974.

Middleton, Simon. *From Privileges to Rights: Work and Politics in Colonial New York City*. Philadelphia: University of Pennsylvania Press, 2006.

Montgomery, David. *Beyond Equality. Labor and the Radical Republicans, 1862–1872*. New York: Alfred A. Knopf, 1967.

Saxton, Alexander. *The Rise and Fall of the White Republic: Class, Politics, and Mass Culture in Nineteenth-Century America*. London: Verso, 1990.

Vickers, Daniel. "Competency and Competition: Economic Culture in Early America." *The William and Mary Quarterly* 47, no.1 (1990): 3–29.

Wilentz, Sean. *Chants Democratic: New York City and the Rise of the American Working Class, 1789–1850*. New York: Oxford University Press, 1984.

CHAPTER 2

SLAVE LABOR IN NEW YORK

Berlin, Ira. *Many Thousands Gone: The First Two Centuries of Slavery in British North America*. Cambridge: Harvard University Press, 1999.

Berlin, Ira, and Leslie M. Harris. *Slavery in New York*. New York: The New Press, 2005.

Burrows, Edwin G., and Mike Wallace. *Gotham: A History of New York City to 1898*. New York: Oxford University Press, 1999.

Christianson, Scott. "Criminal Punishment in New Netherland," in *A Beautiful and Fruitful Place: Selected Rensselaerswijck Seminar Papers*, edited by Nancy Anne McClure Zeller. Albany, N.Y.: New Netherland, 1991.

Clark-Pujara, Christy. *Dark Work: The Business of Slavery in Rhode Island*. New York: New York University Press, 2016.

Curry, Leonard P. *The Free Black in Urban America, 1800–1850: The Shadow of the Dream*. Chicago: University of Chicago Press, 1981.

Davis, Thomas J. *A Rumor of Revolt: The "Great Negro Plot" in Colonial New York City*. New York: Free Press, 1985.

Foote, Thelma Wills. *Black and White Manhattan: The History of Racial Formation in Colonial New York City*. New York: Oxford University Press, 2004.

Gellman, David N. *Emancipating New York: The Politics of Slavery and Freedom, 1777–1827*. Baton Rouge: Louisiana State University Press, 2006.

Goodfriend, Joyce Diane. *Beyond the Melting Pot: Society and Culture in Colonial New York City, 1664–1730*. Princeton: Princeton University Press, 1992.

———. "Burghers and Blacks: The Evolution of a Slave Society at New Amsterdam." *New York History* 59, no. 2 (April 1978): 125–44.

Harris, Leslie M. *In the Shadow of Slavery: African Americans in New York City, 1626–1863*. Chicago: University of Chicago Press, 2003.

Hodges, Graham Russell. *Root and Branch: African Americans in New York and East Jersey, 1613–1863*. Chapel Hill: University of North Carolina Press, 1999.

Lepore, Jill. *New York Burning: Liberty, Slavery, and Conspiracy in Eighteenth-Century Manhattan*. New York: Alfred A. Knopf, 2005.

McKee, Samuel. *Labor in Colonial New York, 1664–1776*. New York: Columbia University Press, 1935.

McManus, Edgar. *A History of Negro Slavery in New York*. Syracuse: Syracuse University Press, 1966.

White, Shane. *Somewhat More Independent: The End of Slavery in New York City, 1770–1810*. Athens: University of Georgia Press, 1991.

CHAPTER 3

SAILORS ASHORE IN NEW YORK'S SAILORTOWN

Fingard, Judith. *Jack in Port: Sailortowns of Eastern Canada*. Toronto: University of Toronto Press, 1982.

Fink, Leon. *Sweatshops at Sea: Merchant Seamen in the World's First Globalized Industry*. Chapel Hill: University of North Carolina Press, 2011.

Gamber, Wendy. *The Boardinghouse in Nineteenth-Century America*. Baltimore: John Hopkins University Press, 2007.

Gilfoyle, Timothy J. *City of Eros: New York City, Prostitution and the Commercialization of Sex, 1790–1920*. New York: W. W. Norton & Company, 1992.

———. *A Pickpocket's Tale: The Underworld of Nineteenth-Century New York*. New York: W. W. Norton & Company, 2006.

Gilje, Paul A. *Liberty on the Waterfront: American Maritime Culture in the Age of Revolution*. Philadelphia: University of Pennsylvania Press, 2004.

Gunn, Thomas Butler. *The Physiology of New York Boarding-Houses*. New York: Mason Brothers, 1857.

Hugill, Stan. *Sailortown*. London: Routledge and K. Paul, 1967.

Jaffe, Steven H. "God Save Poor Jack Ashore: The New York Sailors' Strike of 1869." *Seaport: New York's History Magazine* 34, no. 1 (Spring 1999).

Kverndal, Roald. *Seamen's Missions: Their Origin and Early Growth.* Pasadena: William Carey Library, 1986.

Milne, Graeme. *People, Place, and Power on the Nineteenth-Century Waterfront.* London: Palgrave Macmillan, 2016.

Nelson, Bruce. *Workers on the Waterfront: Seamen, Longshoremen, and Unionism in the 1930s.* Urbana: University of Illinois Press, 1990.

Vickers, Daniel. *Young Men and the Sea: Yankee Seafarers in the Age of Sail.* New Haven: Yale University Press, 2005.

Weintraub, Hyman G. *Andrew Furuseth: Emancipator of the Seamen.* Berkeley: University of California Press, 1958.

CHAPTER 4

HOUSEWORK AND HOMEWORK IN 19TH-CENTURY NEW YORK CITY

Anthony, Katharine. *Mothers Who Must Earn.* New York: Russell Sage Foundation, 1914.

Batlan, Felice. "A Reevaluation of the New York Court of Appeals: The Home, the Market, and Labor, 1885–1905." *Law and Social Inquiry* 27, part 3 (2002): 489–528.

Blackmar, Elizabeth. *Manhattan for Rent, 1785–1850.* Ithaca: Cornell University Press, 1989.

Boris, Eileen. *Home to Work: Motherhood and the Politics of Industrial Homework in the United States.* New York: Cambridge University Press, 1994.

Boydston, Jeanne. *Home and Work: Housework, Wages, and the Ideology of Labor in the Early Republic.* New York: Oxford University Press, 1994.

Campbell, Helen. *Prisoners of Poverty: Women Wage-Workers, Their Trades and Their Lives.* Boston: Little, Brown and Company, 1900.

——. *Women Wage-Earners: Their Past, Their Present and Their Future.* Boston: Roberts Brothers, 1893.

Chapin, Robert Coit. *The Standard of Living among Workingmen's Families in New York City.* New York: New York State Conference on Charities and Correction, 1909.

Cowan, Ruth Schwartz. *More Work for Mother: The Ironies of Household Technology from the Open Hearth to the Microwave.* New York: Basic Books, 1985.

Cromley, Elizabeth. *Alone Together: A History of New York's Early Apartments.* Ithaca: Cornell University Press, 1990.

Dudden, Faye E. *Serving Women: Household Service in Nineteenth-Century America.* Middletown, CT: Wesleyan University Press, 1983.

Faflik, David. Introduction to *The Physiology of New York Boarding-Houses,* by Thomas Gunn. 1857. New Brunswick: Rutgers University Press, 2009.

Folbre, Nancy, and Barnet Wagman. "Counting Housework: New Estimates of Real Product in the United States, 1800–1860." *Journal of Economic History* 53, no. 2 (June 1993): 275–88.

Gamber, Wendy. *The Boardinghouse in Nineteenth-Century America.* Baltimore: Johns Hopkins University Press, 2007.

Hoy, Suellen. *Chasing Dirt: The American Pursuit of Cleanliness.* New York: Oxford University Press, 1995.

Katzman, David M. *Seven Days a Week: Women and Domestic Service in Industrializing America.* New York: Oxford University Press, 1978.

Lubove, Roy. *The Progressives and the Slums: Tenement House Reform in New York City, 1890–1917.* Pittsburgh: University of Pittsburgh Press, 1974.

Sacks, Marcy S. *Before Harlem: The Black Experience in New York City Before World War I.* Philadelphia: University of Pennsylvania Press, 2006.

Sanger, William. *The History of Prostitution.* New York: Harper & Brothers Publishers, 1858.

Stansell, Christine. *City of Women: Sex and Class in New York, 1790–1860.* New York: Alfred A. Knopf, 1986.

Strasser, Susan. *Never Done: A History of American Housework.* New York: Pantheon, 1982.

Vapnek, Lara. *Breadwinners: Working Women and Economic Independence, 1865–1920.* Chicago: University of Illinois Press, 2009.

Watson, Elizabeth C. "Report on Manufacturing in Tenements in New York State." In *Second Report of the Factory Investigating Commission,* Appendix IV. Albany: J.B. Lyon Company, 1913.

CHAPTER 5

VICTIMS, B'HOYS, FOREIGNERS, SLAVE-DRIVERS, AND DESPOTS: PICTURING WORK, WORKERS, AND ACTIVISM IN 19TH-CENTURY NEW YORK

Brown, Joshua. *Beyond the Lines: Pictorial Reporting, Everyday Life, and the Crisis of Gilded Age America.* Berkeley: University of California Press, 2002.

——. "'The Social and Sensational News of the Day': Frank Leslie, *The Days' Doings,* and Scandalous Pictorial News in Gilded Age New York." *New-York Journal of American History* 66, no. 2 (Fall 2003): 10–20.

Edelstein, T. J.. "They Sang 'The Song of the Shirt': The Visual Iconology of the Seamstress." *Victorian Studies* 23, no. 2 (Winter 1980): 183–210.

Reilly, Jr., Bernard F. *American Political Prints, 1766-1876: A Catalog of the Collections in the Library of Congress.* Boston: G.K. Hall, 1991.

Rinear, David L. "F. S. Chanfrau's Mose: The Rise and Fall of an Urban Folk-Hero." *Theatre Journal* 33, no. 2 (May, 1981): 199–212.

Schnapper, M. B. *American Labor: A Pictorial Social History.* Washington, D.C.: Public Affairs Press, 1972.

West, Richard Samuel. *Satire on Stone: The Political Cartoons of Joseph Keppler.* Urbana-Champaign: University of Illinois Press, 1988.

SECTION 2

UNION CITY, 1898–1975

Bernhardt, Debra E., and Rachel Bernstein. *Ordinary People, Extraordinary Lives: A Pictorial History of Working People in New York City,* New York: New York University Press, 2000.

Freeman, Joshua B. *Working-Class New York: Life and Labor Since World War II.* New York: The New Press, 2000.

Wallace, Mike. *Greater Gotham: A History of New York City From 1898 to 1919,* New York: Oxford University Press, 2000.

CHAPTER 6

THE NEEDLE TRADES AND THE UPRISING OF WOMEN WORKERS, 1905–1919

Bao, Xiaolan. *Holding Up More Than Half the Sky: Chinese Women Garment Workers in New York City, 1948–1992.* Urbana and Chicago: University of Illinois Press, 2001.

Bender, Daniel. *Sweated Work, Weak Bodies: Anti-Sweatshop Campaigns and Languages of Labor.* New Brunswick: Rutgers University Press, 2004.

Enstadt, Nan. *Ladies of Labor, Girls of Adventure: Working Women, Popular Culture, and Labor Politics at the Turn of the Twentieth Century.* New York: Columbia University Press, 1999.

"Equality League of Self-Supporting Women of New York City." April 4, 1907. National American Woman Suffrage Association scrapbooks, 1897–1911. Library of Congress.

Katz, Daniel. *All Together Different: Yiddish Socialists, Garment Workers, and the Labor Roots of Multiculturalism.* New York: New York University Press, 2013.

Orleck, Annelise. *Common Sense and a Little Fire: Women and Working-Class Politics in the United States.* 2nd ed. Chapel Hill: University of North Carolina Press, 2017.

Schneiderman, Rose. "A Cap Maker's Story," *The Independent*, April 27, 1905.

Wignot, Jamila. *American Experience, "Triangle Fire,"* 2011. An Apograph Productions Inc. https://www.pbs.org/wgbh/americanexperience/films/triangle/.

CHAPTER 7

SEX WORK AND THE UNDERGROUND ECONOMY

Adler, Polly. *A House Is Not a Home.* Amherst and Boston: University of Massachusetts Press, 2006.

Asbury, Herbert. *The Gangs of New York: An Informal History of the Underworld.* New York: Vintage Books, 2008.

Clarke, Donald. *Billie Holiday: Wishing on the Moon.* New York: Viking, 1994.

Clement, Elizabeth Alice. *Love for Sale: Courting, Treating, and Prostitution in New York City, 1900–1945.* Chapel Hill: University of North Carolina Press, 2006.

Conway, J. North. *Queen of Thieves: The True Story of "Marm" Mandelbaum and Her Gangs of New York.* New York: Skyhorse Publishing, Inc., 2014.

Fronc, Jennifer. *New York Undercover: Private Surveillance in the Progressive Era.* Chicago: University of Chicago Press, 2009.

Gilfoyle, Timothy J. *City of Eros: New York City, Prostitution, and the Commercialization of Sex, 1790–1920.* New York: W. W. Norton & Company, 1994.

Griffin, Farah Jasmine. *If You Can't Be Free, Be a Mystery: In Search of Billie Holiday.* New York: Free Press, 2001.

Harris, LaShawn. *Sex Workers, Psychics, and Numbers Runners: Black Women in New York City's Underground Economy.* Urbana, Chicago, and Springfield: University of Illinois Press, 2016.

Mumford, Kevin J. *Interzones: Black/White Sex Districts in Chicago and New York in the Early Twentieth Century.* New York: Columbia University Press, 1997.

Ogren, Kathy J. *The Jazz Revolution: Twenties America and the Meaning of Jazz.* New York: Oxford University Press, 1992.

CHAPTER 8

HERE COMES THE CIO

Bernstein, Irving. *The Turbulent Years: A History of the American Worker, 1933–1940.* Boston: Houghton Mifflin, 1969.

Fraser, Steve. *Labor Will Rule: Sidney Hillman and the Rise of American Labor.* New York: Free Press, 1991.

Freeman, Joshua B. *In Transit: The Transport Workers Union in New York City, 1933–1966.* New York: Oxford University Press, 1989.

——. *Working-Class New York: Life and Labor Since World War II.* New York: The New Press, 2001.

Opler, Daniel J. *For All White-Collar Workers: The Possibilities of Radicalism in New York City's Department Store Unions, 1934–1953.* Columbus: Ohio State University Press, 2007.

Rosswurm, Steven J., ed. *The CIO's Left-Led Unions.* New Brunswick: Rutgers University Press, 1992.

Zieger, Robert H. *The CIO, 1935–1955.* Chapel Hill: University of North Carolina Press, 1995.

CHAPTER 9

PUERTO RICAN WORKERS AND THE STRUGGLE FOR DECENT LIVES IN NEW YORK CITY, 1910s–1970s

Cruz, José E. *Puerto Rican Identity, Political Development, and Democracy in New York, 1960–1990.* Lanham, MD: Lexington Books, 2017.

Lee, Sonia Song. *Building a Latino Civil Rights Movement: Puerto Ricans, African Americans, and the Pursuit of Racial Justice in New York City.* Chapel Hill: University of North Carolina Press, 2014.

Meléndez, Edgardo. *Sponsored Migration: The State and Puerto Rican Postwar Migration to the United States.* Columbus: Ohio State University Press, 2017.

Ortiz, Altagracia. "'En la aguja y el pedal eché la hiel': Puerto Rican Women in the Garment Industry of New York City, 1920–1980." In *Puerto Rican Women and Work: Bridges in Transnational Labor,* edited by Altagracia

Ortiz. Philadelphia: Temple University Press, 1996.

Thomas, Lorrin. *Puerto Rican Citizen: History and Political Identity in Twentieth-Century New York City.* Chicago: University of Chicago Press, 2010.

Thomas, Lorrin, and Aldo A. Lauria-Santiago. *Rethinking the Struggle for Puerto Rican Rights.* New York: Routledge, 2018.

Whalen, Carmen Teresa. "'The Day the Dresses Stopped': Puerto Rican Women, the International Ladies' Garment Workers' Union, and the 1958 Dressmaker's Strike." In *Memories and Migrations: Mapping Boricua & Chicana Histories,* edited by Vicki Ruiz and John R. Chávez, 121-49. Urbana: University of Illinois Press, 2008.

——. "Sweatshops Here and There: The Garment Industry, Latinas, and Labor Migrations." *International Labor and Working-Class History,* no. 61 (2002): 45–68.

Whalen, Carmen Teresa, and Victor Vázquez-Hernández. *The Puerto Rican Diaspora: Historical Perspectives.* Philadelphia: Temple University Press, 2005.

CHAPTER 10

LABOR AND THE FIGHT FOR RACIAL EQUALITY

Biondi, Martha. *To Stand and Fight: The Struggle for Civil Rights in Postwar New York City.* Cambridge: Harvard University Press, 2003.

Freeman, Joshua B. *Working-Class New York: Life and Labor Since World War II.* New York: The New Press, 2000.

Jones, William P. *The March on Washington: Jobs, Freedom, and the Forgotten History of Civil Rights.* New York: W. W. Norton, 2013.

Taylor, Clarence. ed. *Civil Rights in New York City: From World War II to the Giuliani Era*. New York: Fordham University Press, 2011.

CHAPTER 11

PUBLIC WORKERS

Bellush, Jewel, and Bernard Bellush. *Union Power and New York: Victor Gotbaum and District Council 37*. New York: Praeger, 1984.

Biondi, Martha. *To Stand and Fight: The Struggle for Civil Rights in Postwar New York City*. Cambridge: Harvard University Press, 2003.

Cook, Alice H. "Public Employee Bargaining in New York City." *Industrial Relations* 9 no. 3 (1970): 249-67.

Freeman, Joshua B. *In Transit: The Transport Workers Union in New York City, 1933-1966*. New York: Oxford University Press, 1989.

———. *Working-Class New York: Life and Labor Since World War II*. New York: The New Press, 2000.

Herbert, William A. "Card Check Labor Certification: Lessons from New York." *Albany Law Review* 74 (2010/11): 93-173.

———. "Public Sector Labor Law and History: The Politics of Ancient History?" *Hofstra Labor and Employment Law Journal* 28, issue 2 (2011): 335-61.

Kahlenberg, Richard D. *Tough Liberal: Albert Shanker and the Battles Over Schools, Unions, Race, and Democracy*. New York: Columbia University Press, 2007.

Kramer, Leo. *Labor's Paradox: The American Federation of State, County, and Municipal Employees, AFL-CIO*. New York: John Wiley & Sons, 1962.

Maier, Mark. *City Unions: Managing Discontent in New York City*. New Brunswick: Rutgers University Press, 1987.

Marmo, Michael. *More Profile Than Courage: The New York City Transit Strike of 1966*. Albany: State University of New York Press, 1990.

Milkman, Ruth, and Stephanie Luce. *The State of the Unions 2018: A Profile of Organized Labor in New York City, New York State, and the United States*. New York: CUNY School of Labor and Urban Studies, 2018.

Slater, Joseph. *Public Workers: Government Employee Unions, the Law, and the State, 1900-1962*. Ithaca: Cornell University Press, 2004.

Spero, Sterling Denhard. *Government as Employer*. New York: Remsen Press, 1948.

Taylor, Clarence. *Reds at the Blackboard: Communism, Civil Rights, and the New York City Teachers Union*. New York: Columbia University Press, 2011.

Ziskind, David. *One Thousand Strikes of Government Employees*. New York: Columbia University Press, 1940.

SECTION 3

CRISIS AND TRANSFORMATION, 1975-2018

Thorn, John, ed. *New York 400*. Philadelphia: Running Press, 2009.

Milkman, Ruth, and Stephanie Luce. *The State of the Unions 2017: A Profile of Organized Labor in New York City, New York State, and the United States*. New York: The Joseph S. Murphy Institute for Worker Education and Labor Studies, 2017.

Phillips-Fein, Kim. *Fear City: New York's Fiscal Crisis and the Rise of Austerity Politics*. New York: Metropolitan Books, 2017.

CHAPTER 12

THE FISCAL CRISIS AND UNION DECLINE

DeFreitas, Gregory, and Bhaswati Sengupta. *The State of New York Unions 2017*. Hempstead: Center for the Study of Labor and Democracy, Hofstra University, 2017.

Fitch, Robert. "The Storm at DC 37." *Village Voice*. September 15, 1998.

Freeman, Joshua B. *Working-Class New York: Life and Labor Since World War II*. New York: The New Press, 2000.

Greenhouse, Steven. "Scandals Affirm New York as Union Corruption Capital." *New York Times*. February 15, 1999.

Milkman, Ruth, and Stephanie Luce. *The State of the Unions 2017: A Profile of Organized Labor in New York City, New York State, and the United States*. New York: The Joseph S. Murphy Institute for Worker Education and Labor Studies, 2017.

Milkman, Ruth, and Ed Ott, eds. *New Labor in New York: Precarious Workers and the Future of the Labor Movement*. Ithaca: Cornell University Press, 2014.

Phillips-Fein, Kim. *Fear City: New York's Fiscal Crisis and the Rise of Austerity Politics*. New York: Metropolitan Books, 2017.

Roberts, Sam. "Black Incomes Surpass Whites in Queens." *New York Times*. October 1, 2006.

Soffer, Jonathan, and Themis Chronopoulos. "After the Urban Crisis: New York and the Rise of Inequality." *Journal of Urban History* 43, no. 6 (2017): 855-863.

Steier, Richard. *Enough Blame to Go Round: The Labor Pains of New York City's Public Employee Unions*. Albany: State University of New York Press, 2014.

CHAPTER 13

HEALTH-CARE WORKERS AND UNION POWER

Bellush, Jewell, and Bernard Bellush. *Union Power and New York: Victor Gotbaum and District Council 37*. New York: Praeger, 1984.

Boris, Eileen, and Jennifer Klein. *Caring for America: Home Health Workers in the Shadow of the Welfare State*. New York: Oxford University Press, 2012.

Fink, Leon, and Brian Greenberg. *Upheaval in the Quiet Zone: 1199SEIU and the Politics of Health Care Unionism*. 2nd ed. Urbana: University of Illinois Press, 2009.

Reverby, Susan. "From Aide to Organizer: The Oral History of Lillian Roberts." In *Women of America: A History*, edited by Carol Ruth Berkin and Mary Beth Norton, 289-317. Boston: Houghton Mifflin Company, 1979.

CHAPTER 14

CHINATOWN, THE GARMENT AND RESTAURANT INDUSTRIES, AND LABOR

This chapter is based on Margaret M. Chin's work with Chinese and Latino women garment factory workers and Kenneth J. Guest's work with Chinese restaurant workers and Fuzhounese immigrants.

Bao, Xiaolan. *Holding Up More Than Half the Sky: Chinese Women Garment Workers in New York City 1948-1992*. Urbana and Chicago: University of Illinois Press, 2001.

Chin, Margaret M. *Sewing Women: Immigrants and the New York City Garment Industry*. New York: Columbia University Press, 2005.

———. "The Backbone of Chinatown: Chinese Women and the Garment Industry, 1950–2001." In *Asian American and Pacific Islander Women's History: Local and Global Dimensions*, edited by Shirley Hune and Gail Nomura. New York: New York University Press, forthcoming.

———. "Moving On: Chinese Garment Workers after 9/11." In *Wounded City: The Social Impact of 9/11*, edited by Nancy Foner, 184–207. New York: Russell Sage Foundation, 2005.

Guest, Kenneth J. "All-You-Can-Eat Buffets and Chicken with Broccoli to Go." *Anthropology Now* 1, no. 1 (2009): 21–28.

———. "From Mott Street to East Broadway: Fuzhounese Immigrants and the Revitalization of New York's Chinatown." *Journal of Chinese Overseas* 7, no. 1 (2011): 24–44.

———. *God in Chinatown: Religion and Survival in New York's Evolving Immigrant Community*. New York: New York University Press, 2003.

Guest, Kenneth J., and Peter Kwong. "Ethnic Enclaves and Cultural Diversity." In *Cultural Diversity in the United States: A Critical Reader*, edited by Ida Susser and Thomas C. Patterson, 250–66. Malden, MA and Oxford: Blackwell Publishers, 2001.

Kwong, Peter. *Forbidden Workers: Illegal Chinese Immigrants and American Labor*. New York: The New Press, 1997.

———. *The New Chinatown*. New York: Noonday Press, 1987.

Waldinger, Roger. *Through the Eye of the Needle*. New York: New York University Press, 1989.

Zhou, Min. *Chinatown: The Socioeconomic Potential of an Urban Enclave*. Philadelphia: Temple University Press, 1992.

CHAPTER 15
DOMESTIC WORKERS

Baker, Ella, and Marvel Cooke. "Bronx Slave Market." *The Crisis* 42, no. 11 (November 1935): 330–31.

Bapat, Sheila. *Part of the Family? Nannies, Housekeepers, Caregivers, and the Battle for Domestic Workers' Rights*. New York: Ig Publishing, 2014.

Brown, Tamara Mose. *Raising Brooklyn: Nannies, Childcare and Caribbeans Creating Community*. New York: New York University Press, 2011.

Chang, Grace. *Disposable Domestics: Immigrant Women Workers in the Global Economy*. Chicago: Haymarket Books, 2000.

Cooper, Esther V. "The Negro Woman Domestics in Relation to Trade Unionism." Master's thesis, Fisk University, 1940.

Gornick, Vivian. "There Once Was a Union Maid/Who Never Was Afraid." *Village Voice*. November 29, 1976.

Gray, Brenda Clegg. *Black Female Domestics During the Great Depression in New York City, 1930–1940*. New York: Garland, 1993.

Hondagneu-Sotelo, Pierrette. *Doméstica: Immigrant Workers Cleaning and Caring in the Shadows of Affluence*. Berkeley: University of California Press, 2001.

May, Vanessa. *Unprotected Labor: Household Workers, Politics, and Middle-Class Reform in New York, 1870–1940*. Chapel Hill: University of North Carolina Press, 2011.

Nadasen, Premilla. "Domestic Workers Take it to the Streets." *Ms. Magazine*, fall 2009, 38.

———. *Household Workers Unite: The Untold Story of African American Women Who Built a Movement*. Boston: Beacon, 2015.

Poo, Ai-jen. "A Twenty-First Century Organizing Model: Lessons from the New York Domestic Workers Bill of Rights Campaign." *New Labor Forum* 20, no. 1 (2011): 51–55.

Romero, Mary. *Maid in the U.S.A.* New York: Routledge, 1992.

Van Raaphorst, Donna. *Union Maids Not Wanted: Organizing Domestic Workers, 1870–1940*. New York: Praeger, 1988.

CHAPTER 16
NEW FORMS OF STRUGGLE: THE "ALT-LABOR" MOVEMENT IN NEW YORK CITY

Fine, Janice. *Worker Centers: Organizing Communities at the Edge of the Dream*. Ithaca: Cornell University Press, 2006.

Galvin, Daniel J. "Deterring Wage Theft: Alt-Labor, State Politics, and the Policy Determinants of Minimum Wage Compliance." *Perspectives on Politics* 14, no. 2 (2016): 324–50.

Jenkins, Steve. "Organizing, Advocacy and Member Power: A Critical Reflection." *Working USA* 6, no. 2 (2002): 56–89.

Milkman, Ruth, and Ed Ott, eds. *New Labor in New York: Precarious Workers and the Future of the Labor Movement*. Ithaca: Cornell University Press, 2014.

Ness, Immanuel. *Immigrants, Unions, and the New U.S. Labor Market*. Philadelphia: Temple University Press, 2005.